Basic
Microprocessors
and the 6800

Basic Microprocessors and the 6800

RON BISHOP

Manager, Technical Training
Motorola Semiconductor Group
Phoenix, Arizona

HAYDEN BOOK COMPANY, INC.
Rochelle Park, New Jersey

ISBN 0-8104-0758-2
Library of Congress Catalog Card Number 78-24740

10 11 12 13 14 15 16 17 18 19   PRINTING

81 82 83 84 85   YEAR

Preface

A new device has emerged in the field of electronics over the past eight years that will affect the lives of everyone as much as the transistor did in the fifties and sixties. This device, known as a *microprocessor,* is composed of many thousands of electronic logic elements on one small integrated circuit less than a quarter of an inch square.

As a result of this new technology, microcomputer systems will be included in many homes in the near future to perform such tasks as controlling lights, storing recipes, recording tax information, maintaining security, and the like.

Therein lies the role of this book. One is able to find many books about digital electronics on the market today. Most of them, however, are aimed at the technical person who has a working knowledge of the subject. A large majority of them, moreover, cover the high points of three, four, or even five different microcomputer systems. The reader ends up knowing a little about a lot of systems, but not very much about any one system.

This book is aimed at several categories of students. If one has a solid digital background but wants to learn about microcomputer systems, he can start with Chap. 7. On the other hand, if he has no knowledge of digital systems whatsoever, he should start with Chap. 2. Chapter 1, covering basic electrical theory, is for the many high-school students and other nontechnical people who want to start at "ground zero" and learn some electronics before branching into a study of home computers. This book can also serve as an ideal text for colleges, universities, and technical schools. Each chapter offers a set of problems for students to solve.

Many corporations today manufacture microprocessors. Even though there are differences between brands, all microprocessors are very similar in function and operation. Once a specific microprocessor has been mastered, it is very easy to understand other types. In this book, we will focus on Motorola's M6800 microprocessor and the related family of integrated circuits that can be used to build microcomputer systems. Both the microprocessor and its associated family of parts will be treated as a "black box." Although no attempt will be made to teach the reader how to design a microprocessor, he will be shown how a microcomputer system can be built using a microprocessor and how it can be programmed to perform the functions desired.

I would like to express my appreciation to Ray Doskocil, Bill Johnson, Jasper Norris, Don Aldridge, Dave Van Sant, Brett Richmond, Dennis Pfleger, Ben LeDonne, Clayton Wong, Bob Bratt, Dave Hyder, Jim Bainter, Lucy Brown, Fritz Wilson, Bill Crawford, Don Jackson, and Donald Kesner, each of whom has made significant contributions to the contents of this book. In addition, a much deserved thanks goes to my wife, Mary Jane, who spent many evenings and weekends typing the manuscript, and special thanks to Chuck Thompson, who has supported our training activities over the past several years.

Portions of the material in Chaps. 8, 9, 10, and 11 have been reprinted from the following copyrighted Motorola publications:

1. M6800 Microcomputer System Design Data Sheets
2. M6800 Programming Reference Manual
3. M6800 Course Notes

My thanks to Motorola, Inc., for their permission to make use of these documents.

RON BISHOP

Contents

1

Basic Electronic Principles

Since it is often necessary to interface a computer with other electrical circuits and devices external to the computer itself, a basic understanding of current, voltage, resistance, diodes, and transistors is necessary. This chapter outlines the basic concepts needed and attempts to avoid nonessential information. Examples are presented to illustrate all principles.

1.1 Voltage

Everyone has seen the kind of batteries that are used in flashlights, radios, toys, etc. These batteries are a source of voltage. They provide the power that generates the current (or flow of electrons) in a circuit.

Batteries, or voltage sources, come in many sizes and shapes. A 12-volt automobile battery is quite large, whereas a 12-volt dry cell battery used by hobbyists can be held in the hand. The primary difference between the two types of batteries, other than size, is the amount of energy they make available. A 12-volt battery can also be made by connecting eight 1½-volt batteries together, as shown in Fig. 1.1. Most batteries purchased in drug or department stores for use in flashlights, toys, etc., supply 1½ volts.

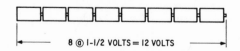

8 @ 1-1/2 VOLTS = 12 VOLTS

Fig. 1.1 Connection of eight 1½-volt batteries

All batteries have a positive (+) terminal and a negative (−) terminal. These terminals determine how you wire the battery in your circuit. It should be emphasized that the batteries themselves are neither positive nor negative. The way the battery is wired in your circuit determines whether it is positive or negative.

The symbol for a battery (power supply) is

$$\underset{\overline{}}{\underline{\underline{}}}\overset{+}{\underset{-}{}}$$

The longest line is the positive terminal, and the shorter line, the negative terminal.

1.2 Resistance

When a battery is connected to a circuit, electrons will start to flow, and this flow is called *current.* The amount of current that flows in any circuit is a function of the resistance in that circuit. Now what exactly does this mean? It means that *anything* which limits or impedes the current flowing in a circuit is called *resistance.* Resistance (R) is measured in units called *ohms* and is symbolized by the capital Greek letter omega (Ω). For example, 10 ohms is often written as 10 Ω.

Resistance values often reach thousands or even millions of ohms. For convenience, it is common practice to specify thousands of ohms as kohms (for kilo, or 10^3) and millions of ohms as Mohms (for mega, or 10^6). For example, 20,000 ohms would be written as 20 kohms and 3,000,000 ohms would be written as 3 Mohms.

Resistance comes in many degrees and forms. However, for the purposes of this discussion, only carbon type resistors will be considered. These are resistors made of carbon and an insulating material that are blended to the correct proportion for the resistance value desired.

Carbon resistors vary in length from approximately ¼ to 1½ in., with diameters up to approximately ¼ in. They have a wire lead attached to the center of each end (Fig. 1.2) which allows them to be connected to a circuit.

Fig. 1.2 Carbon resistor

Notice the bands around the resistor. They represent a color-coding technique that permits the value of the resistor to be determined merely by observation. The color code is given in Fig. 1.3.

The first three bands (A, B, and C) determine the value of the resistor. Band C, the third band, indicates the number of zeros that are to be added to the first two numbers. A black band indicates that *no* zeros are to be added;

Color	Value
Black	0
Brown	1
Red	2
Orange	3
Yellow	4
Green	5
Blue	6
Violet	7
Gray	8
White	9
Gold	5% } on
Silver	10% } Band D only

Fig. 1.3 Color code

BAND D (TOLERANCE)
BAND C (DECIMAL MULTIPLIER)
BAND B (2 ND DIGIT)
BAND A (1ST DIGIT)

Fig. 1.4 Bands

a red band, that two zeros are to be added. The fourth band (D) indicates the *tolerance,* or the extent to which the true value of the resistor may deviate from the color-coded value. For example, a 47k resistor with a silver band ($+$ 10%) may actually be 4.7k higher or lower than the color-coded value of 47k, that is, it may range from 42.3k to 51.7k. See other examples in Fig. 1.5.

Band A	Band B	Band C	Band D	Value
yellow	green	orange	silver	45k $+$ 10%
yellow	green	black	silver	45 $+$ 10%
yellow	green	blue	silver	45M $+$ 10%
red	red	red	gold	2.2k $+$ 5%
orange	red	yellow	silver	320k $+$ 10%
brown	red	orange	gold	12k $+$ 5%
red	black	red	gold	2k $+$ 5%
brown	black	black	gold	10 $+$ 5%

Fig. 1.5 Band values

The symbol used to designate a resistor in a circuit is

10 K

The value of the resistor is often written above the symbol.

Very often it is convenient or necessary to connect two resistors in series, as shown in Fig. 1.6(A), or in parallel, as shown in Fig. 1.6(B).

Fig. 1.6 Series and parallel connections

If two resistors are connected in series, as in Fig. 1.6(A), the total resistance offered is equal to the sum of the two individual resistors. For example, if a 10k and a 2k were connected in series, the total resistance would be 12k. However, when two resistors are connected in parallel, as in Fig. 1.6(B), the total resistance is equal to the product of the values of both resistors divided by the sum of the resistors. In equation form, the total resistance of a parallel branch is written as follows:

$$R_T = \frac{R_1 \times R_2}{R_1 + R_2}$$

For example, if 8k were in parallel with 2k, the total equivalent resistance would be

$$\frac{8k \times 2k}{8k + 2k} = \frac{(8)\,(2)\,(10^3)\,(10^3)}{10\,(10^3)} = 1.6k$$

The equivalent resistance of any parallel branch is *always* less than the smaller of the two resistors. In the above example, the smaller resistor of the parallel branch is 2k. Thus, the equivalent resistance of the parallel branch *must* be less than 2k.

1.3 Current

Current, which is analogous to water flowing in a water pipe, is a flow of electrons through wire and various other devices in a circuit. It is measured in units called *amperes,* abbreviated as A. There is a direct relationship between current and the voltage and resistance just discussed. Ohm's Law states that, given the voltage (V) and the resistance (R), the current flowing in a circuit can be calculated by dividing the resistance into the voltage. In equation form, this law is expressed as:

$$\text{Current (I)} = \frac{V}{R}$$

Very often in computer circuits the amount of current flowing may be much less than an ampere, say .002 A. The term *milliampere* or *milliamp* (mA) is likely to be used. Two milliamps is the same as .002 A or 2×10^{-3} A. Even smaller amounts of current, like .000002 A, are not uncommon. For these, the term *microamp* (μA) is used. Thus, a current of .000002 A is the same as 2×10^{-6} A or 2 μA.

Examples

1. If V = 5 and R = 1k, find I.

$$I = \frac{V}{R} = \frac{5}{1k} = \frac{5}{1000} = .005 \text{ A} = 5 \text{ mA}$$

$$I = \frac{5}{1K} = 5 \text{ mA}$$

2. If V = 5 and R = 1M, find I.

$$I = \frac{V}{R} = \frac{5}{1M} = \frac{5}{1,000,000} = .000005 \text{ A} = 5 \text{ } \mu\text{A}$$

3. If R = 3.5k and I = 1 mA, find V.

$$V = IR = (1)(10^{-3})(3.5)(10^{3}) = 3.5 \text{ V}$$

4. If V = 6 and I = 2 mA, find R.

$$R = \frac{V}{I} = \frac{6}{.002} = 3000 = 3k$$

The question now arises as to the direction of the current flow. In this book we will use what is commonly referred to as *conventional* current flow. Conventional current flows from the positive side of the battery, through the circuit, and back to the negative side of the battery.

1.4 Kirchhoff's Voltage Law

Kirchhoff's Voltage Law states that the *algebraic* sum of all the voltages in any *closed* loop in a circuit is equal to zero. To put this into simpler terms, if a circuit has a single battery and three resistors, the sum of the voltage drops across each of the resistors is equal to the battery voltage. The relationship between the voltage drop across a resistor and the current through the resistor is signified as follows:

The plus sign indicates that that end of the resistor is positive with respect to the other.

Examples

1. Find the voltage drop across each resistor in the circuit shown.

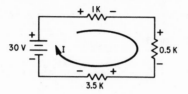

Step 1: Find the equivalent resistance:

1k + .5k + 3.5 k = 5k total

Step 2: Divide the total resistance into the battery voltage to get the total current flowing in the circuit:

$$I = \frac{V}{R} = \frac{30}{5k} = 6 \text{ mA}$$

Step 3: For a current of 6 mA flowing through each resistor, calculate the voltage drop across each resistor. (Recall that **V = IR**.)

V (across 1k) = 6 mA × 1k = 6 V
V (across .5k) = 6 mA × .5k = 3 V
V (across 3.5k) = 6 mA × 3.5k = 21 V

Notice that all voltages across the resistors, when added together, equal the battery voltage.

2. Find the voltage drop across each resistor in the circuit shown.

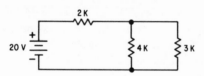

Step 1: Find the equivalent resistance of the parallel branch:

$$R_p = \frac{4k \times 3k}{4k + 3k} = 1.71k$$

Step 2: Draw the new equivalent circuit:

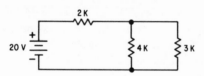

Step 3: Find the total current in the circuit:

$$I = \frac{20}{2k + 1.71k} = \frac{20}{3.71k} = 5.39 \text{ mA}$$

Step 4: Find the voltage drop across each resistor:

V (across 2k) = 2k (5.39 mA) = 10.78 V
V (across 1.71k) = 1.71k (5.39 mA) = 9.22 V

Notice the voltage drop across the 1.71k (which is the equivalent resistance for 4k in parallel with 3k) is the same as the voltage drop across the 3k and the 4k resistors.

The total current flowing through the 2k resistor in Example 2 is 5.39 mA. How much current is flowing in the 3k and 4k resistors? Kirchhoff's current law states that the sum of the currents entering the junction must be equal to the sum of the currents leaving the junction. Therefore, the sum of the currents in the 3k and 4k resistors must be 5.39 mA. As we calculated above, the voltage drop across the 1.71k equivalent resistance is 9.22 V. This, then, is the voltage drop across each resistor. By Ohm's law ($I = V/R$), the current in each resistor can be calculated:

$$I \text{ (in 4k resistor)} = V/R = 9.22/4k = 2.31 \text{ mA}$$
$$I \text{ (in 3k resistor)} = V/R = 9.22/3k = 3.08 \text{ mA}$$

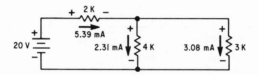

1.5 Diodes

A diode is a device that allows current to flow in one direction only. It is symbolized as follows:

The current flows from the positive ($+$) terminal (anode) of the diode to the negative ($-$) terminal (cathode), as shown by the direction of the arrow. If an attempt is made to make the current flow from the cathode to the anode (opposite the direction of the arrow), nothing will happen.

The voltage drop across a diode is very small when current is flowing through it. In this book, it will be assumed to be zero.

1.6 Transistors

A transistor is a three-lead semiconductor device that may be used in many ways. In this book, it will be used only as an electronic switch.

Transistors are available in two distinct types called *NPN* and *PNP*, depending on the makeup of the semiconductor material. The only real difference between an NPN type and a PNP type is the polarity of the battery used in the circuit. Consequently, only the NPN will be discussed.

Fig. 1.7 Symbol for NPN transistor

The symbol for an NPN transistor is shown in Fig. 1.7. Notice the three leads designated by B, C, and E. The B represents the base of the transistor, the C represents the collector of the transistor, and the E represents the emitter of the transistor. These designations are arbitrary ways of identifying the leads coming out of the transistor.

Using a transistor as an electronic switch is a very simple process. Only the circuit configuration known as the *common emitter* will be used in this book. Figure 1.8 illustrates an NPN transistor in the common emitter mode.

COMMON EMITTER: The emitter lead is common to both the input circuit and the output circuit.

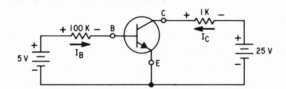

Fig. 1.8 NPN transistor in the common emitter mode

To calculate the current in its base circuit (called the *input circuit*), the voltage drop between the base and the emitter is assumed to be zero (in reality, it is a very small value). Therefore, the base current, I_B, is equal to 5 V divided by 100k:

$$I_B = 5/100k = .05 \text{ mA}$$

In a transistor circuit such as that shown in Fig. 1.8, the collector current, I_C, is found by multiplying the base current, I_B, by the gain, β (called *beta*), of the transistor. The gain of the transistor can usually be found in the data sheet that describes the transistor. A typical value is 100. Therefore, if the typical value is assumed for this transistor, the collector current (I_C) is found by multiplying the base current (I_B) by 100:

$$I_C = \beta I_B = 100 \times .05 \text{ mA} = 5 \text{ mA}$$

Recall the rule discussed previously that the sum of the voltage drops in a closed circuit must equal the battery voltage. In this transistor circuit, the voltage drop across the 1k resistor must equal the product of the current through the resistor and the value of the resistor, or $V = 1k \times 5$ mA $= 5$ V. Therefore, the remaining voltage of 20 V (battery voltage minus drop across resistor, or $25 - 5 = 20$) must be between the collector and the emitter of the transistor. The voltage between the collector and the emitter is called V_{CE}. It is this voltage that is of significance in computer circuits.

If the 5-V battery on the input circuit were changed to 0 V, there would be no base current (I_B). If there were no base current, the collector current (I_C) would also be 0, which means that the voltage drop across the 1k resistor would be 0 as well. Therefore, the voltage drop between the collector and the emitter (V_{CE}) must be 25 V since the voltage drops in any closed circuit must equal the sum of the battery voltage. The V_{CE} of 25 volts is known as the *cutoff voltage*. A transistor in the cutoff state has a voltage between the collector and the emitter (V_{CE}) equal to the battery voltage in the output circuit.

On the other hand, if the 5-V battery on the input circuit were increased to 25 V, the base current (I_B) would be .25 mA (25/100k). A base current of .25 mA would produce a collector current (I_C) of βI_B, or 25 mA (100 $\times$ .25 mA). The voltage drop across the 1k resistor in the output circuit is therefore 25 mA $\times$ 1k, or 25 V. Therefore, the 25 volts from the battery is accounted for by the drop across the 1k resistor. Thus, the voltage across the collector to the emitter (V_{CE}) of the transistor is 0 V. The transistor is now in a state referred to as *saturated*.

A transistor in the saturated state has a voltage between the collector and the emitter (V_{CE}) approximately equal to 0 V.

It should also be noted that any further increases in base current after saturation has no effect on V_{CE} and the output circuit. The maximum collector current possible in the output circuit is the battery voltage divided by the resistance in series with the collector lead. Once the transistor is saturated, the battery and resistance determine the magnitude of the current.

As mentioned previously, transistors come in NPN and PNP types. The above discussion was based on the NPN type. Calculations for the PNP type are identical to those for the NPN type except that the batteries are reversed and the currents flow in the opposite direction. Figure 1.9 illustrates a PNP transistor using the same size batteries and resistors as the NPN circuit mentioned earlier.

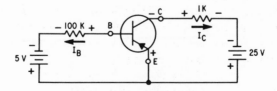

Fig. 1.9 PNP transistor circuit

If the β of this transistor were the same as that for the NPN transistor in Fig. 1.8, the currents in Fig. 1.9 would be of the *same* magnitude as those in Fig. 1.8 but their directions would be opposite. Also notice that the batteries (or power supplies) in the circuit of Fig. 1.9 are opposite those in Fig. 1.8.

Very often, transistors are shown in a circuit in a slightly different way from that illustrated. The circuit in Fig. 1.8 would be as shown in Fig. 1.10.

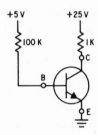

Fig. 1.10 Alternative NPN transistor circuit

These two circuits are identical even though they may appear quite different. In Fig. 1.10, which is just an abbreviated way of showing the same thing as Fig. 1.8, the plus side of the 5-V battery is connected to the 100k resistor. The negative side of the 5-V battery would be connected to the emitter of the transistor. Likewise, the plus side of the 25-V battery is connected to the 1k resistor, and its negative side would be connected to the emitter.

1.7 Example Circuits

Shown below are various circuits and calculations of their basic values.

(a)

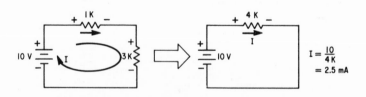

$$I = \frac{10}{4k} = 2.5 \text{ mA}$$

(b)

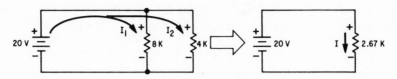

The equivalent resistance $R_T = \dfrac{8k \times 4k}{8k + 4k} = 2.67k$

$I = \dfrac{20}{2.67k} = 7.49$ mA (in direction shown)

(c)

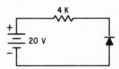

$I = \dfrac{20}{4k} = 5$ mA (in direction shown)

(d)

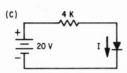

$I = 0$ (current will not flow opposite the diode)

(e) Find I_B, I_C, and V_{CE} when $\beta = 80$.

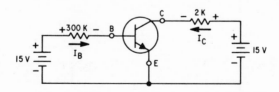

$I_B = \dfrac{15}{300k} = .05$ mA

$I_C = \beta I_B = 80 \times .05$ mA $= 4$ mA

$V_{CE} = 15 - (2k \times 4$ mA$)$

$\quad\;\; = 15 - 8$

$\quad\;\; = 7$ V

Problems

1. Determine the value of each resistor given the color coding indicated below. Also, calculate the possible maximum and minimum value of each resistor.

Band A	Band B	Band C	Band D	Value	Max Value	Min Value
Brown	Brown	Brown	Gold			
White	Gray	Blue	Silver			
Orange	Black	Orange	Silver			
Orange	Orange	Orange	Gold			
Yellow	Red	Black	Silver			
Blue	White	Red	Gold			
Violet	Green	Orange	Silver			
White	Black	Black	Gold			

2. Find the total resistance of each set of resistors below:

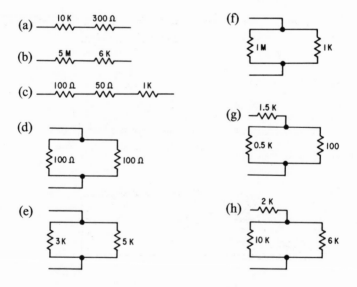

3. Calculate the current flowing in each resistor and the voltage across each resistor in each of the following circuits. Verify that the sum of the voltage drops equals the battery voltage.

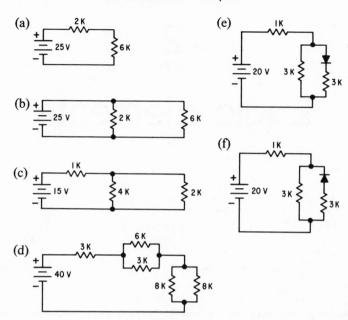

4. Calculate I_B, I_C, and V_{CE} for each of the following circuits. Show the directions of each current. Assume that $\beta = 80$ for each transistor.

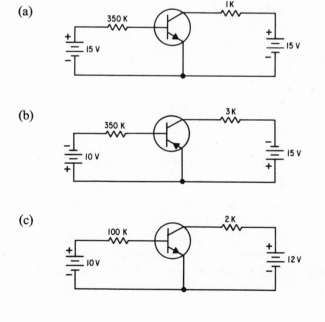

2

Logic Elements

LOGIC ELEMENT: A device consisting of electronic circuitry that provides an output based on the input of one, two, or more variables.

An example of a logic element is the starter in a car. Before the starter will work, the key must be inserted in the ignition and turned, *and* the shifting lever (for automatic shift) must be in "park." An electrical signal is sent to the starter after these two inputs have taken place. The circuit for the starter could be like the one shown in Fig. 2.1.

Many thousands of logic elements make up a computer. This book will not study the internal circuitry of computers in detail. However, it is often necessary to employ logic elements when a computer is used to control or monitor some external device or function. This chapter will discuss several of the basic logic elements often found in computers. Input voltages of +5 V and 0 V have been chosen for the illustrations. Logic gates with other input voltages can also be obtained. As will be shown both in this and later chapters, logic elements are utilized to make decisions and perform various operations.

2.1 "AND" Gate

GATE: A term used synonymously with the term "logic element." Most logic elements are referred to as "gates."

Assume that a circuit has a battery, two switches called S1 and S2, and a resistor in series, as shown in Fig. 2.1.

Notice that if only S1 is closed, current cannot flow. Also, if S2 is closed but S1 remains open, current cannot flow. However, if S1 *and* S2 are closed, current will flow through the 2-Ω resistor. This type of circuit is known as an *"AND" gate* because two conditions must be satisfied simultaneously (S1

Fig. 2.1 AND gate circuit   **Fig. 2.2** Symbol for AND gate

and S2 closed). Symbolically, an "AND" gate is represented as shown in Fig. 2.2.

If a voltage (+5 V) is applied at terminal A but *not* at terminal B (0 V), there will be no voltage at terminal C. Likewise, if a voltage is applied at terminal B but *not* at terminal A, there will be no voltage at terminal C. However, if a voltage is applied at terminals A *and* B, there will be a voltage at terminal C (+5V).

TRUTH TABLE: A table showing all possible combinations of inputs with the respective output for each set of inputs.

The truth table for the "AND" gate is shown in Fig. 2.3.

Voltage at A	and	Voltage at B	=	Voltage at C
0		0		0
+5		0		0
0		+5		0
+5		+5		+5

Fig. 2.3 Truth table for AND gate

"AND" gates may have two or more inputs. For example, if an "AND" gate has four inputs, *each* of the four inputs must have a voltage applied before there can be an output voltage.

2.2 "OR" Gate

Now, assume a circuit such as the one shown in Fig. 2.4 consisting of a battery, two switches (S1 and S2), and a resistor.

Notice that if either S1 or S2 is closed, current will flow through the 4k resistor. If neither one is closed, no current can flow. This type of circuit is known as an *"OR" gate.* Symbolically, an "OR" gate is represented as shown in Fig. 2.5.

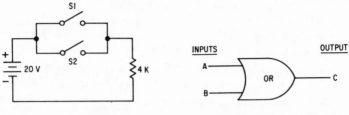

Fig. 2.4 OR gate circuit   **Fig. 2.5** Symbol for OR gate

If a voltage (+5 V) is applied at terminal A *or* at terminal B, there will be a voltage at terminal C (+5 V). A voltage applied at both terminal A and terminal B also results in a voltage at terminal C. The truth table for the "OR" gate is shown in Fig. 2.6.

Voltage at A	and	Voltage at B	=	Voltage at C
0		0		0
+5		0		+5
0		+5		+5
+5		+5		+5

Fig. 2.6 Truth table for OR gate

Again, an "OR" gate may have two or more inputs. A voltage at any or all of the inputs would result in an output voltage.

2.3 "NOT" Gate

Examine the circuit shown in Fig. 2.7. Notice that if S1 is open, current will flow through the 100-ohm resistor and the 4000-ohm resistor. If we calculate the voltage drop across each resistor, we will see that the voltage across the 4k resistor is very large and that the voltage across the 100-ohm resistor is very small.

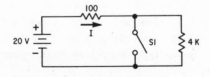

Fig. 2.7 NOT gate circuit

The following values obtain in this circuit:
Total current: $I = 20/4100 = 4.88$ mA
Voltage across 100 Ω: $V = (4.88$ mA$)(100\Omega) = .48$ V
Voltage across 4k: $V = (4.88$ mA$)(4k) = 19.52$ V

Now examine what happens when S1 is closed. Notice that the voltage across the 100-ohm resistor rises to 20 volts and the voltage across the 4k resistor has been "shorted out" (because all current flows through S1 and none through the 4k resistor).

What has happened in each of these cases? When S1 was open, the voltage across the 100-ohm resistor was low and the voltage across the 4k resistor was high. When S1 is closed, the situation is reversed, with the voltage across the 100-ohm resistor high and the voltage across the 4k resistor low (or zero). This type of circuit is referred to as a *"NOT" gate* (also referred to as an inverter). NOT, in computer terminology, refers to an inverted quantity. For example, if A is $+5$ V, NOT A is 0 V. NOT A is shown in shorthand notation as $\overline{A}$. Symbolically, a "NOT" gate is represented as shown in Fig. 2.8.

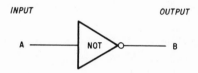

INPUT   *OUTPUT*

A ———————| NOT >○——— B

Fig. 2.8 Symbol for NOT gate

When the voltage at terminal A is high ($+5$ V), the voltage at terminal B is low (0 V). When the voltage at terminal A is low, the voltage at terminal B is high. The truth table for a "NOT" gate is shown in Fig. 2.9.

Voltage at A	Voltage at B
0	+5
+5	0

Fig. 2.9 Truth table for NOT gate

2.4 "NOR" Gate

The "NOR" gate is formed by combining the "OR" gate with the "NOT" gate, as shown in Fig. 2.10. Recall that the "NOT" gate produces an output voltage that is opposite the input voltage.

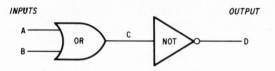

Fig. 2.10 Formation of NOR gate

The truth table for the "NOR" gate is shown in Fig. 2.11.

Voltage at A	Voltage at B	Voltage at C	Voltage at D
0	0	0	+5
+5	0	+5	0
0	+5	+5	0
+5	+5	+5	0

Fig. 2.11 Truth table for NOR gate

Rather than show a "NOR" gate as in Fig. 2.10, the symbol in Fig. 2.12 has been adopted for a "NOR" gate.

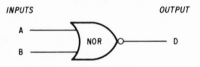

Fig. 2.12 Symbol for NOR gate

Another truth table for the "NOR" gate is shown in Fig. 2.13. This is the same as the truth table in Fig. 2.11 except that the middle terminal (C) is not shown.

Voltage at A	Voltage at B	Voltage at D
0	0	+5
+5	0	0
0	+5	0
+5	+5	0

Fig. 2.13 Truth table for NOR gate

"NOR" represents "NOT"–"OR," which actually describes the gate. The output from the "OR" gate is just inverted (or NOTted).

2.5 "NAND" Gate

The "NAND" gate is formed by combining the "AND" gate with the "NOT" gate just as was done to form the "NOR" gate.

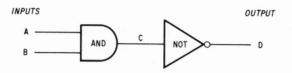

Fig. 2.14 Formation of NAND gate

The truth table for the "NAND" gate is shown in Fig. 2.15.

Voltage at A	Voltage at B	Voltage at C	Voltage at D
0	0	0	+5
+5	0	0	+5
0	+5	0	+5
+5	+5	+5	0

Again, the symbol shown in Fig. 2.16 has been adopted for the "NAND" gate.

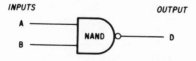

Fig. 2.16 Symbol for NAND gate

Another truth table for the "NAND" gate is shown in Fig. 2.17. This is the same as the truth table in Fig. 2.15 except that the middle terminal (C) is not shown.

Voltage at A	Voltage at B	Voltage at D
0	0	+5
+5	0	+5
0	+5	+5
+5	+5	0

Fig. 2.17 Truth table for NAND gate

"NAND" represents "NOT"–"AND," which actually describes the gate. The output from the "AND" gate is just inverted (or NOTted).

2.6 "EXCLUSIVE OR" Gate

Another logic element often used is called the *"EXCLUSIVE OR"* *gate*. Recall that in the OR gate, an output is realized if one or both inputs are present. In the "EXCLUSIVE OR" gate an output will be realized if one input is present but *not both*. The symbol for this gate is shown in Fig. 2.18 and the truth table in Fig. 2.19.

Fig. 2.18 Symbol for EXCLUSIVE OR gate

Voltage at A	Voltage at B	Voltage at C
0	0	0
+5	0	+5
0	+5	+5
+5	+5	0*

*Notice the difference between this value and its equivalent in "OR" gate truth table.

Fig. 2.19 Truth table for EXCLUSIVE OR

2.7 Notation

If some function A is to be "ANDed" with another function B, the operation would be described as "Function A ANDed with function B results in an output C." As can be seen, this description is rather tedious to write. Fortunately, a shorthand notation that says the same thing has been adopted: $A \cdot B = C$. The two input functions are written with a dot ($\bullet$) between them and then set equal to the output function. Sometimes, the dot is also shown on the AND symbol, although it is not essential.

Figure 2.13 summarizes the logic elements and the shorthand notation describing various functions:

Symbol	Equation	Function
A B — [•] — C	$C = A \cdot B$	AND
A B — [+] — C	$C = A + B$	OR
A — [▷○] — C	$C = \bar{A}$	INVERTER
A B — [⊕] — C	$C = A \oplus B$	EXCLUSIVE OR

Fig. 2.20 Summary of logic elements

In this chapter, $+5$ V was used as the "high" input and 0 V was used as the "low" input. It must be emphasized that the value of the "high" and/or "low" input voltages to any logic element is a function of the device itself. These voltages may be any combination of voltages that the manufacturer may have designed the logic elements for. Therefore, in order to make the truth tables more universal, the high condition is generally represented as a "1" (called a logic one) and the low condition as a "0" (called a logic zero). The truth tables would then appear as follows:

"AND" Function				"OR" Function		
Input A	Input B	Output C		Input A	Input B	Output C
0	0	0		0	0	0
0	1	0		0	1	1
1	0	0		1	0	1
1	1	1		1	1	1

"NOT" Function

Input A	Output B
0	1
1	0

"NOR" Function

Input A	Input B	Output C
0	0	1
0	1	0
1	0	0
1	1	0

"NAND" Function

Input A	Input B	Output C
0	0	1
0	1	1
1	0	1
1	1	0

"EXCLUSIVE OR" Function

Input A	Input B	Output C
0	0	0
0	1	1
1	0	1
1	1	0

2.8 Applications

Now that you know what AND, OR, NAND, and NOR gates are, where can they be used? As previously mentioned, many of these gates are used internally in the microprocessor along with additional elements such as flip-flops, half adders, and full adders. Flip-flops, half adders, and full adders are sometimes used externally to the microprocessor system. However, AND, OR, NAND, and NOR gates are used much more often.

Assume that you have a small computer installed in your home to monitor and control several functions. One of these functions may be to sound an alarm if any door in the house is opened (that is, to serve as a burglar alarm). A mechanical switch can be installed above each door in the house in a position that would cause the contact to close when a door opens, resulting in a voltage to the input of an OR gate, as shown in Fig. 2.21. The output of the OR gate

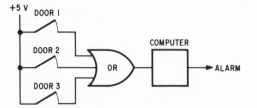

Fig. 2.21 Alarm system

could then be fed into the computer, which would sound an alarm such as a bell, turn on all lights in the house, or even send some kind of a signal to the police. With the use of one OR gate, only one input line to the computer is required. Otherwise, one input line for each door is required. This is not good practice, as the number of input lines to a computer system is usually limited for economic reasons.

The use of logic elements is unlimited. Several other applications will be discussed in a later chapter.

Problems

1. Your computer has only one input line available. However, an alarm must be sounded if one of the two doors in the kitchen, one of the two windows in the kitchen, or the garage door is opened. Show the logic required to implement this function. You may use only two input devices.
2. At a later time, you have decided to also sound an alarm if one of the two doors in the storage room, one of the two windows in the family room, or the patio door is opened. Show how this logic would be added to the logic of Problem 1. Assume that there is only one input to the computer available.

3

Number Systems— Why?

Up to now, the word *computer* has been used without any explanation or definition. There are two primary types of computers, namely digital computers and analog computers. This book is solely concerned with digital computers. However, let us take a very brief look at analog signals and see how they compare with digital signals.

All of us are quite familiar with analog signals, although we may not realize it. When you look at a thermometer, the height of the mercury rises as the temperature increases. As you drive your car, the speedometer needle moves farther to the right as you increase your speed. When you play records on your stereo, the music gets louder as the volume knob is turned to the right. All these devices have one thing in common—they measure one quantity in terms of some other quantity, for example, height of mercury in terms of degrees of temperature.

Digital signals are quite different from analog signals in that they have only two states. When you walk into a room, the switch that controls the light is either "on" or "off." The door to your house is either "open" or "closed." The switch that controls the lights on your car is either "on" or "off." These are all examples of digital states. Such digital concepts are the basis of "digital computers." In each of these examples, we could define the "on" or "open" condition as a logic "1" and the opposite condition as a logic "0." These are referred to as binary states (one of two possible states).

3.1 Binary Numbers

Everyone is familiar with the base 10 number system, that is, the numbers 0, 1, 2, 3, 4, 5, 6, 7, 8, and 9. In all probability, the base 10 number system was established as a result of our having 10 fingers and 10 toes.

However, in digital computers, only two distinct states exist, namely, logic 1 and logic 0. A +5-volt input could be defined as a logic 1 while a 0-volt input would be a logic 0. Consequently, all inputs to a digital computer must be converted to a series of 1's and 0's before the computer can make any use of the data.

3.2 Digital Example

Assume that we have three switches connected between a 9-V battery and three light bulbs, as shown in Fig. 3.1.

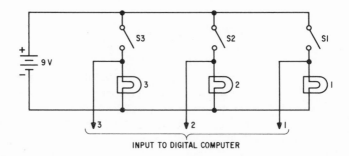

Fig. 3.1 Light bulb analogy

It is desired to have the computer monitor the status of the three lights. With all the switches open, none of the bulbs will glow and the voltage to the computer is 0. This will be defined as the 0 logic level. If any switch is closed, the voltage at the bulb will be 9 V, which is defined as a logic 1.

Assume that switch 3 is closed; then bulb 3 will glow and the computer will detect a logic 1 on that wire. The status of the input wires changes from 000 to 100, since S1 and S2 are still open. Now if S2 is closed, bulb 2 glows, and the input to the computer changes from 100 to 110 (assuming S3 remains closed). If all possible combinations are recorded in a chart, it is seen that the three lines to the computer may have eight different states, as shown below:

Bulb 3	Bulb 2	Bulb 1	Status	Computer Input
0	0	0	All bulbs off	000
0	0	1	Only bulb 1 on	001
0	1	0	Only bulb 2 on	010
0	1	1	Bulbs 1 and 2 on	011
1	0	0	Only bulb 3 on	100
1	0	1	Bulbs 1 and 3 on	101
1	1	0	Bulbs 2 and 3 on	110
1	1	1	All bulbs on	111

The status of each of the three lines to the computer is in digital form, that is, in one of two states or conditions (1 or 0). The computer can read and record the status of the bulbs and make decisions to do other things based on these inputs.

With this in mind, visualize 16, 20, or even 25 such inputs and consider the problems associated with long strings of 1's and 0's if the boss calls and asks for the status of 16 or more individual lines to the computer. Obviously, it is very difficult to convey useful information in digital form. However, if the 1's and 0's could be arranged in groups of 3 or 4, a great deal of chance for confusion and error would be eliminated.

3.3 Base 10 to Binary Conversion

Base 10 number systems have ten distinct numbers, 0 through 9. As one may have guessed by now, since a digital signal must be represented by a 0 or a 1, the base 2 number system will play a very prominent role. Base 2 numbers have only two distinct numbers, 0 and 1.

Before a base 10 number can be used by a digital computer, it must first be converted to 1's and 0's (that is, into a base 2 number). A method of doing this is known as "repeated division by 2." To illustrate, the base 10 number 29_{10} will be converted to a base 2, or binary, number. (The number system base is often written as a subscript.)

Step 1: Divide the base 10 number by 2:

$$\frac{14}{2\overline{)29}} \qquad \text{Remainder } 1 = 1$$

Step 2: Divide answer in Step 1 (14) by 2:

$$\frac{7}{2\overline{)14}} \qquad \text{Remainder } 2 = 0$$

Step 3: Divide answer in Step 2 (7) by 2:

$$\frac{3}{2\overline{)7}} \qquad \text{Remainder } 3 = 1$$

Read remainders in this direction to form answer

Step 4: Divide answer in Step 3 (3) by 2:

$$\frac{1}{2\overline{)3}} \qquad \text{Remainder } 4 = 1$$

Step 5: Divide answer in Step 4 (1) by 2:

$$\frac{0}{2\overline{)1}} \qquad \text{Remainder } 5 = 1$$

Step 6: Stop dividing when the answer is zero. The remainders are then read in the reverse order to form the answer:

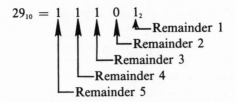

$$29_{10} = 1 \quad 1 \quad 1 \quad 0 \quad 1_2$$

Remainder 1
Remainder 2
Remainder 3
Remainder 4
Remainder 5

Remember that 29_{10} is really $(9 \times 10^0) + (2 \times 10^1)$, or $9 + 20 = 29$. (Any number to the zero power is 1; thus $10^0 = 1$.) To check the base 2 equivalent of 11101, we will convert it back to a base 10 number:

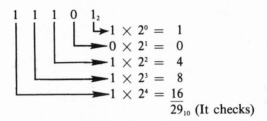

$$1 \quad 1 \quad 1 \quad 0 \quad 1_2$$

$1 \times 2^0 = 1$
$0 \times 2^1 = 0$
$1 \times 2^2 = 4$
$1 \times 2^3 = 8$
$1 \times 2^4 = \underline{16}$
29_{10} (It checks)

Convert 69_{10} to a binary or base 2 number:

$$\begin{array}{ll}
34 & \\
2)\overline{69} & R = 1 \\
17 & \\
2)\overline{34} & R = 0 \\
8 & \\
2)\overline{17} & R = 1 \\
4 & \\
2)\overline{8} & R = 0 \\
2 & \\
2)\overline{4} & R = 0 \\
1 & \\
2)\overline{2} & R = 0 \\
0 & \\
2)\overline{1} & R = 1 \\
\end{array}$$

Read remainders
in this direction
to form answer

Therefore, $69_{10} = 1000101_2$. To check:

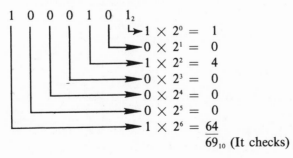

$$1 \quad 0 \quad 0 \quad 0 \quad 1 \quad 0 \quad 1_2$$

$1 \times 2^0 = 1$
$0 \times 2^1 = 0$
$1 \times 2^2 = 4$
$0 \times 2^3 = 0$
$0 \times 2^4 = 0$
$0 \times 2^5 = 0$
$1 \times 2^6 = \underline{64}$
69_{10} (It checks)

3.4 Base 10 to Base 8 (Octal) Conversion

If a base 10 number has been converted to binary, a string of 1's and 0's forms the answer. By dividing the 1's and 0's into groups and using another number to represent each group—for example, a base 8 number—the total number of digits may be reduced. Base 8 is a very convenient number system for digital computers, as a base 8 number represents three binary digits. To illustrate, the base 10 number of 29 can be converted to its base 8 equivalent in basically the same manner as for base 2, that is, by repeated division by 8.

Step 1: Divide the base 10 number by 8:

$$\begin{array}{r} 3 \\ 8\overline{)29} \end{array} \qquad R = 5$$

Step 2: Divide the answer of Step 1 by 8:

$$\begin{array}{r} 0 \\ 8\overline{)3} \end{array} \qquad R = 3$$

The base 8 answer is obtained by reading the remainders in the reverse order as in a base 2 conversion. Therefore, $29_{10} = 35_8$. To check the answer, conversion from base 8 to base 10 is accomplished by multiplying each base 8 digit times its proper weighted value:

$$35_8$$
$$\begin{array}{l} \hookrightarrow 5 \times 8^0 = 5 \\ \hookrightarrow 3 \times 8^1 = 24 \\ \hline 29_{10} \text{ (It checks)} \end{array}$$

We have already seen that $29_{10} = 11101_2$. Therefore, $29_{10} = 35_8 = 11101_2$. There exists a relationship between base 8 and base 2 which permits dividing a base 2 number into groups of three digits, with a single base 8 number representing each group. To show this relationship, it will be necessary to convert each base 10 number of 1, 2, 3, 4, 5, 6, and 7 to the equivalent base 2 and base 8 numbers.

Base 10 numbers converted to base 2:

7_{10}		6_{10}	

$$\begin{array}{r} 3 \\ 2\overline{)7} \end{array} \qquad R = 1$$
$$\begin{array}{r} 1 \\ 2\overline{)3} \end{array} \qquad R = 1 \quad \uparrow \quad 7_{10} = 111_2$$
$$\begin{array}{r} 0 \\ 2\overline{)1} \end{array} \qquad R = 1$$

$$\begin{array}{r} 3 \\ 2\overline{)6} \end{array} \qquad R = 0$$
$$\begin{array}{r} 1 \\ 2\overline{)3} \end{array} \qquad R = 1 \quad \uparrow \quad 6_{10} = 110_2$$
$$\begin{array}{r} 0 \\ 2\overline{)1} \end{array} \qquad R = 1$$

$\boxed{5_{10}}$

$\begin{array}{l}2\\2\overline{)5}\qquad R=1\\1\\2\overline{)2}\qquad R=0\qquad \uparrow\quad 5_{10}=101_2\\0\\2\overline{)1}\qquad R=1\end{array}$

$\boxed{4_{10}}$

$\begin{array}{l}2\\2\overline{)4}\qquad R=0\\1\\2\overline{)2}\qquad R=0\qquad \uparrow\quad 4_{10}=100_2\\0\\2\overline{)1}\qquad R=1\end{array}$

$\boxed{3_{10}}$

$\begin{array}{l}1\\2\overline{)3}\qquad R=1\\0\\2\overline{)1}\qquad R=1\end{array}\qquad \uparrow\quad 3_{10}=11_2$

$\boxed{2_{10}}$

$\begin{array}{l}1\\2\overline{)2}\qquad R=0\\0\\2\overline{)1}\qquad R=1\end{array}\qquad \uparrow\quad 2_{10}=10_2$

$\boxed{1_{10}}$

$\begin{array}{l}0\\2\overline{)1}\qquad R=1\qquad 1_{10}=1_2\end{array}$

$\boxed{0_{10}}$

$0_{10}=0_2$

Base 10 numbers converted to base 8:

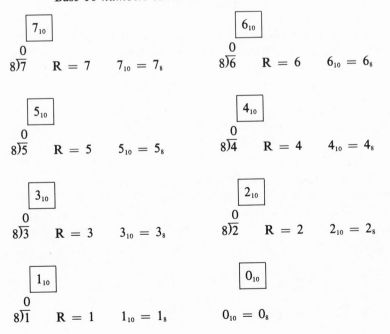

$\boxed{7_{10}}$

$\begin{array}{l}0\\8\overline{)7}\qquad R=7\qquad 7_{10}=7_8\end{array}$

$\boxed{6_{10}}$

$\begin{array}{l}0\\8\overline{)6}\qquad R=6\qquad 6_{10}=6_8\end{array}$

$\boxed{5_{10}}$

$\begin{array}{l}0\\8\overline{)5}\qquad R=5\qquad 5_{10}=5_8\end{array}$

$\boxed{4_{10}}$

$\begin{array}{l}0\\8\overline{)4}\qquad R=4\qquad 4_{10}=4_8\end{array}$

$\boxed{3_{10}}$

$\begin{array}{l}0\\8\overline{)3}\qquad R=3\qquad 3_{10}=3_8\end{array}$

$\boxed{2_{10}}$

$\begin{array}{l}0\\8\overline{)2}\qquad R=2\qquad 2_{10}=2_8\end{array}$

$\boxed{1_{10}}$

$\begin{array}{l}0\\8\overline{)1}\qquad R=1\qquad 1_{10}=1_8\end{array}$

$\boxed{0_{10}}$

$0_{10}=0_8$

The relationship of each base 8 and each base 2 number to the equivalent base 10 number is shown in the following chart:

Base 10	Base 8	Base 2
7	7	111
6	6	110
5	5	101
4	4	100
3	3	011
2	2	010
1	1	001
0	0	000

Notice that each base 8 number has a base 2 equivalent that encompasses three digits of the base 2 number. What this really means is that a base 2 number can be divided into groups of three digits each, starting from the right, and each group may be represented with its base 8 equivalent. In the previous example, $29_{10} = 35_8 = 011 \ 101_2$, notice that the base 2 number may be written directly from each base 8 number or the base 8 number can be written directly from the base 2 number.

$$0 \ 1 \ 1 \ | \ 1 \ 0 \ 1_2$$
$$3 \quad | \quad 5_8$$

To illustrate the advantage of this technique, 150_{10} will be converted to base 8 and base 2. Conversion to base 8 is as follows:

$$\begin{array}{r} 18 \\ 8\overline{)150} \end{array} \qquad R = 6$$

$$\begin{array}{r} 2 \\ 8\overline{)18} \end{array} \qquad R = 2$$

$$\begin{array}{r} 0 \\ 8\overline{)2} \end{array} \qquad R = 2$$

Therefore, $150_{10} = 226_8$. If the base 2 equivalent is written directly from the base 8 answer, we get $150_{10} = 010 \ 010 \ 110_2$. To verify the base 2 answer, let's convert 150_{10} directly to base 2 by repeated division by 2:

$$\begin{array}{r} 75 \\ 2\overline{)150} \end{array} \qquad R = 0$$

$$\begin{array}{r} 37 \\ 2\overline{)75} \end{array} \qquad R = 1$$

$$\begin{array}{r} 18 \\ 2\overline{)37} \end{array} \qquad R = 1$$

$$\begin{array}{ll} \dfrac{9}{2\overline{)18}} & R = 0 \\[2mm] \dfrac{4}{2\overline{)9}} & R = 1 \\[2mm] \dfrac{2}{2\overline{)4}} & R = 0 \\[2mm] \dfrac{1}{2\overline{)2}} & R = 0 \\[2mm] \dfrac{0}{2\overline{)1}} & R = 1 \end{array}$$

Therefore $150_{10} = 10010110_2$

Notice that this answer and the one obtained by first converting 150_{10} to a base 8 number and then converting the base 8 number to a base 2 number are identical. The conclusion to be drawn is that for base 10 to base 2 conversions, it is much easier to convert the number to its base 8 equivalent and then write the base 2 equivalent for each base 8 digit. In this last example, it took three divisions for the base 8 conversion and eight divisions for the base 2 conversion.

This technique also works well in the reverse order. Given a binary number consisting of many digits, what is the base 10 equivalent? For example, what is the base 10 equivalent number for the binary number $1\,101\,011\,101_2$?

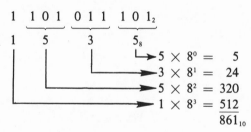

$$1 \quad 1\,0\,1 \quad 0\,1\,1 \quad 1\,0\,1_2$$
$$1 \qquad 5 \qquad 3 \qquad 5_8$$

$$
\begin{aligned}
5 \times 8^0 &= 5 \\
3 \times 8^1 &= 24 \\
5 \times 8^2 &= 320 \\
1 \times 8^3 &= \underline{512} \\
& \;\, 861_{10}
\end{aligned}
$$

3.5 Base 10 to Base 16 (Hexadecimal) Conversion

In the previous section, the convenience of the base 8 system was illustrated. In this section, another convenient number system, base 16, will be studied. The principles of converting from base 10 to any other number system are the same. However, base 16, which will hereafter be referred to as the *hex system,* has a certain mystique about it, since some of the symbols representing the base 16 numbers are letters.

The obvious question one may ask is why use another number system when base 8 works just fine. Most of the microcomputer systems available today utilize up to 16 address lines. In the hex system, each group of four digits is represented by one hex symbol. Hence, 16 binary digits can be represented with four hex symbols, or six base 8 symbols. Four hex symbols are easier to work with.

In the hex system, the letters A, B, C, D, E, and F, in addition to the numbers 0 through 9, are used to represent the hex numbers. The relationship between base 10, base 16, and base 2 is shown in Fig. 3.2. When counting in the hex system, try to forget that there is a base 10 system. After the number 9 come the "numbers" A, B, C, D, E, and F. This will be the hardest part of the system to understand, but with some practice, it will be as comfortable as any of the other number systems.

Base 10 (decimal)	Base 16 (hexadecimal)	Base 2 (binary)
0	0	0000
1	1	0001
2	2	0010
3	3	0011
4	4	0100
5	5	0101
6	6	0110
7	7	0111
8	8	1000
9	9	1001
10	A	1010
11	B	1011
12	C	1100
13	D	1101
14	E	1110
15	F	1111

Fig. 3.2

To illustrate conversion from base 10 to hex, 156_{10} will be converted by repeated division, as in other conversions:

$$\frac{9}{16)156} \qquad R = 12 = C$$

(Remember, 12 in base 10 is C in hex)

$$\frac{0}{16)9} \qquad R = 9$$

Therefore, $156_{10} = 9C_{16}$.

To convert $9C_{16}$ back to base 10, the same procedure used earlier is applied:

9 C_{16}

└──► $C \times 16^0 = 12 \times 16^0 = \quad 12$

└──► $9 \times 16^1 = \qquad\qquad 144$

$\overline{156_{10}}$ (It checks)

To illustrate the usefulness of the hex system further, the number 982_{10} will be converted to binary by repeated division by 2 and then converted to binary by first converting it to a hex number and then to the binary equivalent. Conversion by repeated division by 2 is as follows:

$$\begin{array}{r} 491 \\ \overline{2)982} \end{array} \qquad R = 0$$

$$\begin{array}{r} 245 \\ \overline{2)491} \end{array} \qquad R = 1$$

$$\begin{array}{r} 122 \\ \overline{2)245} \end{array} \qquad R = 1$$

$$\begin{array}{r} 61 \\ \overline{2)122} \end{array} \qquad R = 0$$

$$\begin{array}{r} 30 \\ \overline{2)61} \end{array} \qquad R = 1$$

$$\begin{array}{r} 15 \\ \overline{2)30} \end{array} \qquad R = 0$$

$$\begin{array}{r} 7 \\ \overline{2)15} \end{array} \qquad R = 1$$

$$\begin{array}{r} 3 \\ \overline{2)7} \end{array} \qquad R = 1$$

$$\begin{array}{r} 1 \\ \overline{2)3} \end{array} \qquad R = 1$$

$$\begin{array}{r} 0 \\ \overline{2)1} \end{array} \qquad R = 1$$

Therefore, $982_{10} = 1111010110_2$ (10 divisions required).

Conversion by repeated division by 16 is as follows:

$$\begin{array}{r} 61 \\ \overline{16)982} \end{array} \qquad R = 6$$

$$\begin{array}{r} 3 \\ \overline{16)61} \end{array} \qquad R = 13 = D$$

$$\begin{array}{r} 0 \\ \overline{16)3} \end{array} \qquad R = 3$$

Therefore, $982_{10} = 3D6_{16}$ (three divisions required).

The next step is to write the binary equivalent of each individual symbol in the hex number to arrive at the binary equivalent. From Fig. 3.2, $3_{16} = 0011_2$, $D_{16} = 1101$, and $6_{16} = 0110$. Therefore, $982_{10} = 3D6_{16} =$

001111010110_2. Since the 2 leftmost zeros have no meaning, it is common practice to leave them off. Notice the ease in converting a base 10 number to hex and then writing the binary equivalent of each hex symbol. Only three divisions are required instead of the 10 needed with the direct way.

The hex system is also convenient for converting a 16-digit binary number to its base 10 equivalent. To illustrate, the binary number 1101111101100101_2 will be converted to its base 10 equivalent. The first step is to divide the binary digits into groups of four each, starting from the right, and write the hex equivalent of each group:

$$1\ 1\ 0\ 1 \qquad 1\ 1\ 1\ 1 \qquad 0\ 1\ 1\ 0 \qquad 0\ 1\ 0\ 1_2$$

$$\text{D} \qquad\qquad \text{F} \qquad\qquad 6 \qquad\qquad 5$$

$DF65_{16}$ is the hex equivalent of 1101111101100101_2. The next step is to convert $DF65_{16}$ to base 10.

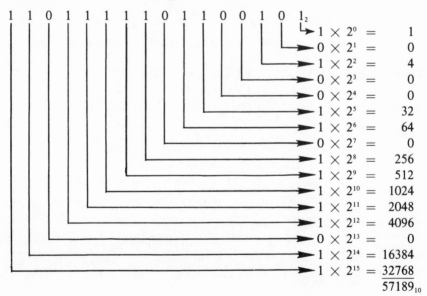

$$
\begin{array}{ll}
\text{D} \quad \text{F} \quad 6 \quad 5_{16} & \\
\;\;\llcorner\!\!\!\rightarrow 5 \times 16^0 = & 5 \\
\;\;\;\;\longrightarrow 6 \times 16^1 = & 96 \\
\;\;\;\;\longrightarrow \text{F} \times 16^2 = 15 \times 16^2 = & 3840 \\
\;\;\;\;\longrightarrow \text{D} \times 16^3 = 13 \times 16^3 = & 53248 \\
\hline
& 57189_{10}
\end{array}
$$

Notice the ease in converting the initial binary number to its base 10 equivalent. To illustrate the other technique, we will convert the binary number, digit for digit, to the base 10 equivalent.

$$1\ 1\ 0\ 1\ 1\ 1\ 1\ 1\ 0\ 1\ 1\ 0\ 0\ 1\ 0\ 1_2$$

$$
\begin{array}{ll}
1 \times 2^0 = & 1 \\
0 \times 2^1 = & 0 \\
1 \times 2^2 = & 4 \\
0 \times 2^3 = & 0 \\
0 \times 2^4 = & 0 \\
1 \times 2^5 = & 32 \\
1 \times 2^6 = & 64 \\
0 \times 2^7 = & 0 \\
1 \times 2^8 = & 256 \\
1 \times 2^9 = & 512 \\
1 \times 2^{10} = & 1024 \\
1 \times 2^{11} = & 2048 \\
1 \times 2^{12} = & 4096 \\
0 \times 2^{13} = & 0 \\
1 \times 2^{14} = & 16384 \\
1 \times 2^{15} = & 32768 \\
\hline
& 57189_{10}
\end{array}
$$

It shall be left to the reader to determine the easiest technique for converting base 10 numbers to their base 2 equivalent.

3.6 Base 10 Fractional Decimals to Binary

Up to now, the only numbers considered have been whole numbers. However, it is often necessary to feed fractional decimal numbers, like .75, into a computer. These must also be in binary form.

To convert a fractional decimal number into binary form, a method known as "repeated multiplication" will be used. To illustrate, we will convert .75 to its binary equivalent:

Step 1: Multiply fractional decimal number by 2:

$$.75$$
$$\underline{\times 2}$$
$$1 \leftarrow \text{①}50$$

Step 2: The 1 or 0 to the left of the decimal point in step 1 is part of the answer. Multiply the remaining numbers to the right of the decimal point by 2:

$$.50$$
$$\underline{\times 2}$$
$$1 \leftarrow \text{①}00$$

Therefore, since the method stipulates stopping when the fractional part of the answer is zero, $.75_{10} = .11_2$. Now remember that

$$.75_{10} = (7 \times 10^{-1}) + (5 \times 10^{-2})$$
$$= .7 + .05$$
$$= .75$$

To convert $.11_2$ back to base 10, the same technique is used (remember that any number to the negative power is the same as that number to the positive power divided into one):

$$.11_2 = (1 \times 2^{-1}) + (1 \times 2^{-2})$$
$$= (1 \times \frac{1}{2}) + (\frac{1}{2^2})$$
$$= (1 \times .5) + (1 \times .25)$$
$$= .5 + .25$$
$$= .75_{10} \quad \text{(It checks)}$$

This all appears relatively straightforward, but, in reality, not all fractional decimal numbers will come out so neatly by continuous multiplication by 2. In these situations, it is common practice to continue until the number of 1's and 0's are equal to the number of individual data lines into the computer. To illustrate, the fractional decimal number $.3017_{10}$ will be converted to binary form:

.3017	.6034	.2068	.4136	.8272
×2	×2	×2	×2	×2
(0).6034	(1).2068	(0).4136	(0).8272	(1).6544
↓	↓	↓	↓	↓
0	1	0	0	1

Therefore, $.3017_{10} = .01001.\ldots$. As can be seen, this answer could continue for many more multiplications, sometimes never coming to an end (fractional part of the answer exactly zero).

3.7 Summary

Any data used by digital computers must be represented in binary notation. In this chapter, several techniques for converting base 10 numbers to binary notation were presented. Also, since data out of the digital computer is in binary form, several techniques were presented to convert the 1's and 0's into fewer symbols so that they can be spoken and written more easily. It is much easier to write the output as $DF65_{16}$ than it is to write 1101111101100101_2.

These binary digits of 1's and 0's are often referred to as *bits* (*bi*nary dig*its*). For example, 11010110 is a binary word consisting of eight bits.

3.8 Examples

1. Convert 1125_{10} to octal (base 8), hex (base 16), and binary (base 2):

1125_{10} to octal:

$$
\begin{array}{ll}
140 & \\
8)\overline{1125} & R = 5 \\
17 & \\
8)\overline{140} & R = 4 \\
2 & \\
8)\overline{17} & R = 1 \\
0 & \\
8)\overline{2} & R = 2
\end{array}
\qquad 1125_{10} = 2145_8
$$

1125_{10} to hex:

$$
\begin{array}{ll}
70 & \\
16)\overline{1125} & R = 5 \\
4 & \\
16)\overline{70} & R = 6 \\
0 & \\
16)\overline{4} & R = 4
\end{array}
\qquad 1125_{10} = 465_{16}
$$

1125_{10} to binary:

$$1125_{10} = 2145_8 = 010001100101_2$$
$$1125_{10} = 465_{16} = 010001100101_2 \text{ (Same result either way)}$$

2. Convert 782_{10} to hex and binary.

782_{10} to hex:

$$\begin{array}{l} 48 \\ 16\overline{)782} \qquad\quad R = 14 = E \\ 3 \\ 16\overline{)48} \qquad\quad\; R = 0 \qquad\quad\uparrow \qquad 782_{10} = 30E_{16} \\ 0 \\ 16\overline{)3} \qquad\quad\;\; R = 3 \end{array}$$

782_{10} to binary:

$$782_{10} = 30E_{16} = 001100001110_2$$

3. Convert the following binary numbers to octal, hex, and decimal.

   (a) 1101011010111100_2

To base 16:
   $1101\quad 0110\quad 1011\quad 1100_2 = D6BC_{16}$
To base 8:
   $1\quad 101\quad 011\quad 010\quad 111\quad 100_2 = 153274_8$
To base 10:
$$\begin{aligned} D6BC &= (C \times 16^0) + (B \times 16^1) + (6 \times 16^2) + (D \times 16^3) \\ &= (12 \times 16^0) + (11 \times 16^1) + (6 \times 16^2) + (13 \times 16^3) \\ &= 12 + 176 + 1536 + 53248 \\ &= 54972_{10} \end{aligned}$$

   (b) 0001011011110101_2:

To base 16:
   $0001\quad 0110\quad 1111\quad 0101_2 = 16F5_{16}$
To base 8:
   $0\quad 001\quad 011\quad 011\quad 110\quad 101_8 = 13365_8$
To base 10:
$$\begin{aligned} 16F5_{16} &= (5 \times 16^0) + (F \times 16^1) + (6 \times 16^2) + (1 \times 16^3) \\ &= (5 \times 16^0) + (15 \times 16^1) + (6 \times 16^2) + (1 \times 16^3) \\ &= 5 + 240 + 1536 + 4096 \\ &= 5877_{10} \end{aligned}$$

4. Convert $.528_{10}$ to binary.

.528	.056	.112	.224	.448	.896
×2	×2	×2	×2	×2	×2
①.056	⓪.112	⓪.224	⓪.448	⓪.896	①.792
↓	↓	↓	↓	↓	↓
1	0	0	0	0	1

Therefore, $.528_{10} = .100001...._2$

Problems

1. Convert the following base 10 numbers to their equivalent binary, octal, and hex numbers:
   (a) 2   (b) 8   (c) 12   (d) 28   (e) 512   (f) 64   (g) 228
   (h) 1156

2. Convert the following base 10 fractional decimal numbers to their equivalent binary numbers:
   (a) .505   (b) .444   (c) .715   (d) .325   (e) .95   (f) .805
   (g) .7   (h) .99

3. Convert the following binary numbers to their octal, hex, and decimal equivalents:
   (a) 110101   (b) 11011101   (c) 10101011   (d) 111111101101
   (e) 111101101   (f) 11000111

4. Convert the following binary numbers to equivalent base 10 numbers:
   (a) 10001011.111   (b) 11000111.011   (c) 11101101.001
   (d) 11100111.101

5. Convert the following octal numbers to decimal numbers:
   (a) 7521   (b) 33   (c) 677   (d) 463   (e) 555

6. Convert the following hex numbers to decimal numbers:
   (a) F6D1   (b) DEF6   (c) 552   (d) 92B   (e) 45FD   (f) FFF1

7. In each case below, add 1 to the number given and write the sum, keeping the answer in the same number system as the problem:
   (a) $99_{10} + 1$ = _____
   (b) $15_{16} + 1$ = _____
   (c) $FF_{16} + 1$ = _____
   (d) $111_2 + 1$ = _____
   (e) $C19_{16} + 1$ = _____

8. Convert the following numbers:
   (a) 48_{10} = _____ (binary)
   (b) 48_{10} = _____ (octal)
   (c) 48_{10} = _____ (hexadecimal)
   (d) $F3_{16}$ = _____ (decimal)
   (e) 1011_2 = _____ (hexadecimal)

9. (a) Express 0111101110000001_2 in both octal and hexadecimal:

Octal: _____   Hexadecimal: _____

4

Digital Arithmetic

In the previous chapter, methods of converting decimal numbers to binary were shown. Emphasis was put on the fact that digital computers can work only in binary 0's and 1's. Now that we have the data in binary, what does the computer do with it? How are these binary numbers added, subtracted, and so forth? These are questions that will be answered in this chapter.

4.1 Binary Addition

Binary numbers are added just as they are in any other number system. In base 10, the one all of us are most familiar with, the rightmost column of numbers is added. If the total exceeds 9, the rightmost digit of the sum is written down and the rest of the total is carried to the next column. For example, if 14 and 19 are added, first the 9 and the 4 are added together, resulting in 13. The 3 is written down, and the 1 (which represents 10) is carried to the second column, which is the tens column. This carry is then added to the numbers in the second column, as follows:

$$
\begin{array}{r}
(1) \quad \text{carry} \\
1\ 9 \\
\underline{1\ 4} \\
3\ 3
\end{array}
$$

Binary numbers are added in much the same way. However, it must be kept in mind that the binary system has only 0's and 1's. When adding binary numbers, four possible combinations exist:

$$
\begin{array}{cccc}
& & & (1) \quad \text{carry} \\
\text{(a)} +0 & \text{(b)} +1 & \text{(c)} +0 & \text{(d)} +1 \\
\underline{+0} & \underline{+0} & \underline{+1} & \underline{+1} \\
+0 & +1 & +1 & +10
\end{array}
$$

In (d), the answer can be verified by converting the answer to base 10:

$$(0 \times 2^0) + (1 \times 2^1) = 0 + 2 = 2_{10}$$

With this in mind, we're now ready to do our first binary addition. If the binary equivalent of 7_{10} and 5_{10} are added, the results, when converted to base 10, will be 12_{10}. Thus, 111_2 (7_{10}) and 101_2 (5_{10}) will be added:

$$(C)(B)(A)$$
$$1\ 1\ 1$$
$$+\underline{1\ 0\ 1}$$

The first step is to add 1 and 1 (column A). The result is 0 with a carry of 1:

$$(1)\quad \text{carry}$$
$$1\ 1\ 1$$
$$+\underline{1\ 0\ 1}$$
$$0$$

The next step is to add 1 and 0 (column B) to the carry of 1 (from column A). The result is 0 with a carry of 1:

$$(1)\quad \text{carry}$$
$$1\ 1\ 1$$
$$+\underline{1\ 0\ 1}$$
$$0\ 0$$

The next step is the most confusing, for 1 and 1 (column C) and 1 (carry from column B) are to be added. We must add just as before, keeping track of the carries in the next column as they occur. Thus, $1 + 1$ is 0 with a carry of 1. Place the carry in the next column, then add the remaining 1 to the 0 just obtained:

$$(1)\quad \text{carry}$$
$$1\ 1\ 1$$
$$+\underline{1\ 0\ 1}$$
$$1\ 0\ 0$$

Since there are no additional numbers to be added, the last 1 (carry from column C) is brought down into the answer:

$$1\ 1\ 1$$
$$+\underline{1\ 0\ 1}$$
$$1\ 1\ 0\ 0$$

To check the answer, 1100_2 is converted back to base 10 by the techniques explained in Chap. 3:

$$1100_2 = (0 \times 2^0) + (0 \times 2^1) + (1 \times 2^2) + (1 \times 2^3)$$
$$= 0 + 0 + 4 + 8$$
$$= 12_{10}$$

To illustrate further, let's add the numbers 421_{10} and 137_{10} in decimal and in binary, then check the binary result by converting to decimal. First, we convert 421_{10} and 137_{10} to binary:

421_{10} to binary

$$
\begin{array}{r}
26 \\
16\overline{)421} \\
1 \\
16\overline{)26} \\
0 \\
16\overline{)1}
\end{array}
\qquad
\begin{array}{l}
R = 5 \\
\\
R = 10 = A \\
\\
R = 1
\end{array}
$$

Therefore, $421_{10} = 1A5_{16} = 000110100101_2$ (the leftmost zeros are insignificant and may be left off).

137_{10} to binary:

$$
\begin{array}{r}
8 \\
16\overline{)137} \\
0 \\
16\overline{)8}
\end{array}
\qquad
\begin{array}{l}
R = 9 \\
\\
R = 8
\end{array}
$$

Therefore, $137_{10} = 89_{16} = 10001001_2$. Now add their binary equivalents:

$$
\begin{array}{l}
(1)(1) \qquad\qquad (1) \\
\ \ 1\ 1\ 0\ 1\ 0\ 0\ 1\ 0\ 1 \quad \leftarrow 421_{10} \\
+\ \ \ \ 1\ 0\ 0\ 0\ 1\ 0\ 0\ 1 \quad \leftarrow 137_{10} \\
\hline
1\ 0\ 0\ 0\ 1\ 0\ 1\ 1\ 1\ 0
\end{array}
$$

The result of 1000101110_2 or $22E_{16}$ can now be converted to decimal to verify the answer:

$$
\begin{aligned}
22E_{16} &= (E \times 16^0) + (2 \times 16^1) + (2 \times 16^2) \\
&= (14 \times 1) + (2 \times 16) + (2 \times 256) \\
&= 14 + 32 + 512 \\
&= 558_{10} \quad \text{(It checks)}
\end{aligned}
$$

Decimal Check

$$
\begin{array}{r}
421 \\
+137 \\
\hline
558_{10}
\end{array}
$$

Often in performing binary multiplication, $1 + 1 + 1$ or $1 + 1 + 1 + 1$ will have to be added. These are added in much the same way except that the number of carries must be carefully determined. To add $1 + 1 + 1$, $1 + 1$ are first added resulting in 0 and a 1 in the carry column. Next, the remaining 1 is added to the 0 from the previous addition resulting in a 1. Since there was only a 1 carry, it is brought down into the answer:

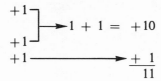

Likewise,

$$
\begin{array}{l}
\left.\begin{array}{l} +1 \\ +1 \end{array}\right\} \!\!\!\!\rightarrow 1 + 1 = +10 \\[2ex]
\left.\begin{array}{l} +1 \\ +1 \end{array}\right\} \!\!\!\!\rightarrow 1 + 1 = \underline{+10} \\
\phantom{\left.\begin{array}{l} +1 \\ +1 \end{array}\right\} \!\!\!\!\rightarrow 1 + 1 = } 100
\end{array}
$$

4.2 Binary Subtraction

The circuitry required for digital computers to add binary numbers is relatively simple. However, since circuitry to subtract binary numbers is very difficult to design and build, another subtraction method (other than that familiar to us) would be desirable. The method is known as "subtraction by addition of the 1's or 2's complements" of the number.

The 1's complement of a binary number is formed by inverting each binary digit of the number, that is, by changing all 1's to 0's and all 0's to 1's. The 2's complement is formed by adding 1 to the 1's complement, as follows:

$$
\begin{array}{lll}
\text{Binary number} & = & 01100100 \\
\text{1's complement} & = & 10011011 \\
\text{2's complement} & = & 10011100
\end{array}
$$

Most computers on the market perform subtraction by "the addition of the 2's complement" of the subtrahend. Subtraction by "the addition of the 1's complement" requires much more hardware to implement. Therefore, we will concentrate only on subtraction by "the addition of the 2's complement."

When a subtraction is performed, the answer can be positive or negative, depending upon the relative value of the minuend and the subtrahend. We must, therefore, in some way account for the sign of the answer. As will become apparent in later chapters, the data in most microprocessors is represented by eight binary digits, called *bits*. The leftmost bit, called the *most significant bit* (MSB), is used as the sign bit. If the MSB is a "1," the number represented by the remaining seven bits is assumed to be negative and is represented by its 2's complement. If the MSB is a "0," the number represented in the remaining seven bits is positive and is equal to the binary equivalent of these seven bits. Thus,

$$0\ 1\ 1\ 1\ 0\ 0\ 0\ 1 = +71_{16} = +113_{10}$$

⎿—Sign bit = +

or

$$1\ 1\ 1\ 0\ 1\ 1\ 0\ 1 = -6D_{16} = -109_{10}$$

⎿—Sign bit = −

Let us illustrate by taking a relatively simple example. The number 5_{10} will be subtracted from the number 15_{10}. The eight-bit number 00000101 is the binary representation of 5_{10}, and 00001111 is the binary representation of 15_{10}:

Decimal Subtraction:

$$\begin{array}{r} 15 \\ -\ 5 \\ \hline +10 \end{array}$$

Subtraction by Addition of 2's Complement:

Since the number 5 will be subtracted from the number 15, 5 must be represented in its 2's complement form:

$$0\ 0\ 0\ 0\ 0\ 1\ 0\ 1 = 5_{10}$$
$$1\ 1\ 1\ 1\ 1\ 0\ 1\ 0 = 1\text{'s complement of } 5_{10}$$
$$1\ 1\ 1\ 1\ 1\ 0\ 1\ 1 = 2\text{'s complement of } 5_{10}$$

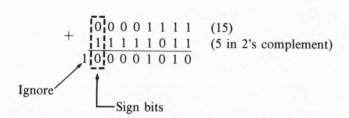

The answer is therefore $+0A_{16}$ or $+10_{10}$.

Included in the M6800 microprocessor, which we will soon be studying in detail, is a Condition Code Register containing several bits that indicate the status of the results of certain operations. One of these bits is an N (for negative) bit. If the arithmetic operation sets the MSB of the answer, indicating a negative answer, the N bit will be set to a "1." Otherwise, it will be a "0."

The Condition Code Register also contains a C bit. If the *absolute* value of the subtrahend is larger than the *absolute* value of the minuend, the C bit will be set to a "1"; otherwise, it will be set to a "0." In this last example, both the C bit and N bit will be a "0."

To illustrate further, let's now reverse the numbers of the first example and subtract the number 15_{10} from the number 5_{10}:

Decimal Subtraction:

$$\begin{array}{r} 5 \\ -15 \\ \hline -10 \end{array}$$

Subtraction by Addition of 2's Complement:

$$0\ 0\ 0\ 0\ 1\ 1\ 1\ 1\ =\ 15_{10}$$
$$1\ 1\ 1\ 1\ 0\ 0\ 0\ 0\ =\ \text{1's complement of } 15_{10}$$
$$1\ 1\ 1\ 1\ 0\ 0\ 0\ 1\ =\ \text{2's complement of } 15_{10}$$

$$+ \begin{array}{l} 0|0\ 0\ 0\ 0\ 1\ 0\ 1 \quad (5) \\ 1|1\ 1\ 1\ 0\ 0\ 0\ 1 \quad (15 \text{ in 2's complement}) \\ 1|1\ 1\ 1\ 0\ 1\ 1\ 0 \quad = -00001010_2 = -0A_{16} = -10_{10} \end{array}$$

∟ Sign bits

In this problem, the N bit and the C bit will be set to a "1." The "1" in the MSB of the answer indicates that the answer is negative, and the value is the 2's complement of the result shown.

As you can see from these two examples, bit 7 serves as the sign bit. A "0" in bit 7 indicates a positive number. Thus, the maximum possible positive number is 01111111, or $+7F_{16}$, which is $+127_{10}$. Likewise, a "1" in bit 7 indicates a negative number. The maximum possible negative number, represented in 2's complement, is 10000000, or -80_{16}, which is -128_{10}. The maximum possible range of numbers is shown in Fig. 4.1, assuming that the data is represented in eight bits.

The next logical question that one may ask is what happens if a number is subtracted from a negative number. It is possible to subtract (or add) two numbers and obtain an invalid answer. This situation is referred to as a 2's complement overflow. In addition to the C and N bits just described, the Condition Code Register also contains a V bit. When a subtraction (or addition) is performed and a 2's complement overflow occurs, the V bit will be set

Number in 2's complement	Binary equivalent number	Hex equivalent number	Decimal equivalent
0111 1111(7F)	0111 1111	7F	+127
0111 1110(7E)	0111 1110	7E	+126
0111 1101(7D)	0111 1101	7D	+125
•	•	•	•
•	•	•	•
•	•	•	•
0000 0010(02)	0000 0010	02	+2
0000 0001(01)	0000 0001	01	+1
0000 0000(00)	0000 0000	00	0
1111 1111(FF)	−0000 0001	−01	−1
1111 1110(FE)	−0000 0010	−02	−2
•	•	•	•
•	•	•	•
•	•	•	•
1000 0010(82)	−0111 1110	−7E	−126
1000 0001(81)	−0111 1111	−7F	−127
1000 0000(80)	−1000 0000	−80	−128

Fig. 4.1 Maximum possible range of numbers

to a "1"; otherwise, it will be cleared. To illustrate, let us subtract the hex number 45 (69_{10}) from the hex number −60 (-96_{10}). The minuend (-96_{10}) must already be in the 2's complement representation:

Decimal Subtraction:

$$
\begin{array}{r}
-\ 96 \\
-\ 69 \\
\hline
-165
\end{array}
$$
(outside of allowable range)

Subtraction by Addition of 2's Complement:

$$
\begin{array}{l}
0\ 1\ 1\ 0\ 0\ 0\ 0\ 0\ (60_{16}) \\
1\ 0\ 0\ 1\ 1\ 1\ 1\ 1\ (\text{1's complement of } 60_{16}) \\
1\ 0\ 1\ 0\ 0\ 0\ 0\ 0\ (\text{2's complement of } 60_{16})
\end{array}
$$

$$
\begin{array}{l}
0\ 1\ 0\ 0\ 0\ 1\ 0\ 1\ (45_{16}) \\
1\ 0\ 1\ 1\ 1\ 0\ 1\ 0\ (\text{1's complement of } 45_{16}) \\
1\ 0\ 1\ 1\ 1\ 0\ 1\ 1\ (\text{2's complement of } 45_{16})
\end{array}
$$

$$
\begin{array}{r}
1\ 0\ 1\ 0\ 0\ 0\ 0\ 0\ (\text{2's complement of } 60_{16}) \\
+\quad 1\ 0\ 1\ 1\ 1\ 0\ 1\ 1\ (\text{2's complement of } 45_{16}) \\
\hline
1\ 0\ 1\ 0\ 1\ 0\ 1\ 1\ 0\ 1\ 1
\end{array}
$$

The above subtraction by the addition of the 2's complement resulted in an answer of $+5B_{16}$, which is $+91_{10}$. Therefore, the V bit will be set to a "1" since the answer should be -165_{10}.

4.3 Binary Multiplication

Binary multiplication is quite similar to decimal multiplication. If the decimal numbers 16 and 12 are multiplied, the first step is to multiply 2 × 6, resulting in 12:

$$
\begin{array}{r}
(1) \quad \text{carry} \\
16 \\
\times \ 12 \\
\hline
2
\end{array}
$$

The 2 is written down, and the 1, which is the ten's unit ($12 = 10 + 2$), is carried to the next digit, as shown above. Then 1 is multiplied by 2, and the carry of 1 from the first multiplication is added to the result:

$$
\begin{array}{r}
16 \\
\times 12 \\
\hline
32
\end{array}
$$

Then the 6 is multiplied by 1, and the answer, 6, is placed under the 3 (shifted one digit to the left):

$$
\begin{array}{r}
16 \\
\times 12 \\
\hline
32 \\
6
\end{array}
$$

After multiplying 1 by 1 and placing the result, 1, to the left of the 6 from the previous step, the final answer is obtained by adding the partial results:

$$
\begin{array}{r}
16 \\
\times \ \ 12 \\
\hline
32 \\
16 \ \\
\hline
192
\end{array}
$$

Just as a multiplication table has to be learned for the decimal system, a multiplication table for binary numbers must also be memorized:

$$
\begin{array}{l}
0 \times 0 = 0 \\
0 \times 1 = 0 \\
1 \times 0 = 0 \\
1 \times 1 = 1
\end{array}
$$

As can be seen, this multiplication table is much easier to remember than the decimal multiplication table drilled into us in our early school days.

To illustrate the ease with which binary numbers can be multiplied, the same two numbers (16_{10} and 12_{10}) used in the previous example will be used again:

$$16_{10} = 10000_2$$
$$12_{10} = 1100_2$$

$$
\begin{array}{r}
10000 \\
\times\ 1100 \\
\hline
00000 \\
00000 \\
10000 \\
10000 \\
\hline
11000000_2
\end{array}
$$

This is a relatively simple example, since there are no carries, but the basic principles are the same. To check:

$$
\begin{aligned}
11000000_2 &= (1 \times 2^6) + (1 \times 2^7) \\
&= 64 + 128 \\
&= 192_{10} \quad \text{(It checks)}
\end{aligned}
$$

Let us look at another example. The binary numbers 101_2 and 11_2 will be multiplied. In decimal notation this would be $5_{10} \times 3_{10}$, which is known to be 15_{10}.

Step 1:

$$
\begin{array}{r}
101 \\
\times\ 11 \\
\hline
101 \quad (1 \times 101 = 101)
\end{array}
$$

Step 2:

$$
\begin{array}{r}
101 \\
\times\ 11 \\
\hline
101 \\
101 \quad (1 \times 101 = 101)
\end{array}
$$

Step 3: Add partial results:

$$
\begin{array}{r}
101 \\
\times\ 11 \\
\hline
101 \\
+\ 101 \\
\hline
1111_2
\end{array}
$$

Therefore, $1111_2 = 15_{10}$.

A more difficult example, illustrating binary multiplication with carries, is $1111_2 \times 111_2$. In decimal, this would be $15_{10} \times 7_{10}$, or 105_{10}.

```
   1111
×   111
   1111
+ 1111
   1111
```

In adding these partial results, one must be very careful:

Step 1: Bring the rightmost 1 down as part of the answer:

```
  1111
  1111
  1111
      1
```

Step 2: Add the 1 and 1, resulting in 0 with a carry of 1:

```
 (1)   carry
 1 1 1 1
 1 1 1 1
1 1 1 1
      0 1
```

Step 3: There are now four 1's to be added to form the next part of the answer. This can be thought of as adding 1 and 1, resulting in 0 with a carry of 1; then adding the next 1 to the 0, resulting in 1; and finally, adding the last 1, resulting in 0 with another carry of 1 (two carries):

```
 (1)
 (1)(1)   carry
 1 1 1 1
 1 1 1 1
1 1 1 1
     0 0 1
```

Step 4: Similar to step 3. Adding $1 + 1 + 1 + 1 + 1$ results in a 1 with two carries:

```
 (1)
 (1)1 1 1 1
 1 1 1 1
1 1 1 1
   1 0 0 1
```

Step 5: Same as step 3 ($1 + 1 + 1 + 1 = 0$ with two carries):

$$\begin{array}{r} (1) \quad 1\ 1\ 1\ 1 \\ (1)\ 1\ 1\ 1\ 1 \\ 1\ 1\ 1\ 1 \\ \hline 0\ 1\ 0\ 0\ 1 \end{array}$$

Step 6: Add last three 1's ($1 + 1 + 1 = 1$ with one carry):

$$\begin{array}{r} 1\ 1\ 1\ 1 \\ \times\quad 1\ 1\ 1 \\ \hline 1\ 1\ 1\ 1 \\ 1\ 1\ 1\ 1 \\ 1\ 1\ 1\ 1 \\ \hline 1\ 1\ 0\ 1\ 0\ 0\ 1_2 \end{array}$$

Checking the result:

$$\begin{aligned} 1101001_2 &= 69_{16} \\ &= 9 \times 16^0 + 6 \times 16^1 \\ &= 9 + 96 \\ &= 105_{10} \quad \text{(It checks)} \end{aligned}$$

Multiplication with digital computers is often accomplished with the program in memory rather than the hardware itself. The theory and basics just covered are implemented by the program to perform a binary multiplication. As was just explained, binary multiplication is nothing more than a series of shifts and adds of the multiplicand. A multiplication program shown in Chap. 11 illustrates these principles.

4.4 Binary Division

Binary division is accomplished in nearly the same way as decimal division. The division table is very simple:

$$\left. \begin{array}{c} \dfrac{0}{0} \\[2em] \dfrac{1}{0} \end{array} \right\} \quad \text{Meaningless, just as it is in the decimal system} \qquad \qquad \begin{array}{c} \dfrac{0}{1} = 0 \\[1.5em] \dfrac{1}{1} = 1 \end{array}$$

To illustrate binary division, the number 18 will be divided by 6. Since $18_{10} = 10010_2$ and $6_{10} = 110$, the problem is written as

$$110\overline{)10010}$$

Step 1: Since 110 is larger than 100, it will not divide into 100. Therefore, 110 is divided into 1001.

$$\begin{array}{r} 1 \\ 110\overline{)10010} \\ \underline{110} \\ 11 \end{array}$$

Subtracting 110 from 1001 can be thought of in the following way. What number, when added to 110, will equal 1001? Obviously,

$$11 + 110 = 1001$$

Step 2: Bring down the last 0 and divide again, just as in the decimal case:

$$\begin{array}{r} 11 \\ 110\overline{)10010} \\ \underline{110} \\ 110 \\ \underline{110} \end{array}$$

The answer, 11_2, checks with the known answer of 3_{10}.

Very often in division, the answer will not come out even. Again, this problem is handled in much the same way as it is in the decimal system. To illustrate, 27_{10} will be divided by 4_{10}. First, we must convert 27_{10} to binary:

$$\begin{array}{r} 1 \\ 16\overline{)27} \end{array} \qquad R = 11 = B$$

$$\begin{array}{r} 0 \\ 16\overline{)1} \end{array} \qquad R = 1$$

$$27_{10} = 1B_{16} = 00011011_2$$

Since $4_{10} = 100_2$, the division proceeds as follows:

Step 1:

$$\begin{array}{r} 1 \\ 100\overline{)11011} \\ \underline{100} \\ 101 \end{array}$$

Step 2:

$$\begin{array}{r} 11 \\ 100\overline{)11011} \\ \underline{100} \\ 101 \\ \underline{100} \\ 1 \end{array}$$

Step 3:

$$
\begin{array}{r}
110 \\
100 \overline{)11011} \\
\underline{100} \\
101 \\
\underline{100} \\
11
\end{array}
$$

Step 4:

$$
\begin{array}{r}
110.1 \\
100 \overline{)11011.0} \\
\underline{100} \\
101 \\
\underline{100} \\
110 \\
\underline{100} \\
10
\end{array}
$$

Step 5:

$$
\begin{array}{r}
110.11 \\
100 \overline{)11011.00} \\
\underline{100} \\
101 \\
\underline{100} \\
110 \\
\underline{100} \\
100 \\
\underline{100}
\end{array}
$$

To convert 110.11_2 to the decimal system as a check, we use the methods of Chap. 3:

$$
\begin{aligned}
110.11_2 &= (1 \times 2^{-2}) + (1 \times 2^{-1}) + (0 \times 2^0) + (1 \times 2^1) + (1 \times 2^2) \\
&= (1 \times \tfrac{1}{4}) + (1 \times \tfrac{1}{2}) + 0 + 2 + 4 \\
&= .25 + .5 + 2 + 4 \\
&= 6.75_{10} \quad \text{(It checks)}
\end{aligned}
$$

Again, as in multiplication, division is usually accomplished in digital computers with a computer program (to be discussed later) rather than with electronic circuitry. However, the principle just discussed must be understood if the computer program is to be understood.

4.5 Binary Coded Decimal

Another method of representing numbers in digital computers is known as *Binary Coded Decimal* (BCD). In the BCD system, *each* decimal digit is represented with its own binary equivalent number. For example, 743_{10} would be represented in BCD as:

0111	0100	0011
7	4	3

It must be emphasized that BCD and binary are not the same; for example, 49_{10} in binary is 110001_2, but in BCD it is 01001001.

Many devices use BCD format for data transmitted and received. Consequently, we must know how to handle this data. Adding numbers in BCD can cause problems if we are not fully aware of the possibility of invalid results. To illustrate, let us add the numbers 60_{10} and 55_{10} in BCD:

$$60_{10} = 0110\ 0000$$
$$55_{10} = \underline{0101\ 0101}$$
$$1011\ 0101$$

As you can see, the answer is invalid since 1011 is not a valid BCD number. We know that the decimal answer is 115. Therefore, a correction must be made. Notice what happens when 60 is added to the above result:

$$1011\ 0101$$
$$\underline{0110\ 0000}$$
$$1\ \ 0001\ 0101$$
$$1\ \ \ \ 1\ \ \ \ \ 5$$

We now have the correct answer, 115. The M6800 Microprocessor has an instruction (DAA) that will make whatever adjustments are necessary to correct an invalid result.

A "Binary to BCD Conversion" program is presented in Chap. 11. This program takes binary numbers and structures them into the BCD format:

Decimal number	BCD representation
0	0000
1	0001
2	0010
3	0011
4	0100
5	0101
6	0110
7	0111
8	1000
9	1001

Problems

1. Perform the following additions in binary (numbers given are in decimal). Verify the results in decimal.

  (a)   9   (b)   28   (c)   158
      +3   +21   + 72

  (d)   128   (e)   16   (f)   178
     +128   +22   +642

2. Perform the following subtractions (numbers given are in decimal) by "addition of 2's complement." Verify your answer in decimal.

  (a)   10   (b)   26   (c)   142
     − 3   − 5   − 73

  (d)   17   (e)   50   (f)   33
     −16   −42   −11

3. Perform the following multiplications in binary (numbers given are in decimal). Verify your answers in decimal.

  (a)   5   (b)   12   (c)   13   (d)   125
    ×6   × 8   × 2   × 3

  (e)   123   (f)   12   (g)   8   (h)   17
    × 12   ×12   ×4   ×17

4. Perform the following division in binary (numbers given are in decimal). Verify your answers in decimal.

  (a) 6)$\overline{36}$ (b) 6)$\overline{40}$ (c) 8)$\overline{46}$ (d) 26)$\overline{78}$

  (e) 24)$\overline{108}$ (f) 25)$\overline{179}$ (g) 3)$\overline{47}$ (h) 7)$\overline{60}$

  (i) 10)$\overline{105}$

5. Show the following decimal numbers in binary and BCD:

  (a) 9   (b) 13   (c) 42   (d) 92

  (e) 103   (f) 783   (g) 1243   (h) 9436

5

Microcomputers—
What Are They?

At this point, we've learned how to convert decimal numbers to binary numbers (1's and 0's); how binary numbers can be added subtracted, multiplied, and divided; and what logic elements are. Where does all this fit into a computer system? What can a computer do? How does a computer work? How does it know what to do? Does it think for itself? These are some of the questions that will be addressed in this chapter.

5.1 History

Computers are not new. The abacus, which originated many centuries ago, is a form of digital computer. This calculating device, illustrated in Fig. 5.1, can be used to add, subtract, multiply, and divide. Each column contains two beads above the crossbar and five beads below it. Each bead above the cross bar represents five units, and each bead below it represents one unit. Notice the value of each column as shown below the abacus. The number depicted is 10201. If the number 60201 were to be illustrated, a bead above the cross bar in the 10,000 column would also be raised. Details of "abacus arithmetic" will not be shown here. However, with a little imagination, partic-

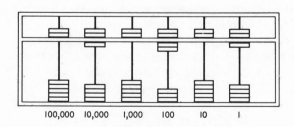

100,000   10,000   1,000   100   10   1

Fig. 5.1 Abacus

ularly after reviewing the chapters on number systems, one can understand how the abacus is a form of computer.

The first mechanical adding machine was developed in the 1600s. Several other types of adding machines and various rudimentary forms of digital computers were invented over the next 350 years. In the late 1940s, the first real "electronic" computers were introduced, but they used vacuum tubes. Such tubes were not really the answer, since they are quite large (1 to 3 in. high), require large amounts of power as well as space, and generate tremendous amounts of heat.

With the invention of the transistor, a semiconductor device, in the late 1940s and early 1950s, many of the problems associated with tubes were solved. Transistors are small compared to tubes (¼ in. high) and require relatively little power. They made it possible to design and build digital computers which could be housed in cabinets and racks that would easily fit in a modestly sized room.

Then in the late 1960s and early 1970s, the microprocessor was born. With this new technology, we were able to replace a module containing 5 to 10,000 transistors with a small piece of semiconductor material less than ¼-inch square; thus, the term *micro*processor. Although the basic principles of digital computing changed very little, this small chip of semiconductor material, often referred to as an "integrated circuit," opened the door to a whole new era of microelectronics. New computer-controlled applications that were beyond our wildest dreams several years earlier now started to emerge. Hand-held electronic calculators—a luxury item for the average person only several years ago—are now available to everyone. Electronic TV games, such as ping-pong, are also a by-product of the microprocessor. The list is endless.

"MPU" and "MICROPROCESSOR": These terms are used interchangeably.

Even though the microprocessor has already affected our lives, its full impact is yet to come. By 1985, a large number of homes in the U.S. will have some kind of computer-based system containing, in all probability, a microprocessor. These microprocessor-based systems will control lights, pool motors, monitor a security system, keep tax records, store recipes, and so forth. The only limitation is one's own imagination. Functions previously performed by computers costing thousands of dollars in the 1960s can now be handled by a microprocessor-based system costing less than $1,000 and occupying much, much less space. A microcomputer kit, which can be assembled in less than 10 hours, can be purchased for less than $200 today.

We are indeed entering a new era.

5.2 Computer Model

Before the microcomputer system is studied in detail, let us first develop a computer model to illustrate its basics.

Picture yourself sitting at a large desk. The shirt you are wearing has a pocket on each side. To your left is a stack of cards, face down, each with an instruction printed on its face. To your right is a small blackboard, a piece of chalk, and an eraser. Directly in front of you are two trays, an input tray and an output tray. On the wall is a large clock.

We have now created a a situation which is analogous to a microcomputer system. *You* will act as the MPU. You will pick a card off the deck of cards once each minute and execute the instruction printed on its face. The deck of cards can be referred to as a *"Read Only Memory" (ROM)*, since its contents cannot be changed. Each card in this ROM represents an "instruction" in memory.

The blackboard, chalk, and eraser to your right may also be referred to as a type of memory. However, in this memory, you can write things down and erase them later on. Such a memory can be referred to as a *"Random Access Memory" (RAM)*, since it may be written on or changed at random. It can be used for storing data (writing information).

Time (each minute) will be determined by the clock on the wall. Any operation performed by you (the MPU) must be done in an orderly, timed sequence.

The two trays in front of you are the "input" and "output" trays. Information to you (the MPU) must come through the input tray. Likewise, output from the MPU must go through the output tray. The input tray, in this system, is filled with cards containing random numbers from 1 to 10.

The pockets in your shirt each contain a sheet of paper large enough to write one number on and a pencil with an eraser. Your left pocket may be referred to as an "A accumulator." An accumulator is similar to the RAM (Random Access Memory) except that it can hold only one number whereas the RAM can store several numbers. Your right pocket may be referred to as your "B accumulator." Both accumulators are identical and perform identical functions, that is, providing temporary locations for the storage of numbers.

The instructions in your program (ROM) will direct you (the MPU) to accumulate, by the addition of numbers from the input tray, five odd numbers greater than 100 on your blackboard (RAM). The instructions on the first eight cards read as follows:

Card 1:   Read a number from the input basket and write this number on the paper in your left pocket (A accumulator).

Card 2:   Is the number odd? If yes, skip cards 3, 4, and 5.

Card 3:   Read a number from the input basket and write this number on the paper in your right pocket (B accumulator).

Card 4:   Add the numbers from your right and left pocket and put the result
           on the paper in your left pocket.
Card 5:   Is the number odd? If not, go back to card 3.
Card 6:   Is the number greater than 100? If not, return to card 3.
Card 7:   Write the number located in your left pocket on your blackboard.
Card 8:   Are there five numbers on your blackboard? If not, return to card 1.

Just as an instruction from your deck of cards—the program in memory (ROM)—is read and executed by you in sequence (unless you—the MPU —are told to *branch* to some other instruction) during some time interval, so does a microcomputer system execute *its* instructions. In our analogous system, data is stored in temporary locations (pockets and blackboard). A microcomputer system also contains temporary storage locations, called *accumulators* and *RAMS,* that function in much the same way. Microcomputer systems also have a clock to control the sequence of events, and the input and output trays of our model system are similar in function to those of a microcomputer system.

Notice that as each instruction is read, you must either make a logical decision based on the contents of the instruction or perform some calculation. These actions are the function of the microprocessor in a microcomputer system. However, in the latter, the instructions have to be coded in some manner. Remember that digital computers respond only to a binary (1's and 0's) language. Therefore, each instruction in our analogous system must be represented by a binary number. For example, card 4 might contain the binary number 00011011 ($1B_{16}$), which would be interpreted by the MPU as "add the contents of the A accumulator to the contents of the B accumulator and put the results in the A accumulator."

As you probably have concluded by this time, a microcomputer system consists of five elements: (1) a microprocessor (MPU), (2) a random access memory (RAM), (3) a read only memory (ROM), (4) a clock, and (5) some technique for getting data in and out of the system (input and output).

5.3 The Microprocessor (MPU)

The role of a microprocessor chip is analogous to the role you played in the computer model just discussed. It is so small that it can be held in your hand, yet it contains all the electronics necessary to perform arithmetic, control, and logical functions. Since the MPU must communicate with other devices in the system, it must have some way to decide which one of them— RAM, ROM, input, output—it wishes to "address." This problem is solved by attaching several wires, called *lines,* to each device in the system. Since these lines "address" the device the MPU wishes to communicate with, they are referred to as an "address bus." Most MPUs today contain 16 address lines. By charging some of them at a high voltage (logical 1's) and some at a low voltage (logical 0's) an address is generated. The device with that address will then communicate with the MPU. (Multiple device addressing will be covered in Chap. 10.) For example, consider the 16 lines (wires) that make up the address bus in Fig. 5.2. Assume that we wish to communicate with a device whose address is 8321_{16}. The binary pattern of 8321_{16} is 1000 0011 0010 0001. If each line that represents a "1" in this binary number were charged at 5 V and each line that represents a "0" were charged at 0 V, only one device at the other end of these wires (bus) would answer to that address and communicate with the MPU. Notice that the arrows of the address bus in Fig. 5.2 all lead from the MPU in the direction of the devices, thereby indicating that all addresses are generated by the MPU. Notice also that the individual lines are numbered 0 through 15. Since each line will have either a high or low voltage to represent a binary "1" or "0," the lines will be collectively referred to as "bits," a term derived from the words bi*nary digi*ts. The 16 lines, then, are referred to as "16 bits." Standard practice is to refer to the first line (the least significant bit when treated as a binary number) as bit 0, the second line as bit 1, and so on to the sixteenth line (the most significant bit when treated as a binary number), which is referred to as bit 15. It is also common practice to refer to a group of eight bits as one "byte." Therefore, the address bus of 16 bits wide would be two bytes wide. Bits 0 through 7 make up the *least significant* byte, and bits 8 through 15 make up the *most significant* byte (see Fig. 5.3).

Just as the MPU must address the device that it wishes to communicate with, it must also have some channel through which it can send data to, or receive data from, the device after it has been addressed. Similarly, when you dial an address (number) on your phone, there must be some way of sending and receiving data (talking and listening). In a computer, this transaction takes place on a series of wires (lines) referred to as a "data bus." Most

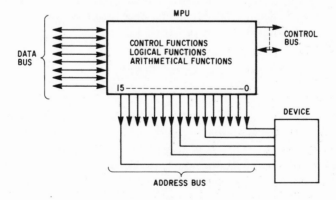

Fig. 5.2 MPU

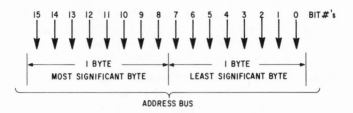

Fig. 5.3 Address bus

MPUs today use a data bus consisting of eight data lines (bits) although there are some MPUs with 16 data lines. Notice the doubly directed arrows of the data lines in Fig. 5.2, indicating that data can be sent or received by the MPU. Again, a high voltage on a data line indicates a binary "1," and a low voltage indicates a "0."

The third type of microcomputer "bus" is the "control bus." Its lines control the sequence of events for the total system. For example, when there is data on the data bus, it is the job of the control bus to inform a device whether the MPU is just trying to get data from it or whether the device should store the data on the data bus, that is, whether it should "read" or "write." Several separate functions are performed by the control bus of any microcomputer system, varying from one type of microprocessor to the next. These differences will be discussed in detail in Chap. 9.

As was shown in our model, the MPU must provide areas for temporary storage of data. Some MPUs have one accumulator, but many have two or more. The system we will be studying in Chap. 9 uses two accumulators, an A accumulator and a B accumulator. Accumulators are often referred to as "registers," for example, the A register or the B register.

Other registers also found in MPUs are the *program counter,* the *index register,* the *stack pointer register,* and the *condition code register.* These will be discussed in detail in later chapters, since their characteristics are often a function of the individual type of MPU.

5.4 Random Access Memory (RAM)

As was illustrated in the computer model presented earlier, a RAM is an area where data may be stored; this data may be erased at any time and new data stored in its place.

The data bus in Fig. 5.4 is the same as that shown in Fig. 5.2 for the MPU. In this simplified example, notice the three "chip selects" marked S1, S2, and S̄3. Also notice the "word select" lines marked A0 through A6. It is through these sets of lines that a RAM memory location is addressed. The function of the "chip select" might be compared to selecting a page in a book whereas that of the "word select" might be compared to selecting a line on that

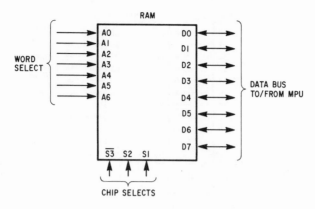

Fig. 5.4 RAM

page. Both "chip selects" and "word selects" are means of specifying an address on the RAM. These lines will therefore be connected to the address bus from the MPU, but a set of rules must be observed to achieve the desired address.

When a high signal ("1") is applied to S1 and S2 of Fig. 5.4 and a low signal ("0") is applied to $\overline{S3}$, this particular RAM will be addressed. As you can see, then, the address of a RAM is determined by the way S1, S2, and $\overline{S3}$ are connected to the address bus. For example, if S1 and S2 were connected to bit 14 and bit 15 of the address bus, respectively, and $\overline{S3}$ were connected to bit 13, the address of this RAM would be 1100 0000 0XXX XXXX. (The assumption is made that this address is for one device only.) The X's shown in the address will be connected to the word select lines to address an individual word in *this* RAM.

Since there are seven word select lines, the number of words that may be addressed on this particular RAM range from 000 0000 (all lines with 0 volts) to 111 1111 (all lines to a high voltage). This binary range is equivalent to 00–7F (base 16), which is the same as 128 locations. As you probably have realized by now, the data word length acceptable to the RAM is eight bits (one byte), which can be put directly on the data bus.

The relationship between the MPU and the RAM is illustrated in Fig. 5.5. The R/W line shown is a signal line from the MPU to inform external devices that the MPU wants (1) to read data, if this line is high, or (2) send (write) data, if it is low.

To expand on the word selection process of a RAM, let's assume that the chip selects and word selects are tied to the MPU address bus as shown in Fig. 5.5. If A14 and A15 are put in a high state and A13 in a low state while A0–A6 are in a low state, the contents of memory location 000 0000 will be gated to the data bus if the MPU requests the contents of that location (the R/W line will be high). If the MPU desires to read the contents of location

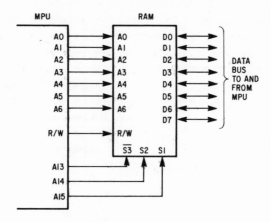

Fig. 5.5 MPU connections with RAM

0011 0111 (37_{16}), the R/W line will be in the high state; address lines A14 and A15 will be high and A13 will be low; and address lines A0, A1, A2, A4, and A5 will be high (see Fig. 5.6). The contents of this location would then be placed on the data bus to be transferred to the MPU.

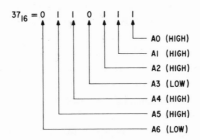

Fig. 5.6 Memory location 37_{16}

The range of addresses for this RAM, as it is presently connected to the address bus, is from 1100 0000 0000 0000 (location 000 0000 of this RAM) to 1100 0000 0111 1111 (location 111 1111 of this RAM), or from $C000_{16}$ to $C07F_{16}$.

It should be obvious by now that all A0's through A6's would be tied to A0 through A6 of the address bus if there were more than one RAM in the system. However, chip select lines S1, S2, and $\overline{S3}$ would be tied to different address lines to provide each RAM with its own unique address. This matter will be covered in greater detail in Chap. 10.

The RAM we have just considered has 128 memory locations, each eight bits wide. Other types of RAMs vary from 1024 bits each to 16,384 bits each. However, the principles discussed are still applicable.

RAMs come in two basic types, referred to as *static* and *dynamic.* Dynamic RAMs usually have more storage capability than static RAMs since their storage cells are smaller. However, what is known as a "refresh signal" must be applied to their cells as frequently as once every millisecond, or the data will be lost. This signal often comes from the MPU clock, which causes the MPU to run at a slightly slower rate. Static RAMs do not need this refresh signal. As long as the main power source is applied, the static RAM will retain its data.

5.5 Read Only Memory (ROM)

Read only memories (ROMs) have an address scheme much the same as that of the RAM. The program to tell the MPU what to do is stored in consecutive locations in the ROM, but the MPU cannot change the contents of ROM locations as it can RAM locations.

Programs are fixed in ROM memories by several different techniques. One is called "mask programmable." After a user has written his program, he supplies it to a ROM manufacturer. The manufacturer will then produce the ROM, usually in large quantities, with the program built in. ROMs obviously do not need to have power continually applied or to be refreshed to hold their program. This state is referred to as "nonvolatile." A typical ROM containing 1024 separate locations, each eight bits wide (1024 × 8), is shown in Fig. 5.7. ROMs vary in size just like RAMs.

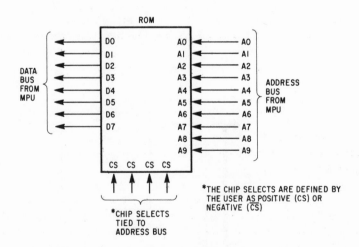

Fig. 5.7 ROM

Notice that the data lines are directed toward the MPU. Data can flow *only* from the ROM to the MPU. As one can see, the required ROM must be selected by the proper signal on the chip selects from the address bus, after which the individual memory location must be addressed through A0–A9 of the address bus. The addressing scheme will be covered in detail in Chap. 10.

5.6 Input/Output

All microcomputer systems must provide a way of getting data loaded into and out of the system, usually by means of one or two chips called *I/O ports* or *peripheral interface chips.* The program can then direct the MPU either to read the status of the input lines on these chips or to send some data to their output lines. The details of the I/O chip for the M6800 system will be discussed in Chap. 9.

5.7 Clock

Just as the computer model developed earlier depended on the clock on the wall to determine when events were to happen, all microcomputer systems are also regulated by clock signals. These signals are routed through the MPU to allow it to execute instructions from the ROM in a timely, orderly manner.

5.8 Microcomputer System

It is now time to consider all the computer elements discussed in this chapter as they relate to the overall system. This interrelationship is shown in Fig. 5.8.

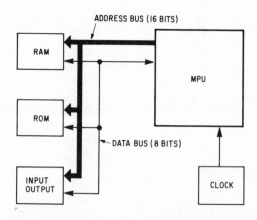

Fig. 5.8 Microcomputer system

Remember that the MPU does only what the program in the ROM directs it to do. A common misconception many people have is that computers are superbeings, that they have brains and can "think." That belief, of course, is false, as you already know. They do exactly what they are told to do and only that, although they do it very fast. The contents of two accumulators can typically be added in 2 or 3 microseconds (.000002 sec). That's fast!

5.9 Interrupts

In the control bus to and from the MPU shown in Fig. 5.2, one of the lines is called an "interrupt line." This section will illustrate the purpose of "interrupts."

Interrupts, as the term indicates, refer to a technique in which the microprocessor is interrupted from doing its primary duties so that it may perform a task much more important. The MPU may be monitoring some rather routine input lines, doing calculations, storing data, and the like, when an emergency type situation occurs. When the MPU is made aware of this emergency situation by an interrupt, it finishes the instruction it is presently executing, stores the contents of its internal registers, and goes to an internal program to solve the difficulty.

Before we can obtain a thorough understanding of interrupts, it is essential to understand what a "real time computer system" is. We're all familiar with the many hand calculators available. These calculators just sit around until you need them, at which time you punch in some numbers, perform some arithmetical calculations, and read the results in the display. A "real time operating system" is similar to the calculator, except that data is continually being fed into the MPU and compared against known data so that output decisions can be made.

To extend the illustration, let us create a "real time situation." The automobile that you have just purchased has a microprocessor system that controls and monitors the following functions:

1. Sounding an alarm if water temperature rises above a certain predetermined limit
2. Maintaining speed at a value you select
3. Maintaining the interior temperature at a value you select.

In reality, it could, and would, perform many more functions, but for the sake of simplicity, these will be enough to illustrate a "real time operating system."

An indicator on the dash of your car allows you to select the speed and inside temperature desired, and a button on the dash, when pressed, places the above functions under microprocessor control.

Let's assume that you are driving down the highway and elect to place these three functions under computer control. You press the button that turns the computer on. The microprocessor will branch to a program in its memory that tells the MPU to read the speed selector. The program will next direct the MPU to check the actual speed; it does so by reading a sensor that generates a signal proportional to the speed. If the actual speed has not yet reached the selected speed, a signal will be generated and transmitted to an electromechanical device that will effectively "push on the gas." The program then directs the MPU to "read in" the temperature selected. The MPU will check the actual temperature inside the automobile through another sensor. If the temperature needs to be raised or lowered, the MPU will send a signal to the appropriate device (either the heater or the air conditioner). The above events will have occurred in much less than a second. The program will now alternately check the speed and temperature, making sure that they reach the desired values. After the desired values are reached, the MPU will continually monitor them to keep both at the desired values.

This is a very simplified example of a real time computer system. Now, you may ask, what about the third function? The alarm that will sound if the water temperature rises above some predetermined value? This is where the need for an interrupt arises. As we have seen, the MPU has a separate input data line to serve as an interrupt line. The voltage on this line, in a normal situation, may be +5 V. However, when the water temperature exceeds the predetermined limit, a sensor will cause the voltage on the interrupt line to drop to zero: When this happens, the MPU will finish the instruction it is executing very quickly, store the contents of its internal registers in memory so that they will be available at a later time if needed, and branch to another program in memory that has been specifically written for situations in which the interrupt line goes low. This program may sound an alarm, put speed and temperature under manual control, or perform any other function desired. Such reactions are often described as "servicing the interrupt." The water temperature rising above limits is much more important than maintaining a constant speed or temperature.

In reality, a real time computer system may have several input functions that may cause an interrupt, even though there is only one interrupt line. Techniques that allow the MPU to determine what function caused an interrupt when more than one function is tied to one interrupt line will be discussed in a subsequent chapter.

5.10 Three-State Control

"Three-state control" is a term used frequently, although often not clearly understood. Three-state control is a technique that allows more than one device to share a common bus, but not at the same time.

In Fig. 5.9, device No. 1 is normally tied to the bus that serves as an input to the MPU. Now assume that the output status of devices Nos. 2 and 3 are needed by the MPU. If S1 is opened and S2 closed, the status of device

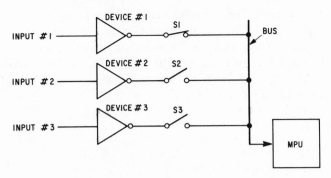

Fig. 5.9 Three-state control

No. 2 can be fed into the MPU. Likewise, if S1 and S2 are open and S3 closed, the status of S3 can be read by the MPU. As far as the MPU is concerned then, each device has three states, "1", "0", and an open circuit. By controlling S1, S2, and S3, the device tied to the bus can be controlled. Fortunately, three-state gates (Fig. 5.10) are available on the market today. The device will appear as an open circuit to the bus when the three-state input is low ("0"). However, if the three-state input goes high ("1"), the output of that device ("1" or "0") can then be tied to the bus. Figure 5.10 shows only one line. Device No. 1, for example, could represent a piece of equipment (such as a typewriter) that in reality has eight output lines tied to the eight lines of the data bus. In this situation, there could be eight identical gates for each line of device No. 1, of which the three-state control lines of each gate would be controlled by the same source so that the output of all eight lines would be gated to the data bus simultaneously.

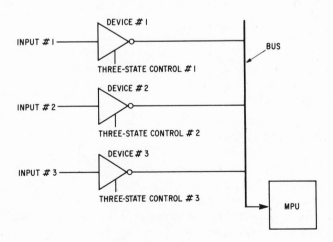

Fig. 5.10 Three-state control (cont'd)

Most microprocessors on the market today have an input pin available on the MPU for this very purpose. The M6800, which we will be reviewing shortly, has a pin called the "TSC" (Three-State Control). When this pin is in the low state, the address bus and the read/write line are in their normal state. However, when a high signal is applied to this pin, the address bus and the read/write line are floating (open).

Problems

1. What is the difference between a RAM and a ROM?
2. Describe the function of the address bus.
3. Do all address lines have to be tied to each device?
4. Do all data lines have to be tied to each device?
5. How many bytes in a 16-bit address bus?
6. What is an interrupt?
7. What does "three state" mean?
8. If an MPU has a 16-bit address bus and it is desired to address a device that responds to the address FB76, what address lines must be tied to this device?
9. When is an interrupt used?
10. Why is three-state capability desirable?
11. What MPU address lines would be tied to the RAM below for the RAM to have an address range from 0300 to 037F?

MPU	RAM
A0	A0
A1	A1
A2	A2
A3	A3
A4	A4
A5	A5
A6	A6
A7	
A8	$\overline{S3}$ S2 S1
A9	
A10	
A11	
A12	
A13	
A14	
A15	

6

Programming
Concepts

In the last chapter, it was shown that a program is nothing more than a series of instructions in memory that direct the activities of the microprocessor. Computer programs are often referred to as "software." Writing a program requires only a paper and pencil. After the program has been written, it can then be manufactured on a ROM as was discussed in the last chapter. The ROM that contains the program may be referred to as "firmware." Once the program has been "burned" into a ROM, it is very difficult to alter. Think of a ROM as you would of a "punched" card. Once the holes have been punched in a card, it is very difficult to alter the contents without making a new one.

6.1 Flowcharting

Before someone actually starts writing a program, it is common practice to generate what is known as a "flowchart" of the activities he wishes his program to accomplish.

FLOWCHART: A graphical representation illustrating the logical steps, calculations, and decisions, in sequence, that must be performed to accomplish a specific task.

The flowchart in Fig. 6.1 illustrates the steps and decisions taken by the computer model described in Chap. 5. Notice the arrows indicating the direction taken after each instruction or decision block. The basic symbols used in writing flowcharts are shown in Fig. 6.2

After a flowchart has been generated, writing the program is relatively simple. However, you will have to prove this fact to yourself.

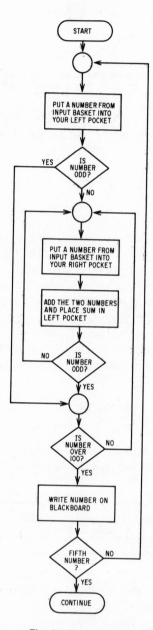

Fig. 6.1 Flowchart

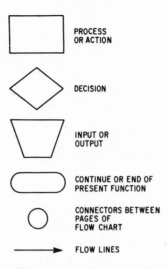

PROCESS
OR ACTION

DECISION

INPUT OR
OUTPUT

CONTINUE OR END OF
PRESENT FUNCTION

CONNECTORS BETWEEN
PAGES OF
FLOW CHART

FLOW LINES

Fig. 6.2 Assembler conversion

6.2 Mnemonics

As we have stressed throughout this book, all digital computers operate with binary numbers only. They do not understand statements in English
or any other type of language. However, most manufacturers of microprocessors do define a two-, three-, or four-letter code that describes the function of
each instruction. This code, known as a "mnemonic," has an equivalent hex
(or binary) number to represent the function. In the computer model developed in Chap. 5, one of the instructions was to "add the A accumulator to the
B accumulator and place the result in the A accumulator." If you are writing
even a simple program, and each instruction requires that much definition, the
program would take forever to prepare. Thus, the manufacturer may assign
a mnemonic code to describe such instructions. The mnemonic in this case is
ABA (add B to A). Again, keep in mind that this mnemonic is only an aid
to the programmer. The ABA operation may be represented by the hex code
1B, which appears in the ROM memory as 0001 1011. Thus, when the MPU
decodes the instruction, it says, "I must add the A and B accumulators
together, place the result in the A accumulator, and then go to the next
sequential location in memory for my next instruction."

MNEMONIC: A simple code, usually alphabetic, that is repre-
sentative of the function of the instruction it represents.

6.3 Assemblers

The question you may now have is, "How do I go from the mnemonic coding to the binary language the computer knows?" Programs written with mnemonic codes are called "source programs." It is from these source programs that the binary code is generated.

> **MACHINE LANGUAGE:** Another term for the binary language (1's and 0's), which is the *only* language a digital computer recognizes.

Once the source code has been written to perform a task, converting to machine language can be accomplished in two ways. One is to refer to the manufacturer's programming manual and manually look up the machine language equivalent for each mnemonic code in the source listing. This can be rather tedious, since calculating the branches (going to an instruction other than the next sequential one) is time-consuming and requires calculations of a very high accuracy. This manual technique, referred to as "hand assembling," is very often used by the hobbyist today but is not suitable for professional applications.

The second method of converting from mnemonic code to machine language is with an "assembler." An assembler is an independent program designed to convert a source program (made up of mnemonic codes) into a machine language program (see Fig. 6.3). Each type of microprocessor available on the market today must have an assembler specifically tailored for its MPU, since its hardware architecture and mnemonic codes will be different. Assemblers for different microprocessors, however, are often able to run on the same system. The assembler to convert M6800 source language to machine language can be run on an IBM 360 computer. The IBM 360 can also run an assembler written by Company X to convert its source programs to machine language. (A more detailed discussion of the M6800 assembler will be presented in Chap. 8.)

Fig. 6.3 ASCII codes

6.4 ASCII

A term you will certainly run across sooner or later is "ASCII," which stands for *A*merican *S*tandard *C*ode for *I*nformation *I*nterchange. This is a standard code used for the interchange of information, both input and output, to or from such devices as typewriters and line printers. Notice in Fig. 6-4 that the ASCII code for an "A" is "1000001." This means that if you wish the typewriter that is tied to your system to type an "A," you must transmit the signal "1000001" on the data lines to the typewriter.

Character	ASCII Code	Character	ASCII Code
@	1000000	FORM FEED	0001100
A	1000001	CARRIAGE RETURN	0001101
B	1000010	RUBOUT	1111111
C	1000011	SPACE	0100000
D	1000100	!	0100001
E	1000101	"	0100010
F	1000110.	#	0100011
G	1000111	$	0100100
H	1001000	%	0100101
I	1001001	&	0100110
J	1001010	'	0100111
K	1001011	(	0101000
L	1001100	)	0101001
M	1001101	*	0101010
N	1001110	+	0101011
O	1001111	,	0101100
P	1010000	−	0101101
Q	1010001	.	0101110
R	1010010	/	0101111
S	1010011	0	0110000
T	1010100	1	0110001
U	1010101	2	0110010
V	1010110	3	0110011
W	1010111	4	0110100
X	1011000	5	0110101
Y	1011001	6	0110110
Z	1011010	7	0110111
[	1011011	8	0111000
\	1011100	9	0111001
]	1011101	:	0111010
↑	1011110	;	0111011
NULL	0000000	<	0111100
HORIZ TAB	0001001	=	0111101
LINE FEED	0001010	>	0111110
VERT TAB	0001011	?	0111111

Fig. 6.4 ASCII Codes(7-bit)

Problems

1. What is a flowchart?

2. Draw a flowchart of the logical steps involved in making the Easy Pound Cake described below:

Ingredients

6   eggs, beaten
4   cups powdered sugar
1½   cups soft butter
4   cups flour
½   cup pineapple juice
1   teaspoon vanilla flavoring

Combine eggs and sugar; beat in butter. Add flour to mixture; beat well. Add pineapple juice; mix well. Stir in vanilla flavoring. Place in cold oven; turn heat to 325 degrees. Bake for 1 hour and 15 minutes.

3. Describe the difference between machine language program, source language program, and assembler program.

7

Addressing Modes

In Chap. 5, an oversimplified computer model was developed to illustrate the basics of a microcomputer system. Recall that instructions are executed in sequence, one by one, unless told to branch to some instruction at a different location in memory. As instructions are executed, they often require data. This data is usually found somewhere in memory, but it may be found immediately following the instruction.

All memory locations in the M6800 system, the system we shall be studying, are eight binary digits wide. Thus, as one may guess, each instruction in the M6800 system is eight bits wide and occupies one memory location. However, even though each instruction is eight bits, or one byte, wide, it often requires use of the next one or two memory locations.

BIT: One binary digit (thus eight binary digits comprise eight bits)
BYTE: A unit composed of eight binary digits (eight bits)

If an instruction requires the use of the next memory location, it is referred to as a two-byte instruction. For example, assume that the number 10011101 immediately following the load A accumulator instruction is to be loaded into the A accumulator. In the ROM memory, it would appear as illustrated in Fig. 7.1. After the MPU has executed the instruction at location 8000, assuming that it is a one-byte instruction, it will execute the instruction at location 8001.

ADDRESSES: Common term for memory locations. Memory location 8001 would be referred to as "address 8001." *Note:* All addresses in this chapter will be in hex unless otherwise specified.

Of course, don't forget that the instruction at address 8001 is in binary. When the MPU decodes this instruction, it will interpret it as "I am to take the number located in the next location (8002) and place it in the A accumulator, after which I am to go to address 8003 for my next instruction."

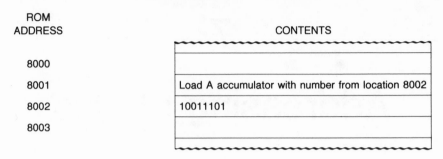

ROM
ADDRESS   CONTENTS

8000	
8001	Load A accumulator with number from location 8002
8002	10011101
8003	

Fig. 7.1 ROM address

Now, you may ask, how did the MPU know to go to address 8003 rather than 8002 for its next instruction? When the MPU decoded the instruction at address 8001, part of the information found there told it to go to 8003.

An instruction may require the next two memory locations (bytes) for execution of the instruction. For example, the next two bytes may contain the address where the data can be found. If the number 11100111 is to be placed in the A accumulator but is located at address (memory location) 9150, it might appear in ROM as shown in Fig. 7.2.

The MPU would decode the instruction at address 8001 to say, "I am to take the number located at address 9150 and put that number in the A accumulator, after which I am to go to address 8004 for my next instruction."

ROM
ADDRESS   CONTENTS

8000	
8001	Load the A accumulator with the number found at the address specified by the next two bytes
8002	91
8003	50
8004	

| 9150 | 1 1 1 0 0 1 1 1 |

Fig. 7.2 ROM address (cont'd)

As you can see, the instruction shown in Fig. 7.2 is a 3-byte instruction, even though the instruction itself only requires one byte in memory.

Both examples just discussed accomplish the same end result, that is, load data into the A accumulator. Yet each found the data in a different area. Each operated in a different "mode" to accomplish the same end result. In this chapter, each of the "addressing modes" of the M6800 will be illustrated. Many instructions may operate in one, two, three, or four different modes to accomplish the same end result.

The M6800 has seven addressing modes:

1. Inherent (or Implied)
2. Accumulator
3. Immediate
4. Direct
5. Extended
6. Indexed
7. Relative

Each of these modes will be illustrated with examples.

7.1 MPU Registers

Before discussing the addressing modes of the M6800, let us review the internal registers and accumulators available in the MPU. These will be discussed in much greater detail in Chap. 9, but a familiarity with them is needed to understand the addressing modes employed in this chapter.

A and B Accumulator

Accumulator: Often referred to as a "register." Thus, A accumulator or A register means the same thing.

The A and B accumulators are eight-bit registers located in the MPU and used for data manipulation, temporary storage locations for the MPU, and other logic functions performed by the MPU.

Index Register (IR)

The index register contains 16 bits (two bytes). It is used primarily to modify addresses.

Program Counter (PC)

The program counter is a 16-bit (two-byte) register that contains the address of the next byte to be fetched from memory. It is used to maintain program control.

Stack Pointer (SP)

The stack pointer is a 16-bit (two-byte) register that contains an address of a location where the status of the MPU registers may be stored under certain conditions.

Condition Code Register (CC)

The condition code register is an eight-bit register used to test the results of certain instructions.

7.2 Inherent (or Implied) Addressing Mode

In the inherent addressing mode, the instruction does not require an address in memory. These are always one-byte instructions. They may also be referred to as "inherent instructions." An example of an implied instruction is the "INX" instruction. This instruction says "add one to the index register." After execution of this instruction, the 16-bit index register will have been increased by one.

7.3 Accumulator Addressing Mode

Instructions in the accumulator addressing mode are 1-byte instructions that address either accumulator A or accumulator B. An example is the COM A (COMplement the Accumulator) instruction. After execution of the COM A instruction, each of the eight bits in the A register will have been inverted, that is, all 1's become 0's and all 0's become 1's.

7.4 Immediate Addressing Mode

In the immediate addressing mode, already mentioned, the "actual" data is found in the next one or two locations immediately following the instruction.

An example would be an instruction to load a B register with the number FO (11110000). The instruction to do this will be coded in memory as hex C6 (11000110). Notice in Fig. 7.3 that whatever was originally in the B register will be lost since the number FO replaces it. Also notice that after the number FO is loaded into the B register, the MPU knows that its next instruction is located at address 202. When it decoded the contents of location 200, the C6 (11000110) code told the MPU to go to location 202 for its next instruction. This could also be a 3-byte instruction. If a number is to be loaded into the stack pointer or index register, it requires two bytes since both the stack pointer and the index register are two bytes wide.

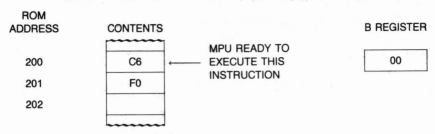

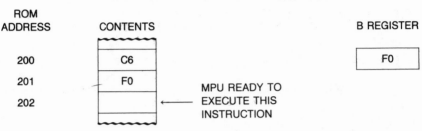

Fig. 7.3 Immediate addressing mode

7.5 Direct Addressing Mode

In the direct addressing mode, the *address* where the data can be found (the "target address") is in the next memory location. This is a two-byte instruction. To illustrate, the number FO, which is stored in location 78 of Fig. 7.4, will be loaded in the B register. This instruction will be coded in memory as D6, or 11010110.

Again, notice that the information that was in the B register has been lost. Also, just as in the immediate mode, when the MPU interprets the instruction represented by the binary number 11010110 (D6), it directs the MPU to go to location 203 for its next instruction after executing the instruction at location 201. Also notice that executing this instruction does not destroy the data (FO) at address 78. It should be emphasized that the address of the data must be specified in one byte (eight bits). Therefore, in the direct mode, the lowest target address is 00000000, and the highest is 11111111 (FF).

7.6 Extended Addressing Mode

The direct mode requires that addresses be specified in eight bits (one byte). This is often not possible because some addresses may require two bytes. In such cases, the extended addressing mode is used. The extended addressing mode is very similar to the direct mode except that it uses three bytes of

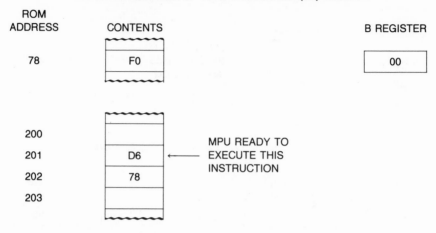

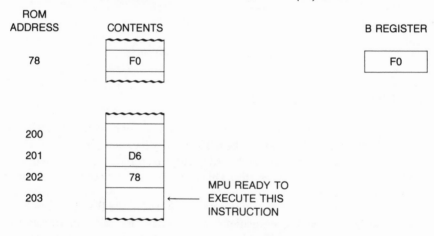

Fig. 7.4 Direct addressing mode

memory instead of two, one for the instruction and the next two for the target address. To illustrate, the number FO located at location 9051_{16} is to be loaded into the B register. The code for this instruction is F6 (11110110). Notice in Fig. 7.5 that the data address in this mode is specified in the two bytes following the instruction. The first of these bytes contains the most significant half of the address (90_{16}) and the second, the least significant half (51_{16}).

Again, after the MPU decodes instruction F6 (11110110), it knows that its next instruction, upon completion of loading the data from location 9051 into the B register, will be found at address 203. Also notice that the data in location 9051 is not destroyed.

BEFORE EXECUTION OF LOAD B REGISTER (F6) EXTENDED

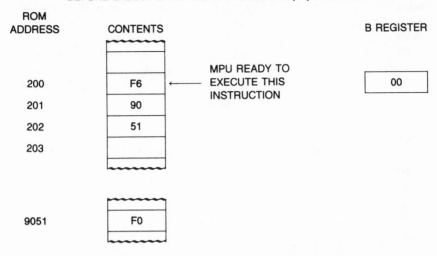

AFTER EXECUTION OF LOAD B REGISTER (F6) EXTENDED

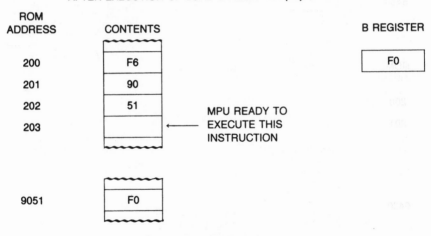

Fig. 7.5 Extended addressing more

7.7 Indexed Mode of Addressing

The indexed mode of addressing uses a 2-byte instruction. The next location from the instruction contains a number (often referred to as an "offset") that is added to the contents of the index register to form an address. This new address, as in the extended mode, contains the data. As an example (Fig. 7.6), assume that the index register contains the number 5430 (in hex). It is desired to put the data found in location 5453, FO, in the B register. The instruction to load the A register from the address that is formed by adding the contents of the next location to the contents of the index register is hex E6 (11100110). The next memory location contains the number 23 (in hex) since 5430 when added to 23 forms the address 5453. Recall that since the index register is 16 bits long, a 16-bit address can be generated.

    The MPU decodes the instruction just as before and knows it is to get its next instruction at location 202. At first, it would appear that this mode of generating an address is the same as the extended mode, but such is not the case. Since the index register can be incremented or decremented by 1, data

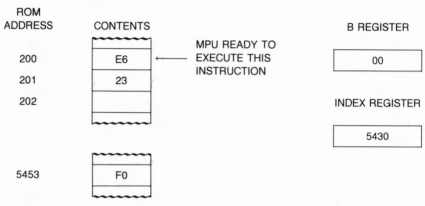

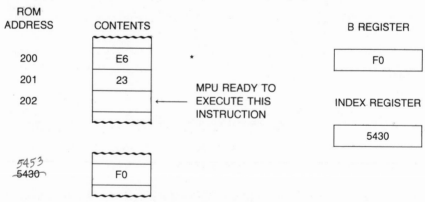

*Remember that the effective address is formed by adding the contents of the index register to the contents of the next byte after the instruction. In this case, the address equals 5430 plus 23, or 5453.

Fig. 7.6 Index addressing mode

can be stored in consecutive memory locations by incrementing or decrementing that register. This feature will be used in sample programs later on. Additionally, the index mode requires only one byte after the instruction whereas the extended mode requires two.

7.8 Relative Addressing Mode

In this mode of addressing, the next instruction to be executed by the MPU is located at some other address than the one following. These will be categorized as "branch" instructions. Such instructions cause the MPU to go to some other address for its next instruction in accordance with some condition within the "condition code" register. These conditions will be studied as each instruction is reviewed in a later chapter. For now, only the mechanics of calculating where the MPU is to get its next instruction will be shown.

Branch instructions are two bytes long. The next location following the branch instruction tells the MPU where it is to get its next instruction, providing certain conditions are met. Since the MPU is capable of branching both forward and backward, each operation will be reviewed separately.

Branching Forward from Present Location

As mentioned above, the next location after the branch instruction contains the information telling the MPU how it is to branch for its next instruction. When the MPU interprets an instruction as a branch instruction, it will decode it as a two-byte instruction. If it didn't branch to a different location, it would next execute the instruction at its present location plus two. Therefore, the branch must be referenced from its present location plus two. Consequently, the MPU will take the contents of the memory location immediately following the branch instruction and add it to the present location plus two. The result of this addition is the address where the MPU is to get its next instruction. The MPU will then continue executing instructions from this new location.

To illustrate with an example, assume that the "branch always" instruction, at memory location 0200, is to be executed (Fig. 7.7). It is desired to branch forward to location 0225. The hex code for the "branch always" instruction is 20, which will be at location 0200. The number located at memory location 0201 will be hex 23. Therefore, the address for the next instruction will be at location 0225 (present location of 200 + 2 + 23).

There is a maximum number of forward memory locations which can be branched over since there is only one byte which can be used for this purpose. The leftmost bit must be kept as a "0" since it is this bit that tells the MPU to branch forward. Therefore, if all the remaining seven bits are a "1," the maximum number of locations that can be branched forward is 1111111, or 7F, or 127_{10} locations.

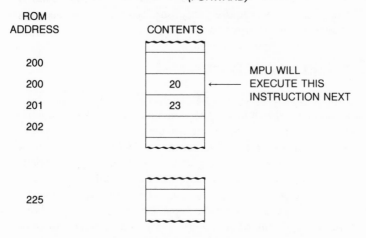

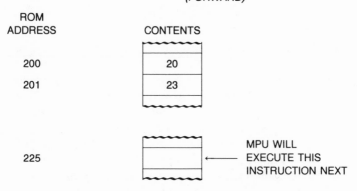

Fig. 7.7 Relative addressing mode (branch forward)

Branching Back from Present Location

The MPU is capable of branching back from its present location just as easily as it can branch forward. Again, the branch is referenced from its present location plus 2. The number immediately following the branch instruction, just as before, tells the MPU how far it is to branch. However, the number must be expressed in 2's complement. For example, assume that we are to branch to memory location 0195 from our present location, 0200. The calculations for the offset are as follows:

$$\begin{array}{r} \text{Present location} + 2 = 0202 \text{ (hex)} \\ \text{Final location} = \underline{0195} \text{ (hex)} \\ 6D \text{ (hex)} \end{array}$$

(You may wish to verify this subtraction in binary if the subtraction in hex is confusing.)

$$6D \text{ (hex)} = 01101101$$
$$1\text{'s complement} = 10010010$$
$$2\text{'s complement} = 10010011$$

————————————This "1" tells the MPU
the branch is backwards

Therefore, the number immediately following the branch instruction would be 10010011, or 93_{16}. The next instruction to be executed will be at location 0195 (Fig. 7.8).

BEFORE EXECUTION OF BRANCH ALWAYS (20) INSTRUCTION
(REVERSE)

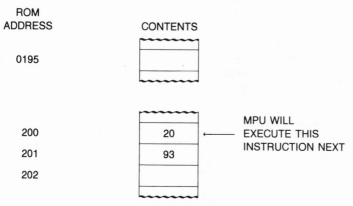

AFTER EXECUTION OF BRANCH ALWAYS (20) INSTRUCTION
(REVERSE)

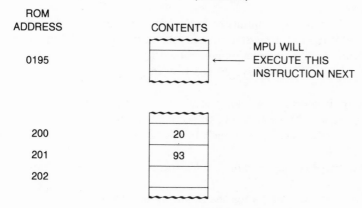

Fig. 7.8 Relative addressing mode (branch back)

7.9 Summary

The instruction to "Load the B register" was described in four different modes: *immediate, direct, extended,* and *indexed.* Notice that the hex code for each mode was different. The whole exercise simply means this: If, while writing your program, the actual data is in the next one or two bytes, then use the instruction code for the *immediate* mode. If the data is located at an address that is one byte wide, then use the instruction code for the *direct* mode. If the data is found at an address that requires two bytes to specify, then use the instruction code for the *extended* mode. If the data is at an address which is specified by adding the next byte to the index register to form a new address, then use the instruction code for the *indexed* mode. The *branch* instructions are self-explanatory. As can be seen in Fig. 7.9, the codes for the "Load B Register" instruction are quite different.

Mode	Instruction code
LOAD B IMMEDIATE	C6
LOAD B DIRECT	D6
LOAD B EXTENDED	F6
LOAD B INDEXED	E6

Fig. 7.9 Load B register addressing modes

Problems

1. What addressing mode is used for all branches?
2. What is the difference between the immediate addressing mode and the direct addressing mode?
3. If it is desired to load the A accumulator in the indexed mode, what location will be addressed if the index register contains the hex number 4201 and the next byte from the load A instruction contain a 10?
4. How many locations is it possible to branch over in the forward and reverse direction?
5. If a branch always instruction were located at address 4050 and it was desired to branch to address 4080, what would the contents of 4051 be?
6. If in problem 5, it was desired to branch to address 4000, what would the contents of 4051 be?
7. What is the difference between the direct mode and extended mode of addressing?
8. Calculate the destination address for the following branch instructions:

Hex Address	Hex Contents	Destination Address
4014	20	
4015	F8	_____
5535	20	
5536	14	_____
800F	20	
8010	E6	_____
99AB	20	
99AC	F2	_____

8

M6800 Software

As we observed in Chap. 7, a single instruction may have one, two, three, or four different addressing modes. Yet although there may be up to four modes for a single instruction, the end result of an instruction is the same. Each addressing mode is just a different manner of telling the MPU where to find the data.

The M6800 instruction set includes 72 separate instructions; however, since each instruction can have more than one addressing mode, there are 197 valid machine codes. For example, the ADD A instruction has an 8B operation code for the immediate mode, 9B operation code for the direct mode, BB operation code for the extended mode, and an AB operation code for the indexed mode. In the immediate mode, the data is in the next byte of memory, yet in the other three modes the data is at some other memory address.

In this chapter, each instruction of the M6800 will be reviewed. All addressing modes for each instruction will be summarized, and the hex operation code for each addressing mode listed. Many examples will be presented to illustrate the contents of applicable registers before and after execution of an instruction. A sample source listing is also shown for all 72 instructions in each mode. When a # sign is shown, the instruction is in the immediate mode, and the number following the # sign is located in the next byte of memory. When a $ sign is shown, it indicates that the next number is in hex. If a # sign is not present, then the number following the $ is a hex address in memory. The indexed addressing mode is shown with a hex number, followed by a comma, and an X ($10,X). The number following the $ sign is added to the contents of the index register to form a new effective address. For example,

1. *LDA A #$25* indicates that the data of 25 is in hex *(immediate mode)*.

2. *LDA A $25* indicates that hex 25 is an address *(direct mode)*.

3. *LDA A $2525* indicates that hex 2525 is an address *(extended mode)*.

4. *LDA A $25,X* indicates that the address is formed by adding hex 25 to the contents of the index register to form a new address *(indexed mode)*.

The M6800 microprocessor has a "condition code register" that has certain bits set or cleared in accordance with the results of certain instructions. The eight bits of the condition code register are as follows:

Bit 0:	C	(carry–borrow)
Bit 1:	V	(2's complement overflow indicator)
Bit 2:	Z	(zero indicator)
Bit 3:	N	(negative indicator)
Bit 4:	I	(interrupt mask)
Bit 5:	H	(half-carry)
Bits 6 and *7:*	Always "1"	

Included in the description of each instruction is a listing of the condition code register bits affected. If the letter of the condition code register bit is shown, refer to Fig. 8.1 for the explanation of that letter. Should any of these explanations be inapplicable for a particular instruction, the correct explanation will be given at the end of the instruction.

H: Set if there was a carry from bit 3; cleared otherwise.
I: Cleared.
N: Set if the most significant bit of the result is set; cleared otherwise.
Z: Set if all bits of the result are cleared; cleared otherwise.
V: Set if there was a two's complement overflow as a result of the operation; cleared otherwise.
C: Set if there was a carry from the most significant bit of the result; cleared otherwise.

Fig. 8.1 Condition code register

8.1 M6800 Instruction Set

This section contains the complete instruction set for the M6800 microprocessor. All addresses and examples used, including.register and memory contents, have been randomly selected and are shown for illustrative purposes only. Parentheses are used to indicate "contents of." For example, the expression (A accumulator) means "the contents of the A accumulator." *An arrow is shown in many examples to indicate the next instruction that will be executed by the MPU.* The three letters in quotation marks at the beginning of each instruction comprise the mnemonic for that instruction.

"ABA": Add Accumulator B to Accumulator A

The contents of the A accumulator are added to the contents of the B accumulator, the sum going into the A accumulator. The B accumulator is not changed.

Execution Time (Cycles)	Instruction Code (Hex)	Source Listing Example
2	1B	ABA

The condition code register bits affected are as follows: H, N, Z, V, C (see Fig. 8.1).

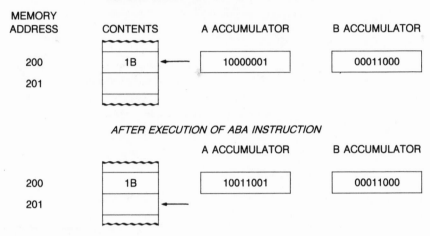

BEFORE EXECUTION OF ABA INSTRUCTION

MEMORY ADDRESS — CONTENTS — A ACCUMULATOR — B ACCUMULATOR

200   1B ← 10000001   00011000

201

AFTER EXECUTION OF ABA INSTRUCTION

A ACCUMULATOR — B ACCUMULATOR

200   1B   10011001   00011000

201

"ADC": Add with Carry

The contents of the C bit in the condition code register are added to the contents of either the A accumulator or the B accumulator and a memory location, the result being placed in that same A or B accumulator.

Mode	Execution Time (Cycle)	Instruction Code (Hex)	Source Listing Example	Explanation
A IMMEDIATE	2	89	ADC A #$25	Note 1
A DIRECT	3	99	ADC A $25	Note 2
A EXTENDED	4	B9	ADC A $7168	Note 3 (see example)
A INDEXED	5	A9	ADC A $25,X	Note 4
B IMMEDIATE	2	C9	ADC B #$CE	Note 5
B DIRECT	3	D9	ADC B $AD	Note 6
B EXTENDED	4	F9	ADC B $CCCC	Note 7
B INDEXED	5	E9	ADC B $D2,X	Note 8

The condition code register bits affected are as follows: H, N, Z, V, C (see Fig. 8.1).

NOTES:

1. (C) + (A accumulator) + hex 25 ⎫
2. (C) + (A accumulator) + (hex address 25) ⎪ Result is placed
3. (C) + (A accumulator) + (hex address 7168) ⎬ in A
4. (C) + (A accumulator) + (address specified ⎪ accumulator
   by index register + hex 25) ⎭
5. (C) + (B accumulator) + hex CE ⎫
6. (C) + (B accumulator) + (hex address AD) ⎪ Result is placed
7. (C) + (B accumulator) + (hex address ⎬ in B
   CCCC) ⎪ accumulator
8. (C) + (B accumulator) + (address specified ⎭
   by index register + hex D2)

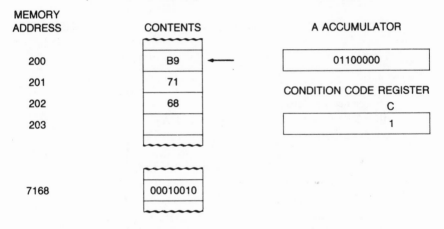

*BEFORE EXECUTION OF ADC INSTRUCTION
(EXAMPLE USING A EXTENDED MODE—ADC A $7168)*

MEMORY
ADDRESS   CONTENTS   A ACCUMULATOR

200   B9   ◄——   01100000

201   71   CONDITION CODE REGISTER
                                                                C
202   68

203   1

7168   00010010

AFTER EXECUTION OF ADC INSTRUCTION

MEMORY
ADDRESS   CONTENTS   A ACCUMULATOR

200   B9   01110011

201   71   CONDITION CODE REGISTER
                                                                C
202   68

203   ◄——   0

7168   00010010

"ADD": Add Without Carry

The contents of the A accumulator or the B accumulator are added to the contents of a memory location, the sum going into that same accumulator.

Mode	Execution Time (Cycles)	Instruction Code (Hex)	Source Listing Example	Explanation
A IMMEDIATE	2	8B	ADD A #$DA	Note 9
A DIRECT	3	9B	ADD A $DA	Note 10
A EXTENDED	4	BB	ADD A $DA53	Note 11
A INDEXED	5	AB	ADD A $DA,X	Note 12
B IMMEDIATE	2	CB	ADD B #$21	Note 13 (see example)
B DIRECT	3	DB	ADD B $4D	Note 14
B EXTENDED	4	FB	ADD B $ADFF	Note 15
B INDEXED	5	EB	ADD B $55,X	Note 16

The condition code register bits affected are as follows: H, N, Z, V, C (see Fig. 8.1).

NOTES:

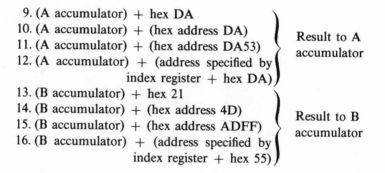

9. (A accumulator) + hex DA
10. (A accumulator) + (hex address DA)
11. (A accumulator) + (hex address DA53)
12. (A accumulator) + (address specified by index register + hex DA)

⎫ Result to A accumulator

13. (B accumulator) + hex 21
14. (B accumulator) + (hex address 4D)
15. (B accumulator) + (hex address ADFF)
16. (B accumulator) + (address specified by index register + hex 55)

⎫ Result to B accumulator

*BEFORE EXECUTION OF ADD INSTRUCTION
(EXAMPLE USING ADD B #21)*

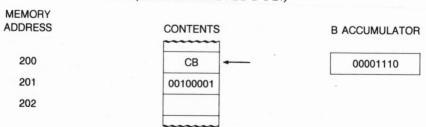

MEMORY ADDRESS	CONTENTS	B ACCUMULATOR
200	CB ◄──	00001110
201	00100001	
202		

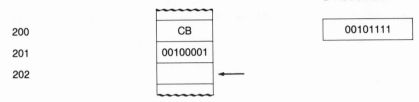

AFTER EXECUTION OF ADD INSTRUCTION

B ACCUMULATOR

200	CB
201	00100001
202	

B ACCUMULATOR: 00101111

"AND": Logical AND

Each bit of the A or B accumulator is logically "ANDed" with each corresponding bit of a memory location, the result going into that same accumulator.

Mode	Execution Time (Cycles)	Instruction Code (Hex)	Source Listing Example	Explanation
A IMMEDIATE	2	84	AND A #$C2	Note 17
A DIRECT	3	94	AND A $6F	Note 18
A EXTENDED	4	B4	AND A $3DCA	Note 19
A INDEXED	5	A4	AND A $F1,X	Note 20
B IMMEDIATE	2	C4	AND B #$10	Note 21
B DIRECT	3	D4	AND B $10	Note 22
B EXTENDED	4	F4	AND B $1000	Note 23
B INDEXED	5	E4	AND B $10,X	Note 24
				(see example)

The condition code register bits affected are as follows: N, Z (see Fig. 8.1); V will be cleared.

NOTES:

17. (A accumulator) "ANDed" with hex C2
18. (A accumulator) "ANDed" with (hex address 6F)
19. (A accumulator) "ANDed" with (hex address 3DCA)
20. (A accumulator) "ANDed" with (address specified by index register + hex F1)

⎫ Result in A accumulator

21. (B accumulator) "ANDed" with hex 10
22. (B accumulator) "ANDed" with (hex address 10)
23. (B accumulator) "ANDed" with (hex address 1000)
24. (B accumulator) "ANDed" with (address specified by index register + hex 10)

⎫ Result in B accumulator

BEFORE EXECUTION OF AND INSTRUCTION
(EXAMPLE USING AND B $10,X)

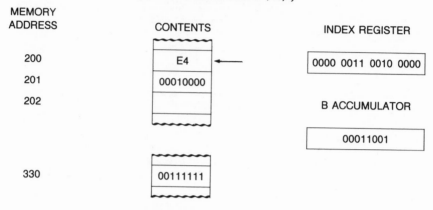

AFTER EXECUTION OF AND INSTRUCTION

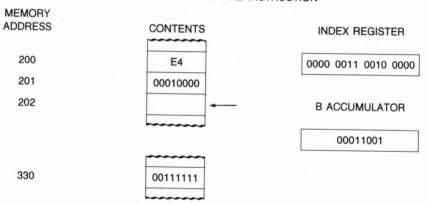

Notice that the address is formed by adding the contents of the index register to the hex number specified in the program (0320 + 10 = 0330). At hex address 330 is the number (00111111), which is to be "ANDed" with the contents of the B accumulator (00011001) to produce the result 00011001.

"ASL": Arithmetic Shift Left

All bits of the A accumulator, B accumulator, or a memory location are shifted one place to the left with the most significant bit (bit 7) loaded into the "C" bit of the condition code register. A zero will be loaded into the least significant bit (bit 0) of the location being shifted.

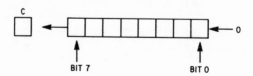

Mode	Execution Time (Cycles)	Instruction Code (Hex)	Source Listing Example	Explanation
A ACCUMULATOR	2	48	ASL A	Note 25
B ACCUMULATOR	2	58	ASL B	Note 26
EXTENDED ADDRESS	6	78	ASL $67AD	Note 27 (see example)
INDEXED ADDRESS	7	68	ASL $25,X	Note 28

The condition code register bits affected are as follows:

N,Z   See Fig. 8.1.   p. 89
V   Set if, after the completion of the shift operation, either (N is "1" and C is "0") or (N is "0" and C is "1"); cleared otherwise.
C   Set if, before the operation, the most significant bit of the location being shifted was set; cleared otherwise.

NOTES:

25. (A accumulator) shifted left one place
26. (B accumulator) shifted left one place
27. (Hex address 67AD) shifted left one place
28. (Address specified by index register + hex 25) shifted left one place

(Bit 7) is loaded into the C bit; a "0" is loaded into bit 0

EXECUTION OF ASL INSTRUCTION
(EXAMPLE USING ASL $67AD)

BEFORE EXECUTION

MEMORY ADDRESS   CONTENTS
200   78 ←
201   67
202   AD
203

67AD   11111111

CONDITION CODE REGISTER
C
0

AFTER EXECUTION

MEMORY ADDRESS   CONTENTS
200   78
201   67
202   AD
203   ←

67AD   11111110

CONDITION CODE REGISTER
C
1

Notice that bit 7 of hex address 67AD is shifted into the C bit and that a "0" is loaded into bit 0 of hex address 67AD.

"ASR": Arithmetic Shift Right

All bits of the A accumulator, B accumulator, or a memory address are shifted one place to the right. Bit 0 will be loaded into the C bit of the condition code register. The contents of bit 7 will not be changed.

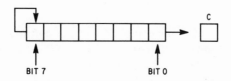

BIT 7   BIT 0

Mode	Execution Time (Cycles)	Instruction Code (Hex)	Source Listing Example	Explanation
A ACCUMULATOR	2	47	ASR A	Note 29 (see example)
B ACCUMULATOR	2	57	ASR B	Note 30
EXTENDED ADDRESS	6	77	ASR $ABF1	Note 31
INDEXED ADDRESS	7	67	ASR $14,X	Note 32

The condition code register bits affected are as follows:

N,Z See Fig. 8.1.

V   Set if after the completion of the shift operation, either (N is "1" or C is "0") or (N is "0" and C is "1"); cleared otherwise.

C   Set if, before the operation, the least significant bit of the location being shifted was set; cleared otherwise.

NOTES:

29. (A accumulator) shifted right one place   Bit 0 will be
30. (B accumulator) shifted right one place   loaded into the
31. (Hex address ABF1) shifted right one place   C bit; bit 7
32. (Address specified by index register + hex   remains the
              14) shifted right one place   same

Notice that bit 0 of the A accumulator is shifted into the C bit. Also notice that the contents of bit 7 remained the same, yet the contents of bit 6 were changed to match bit 7.

EXECUTION OF ASR INSTRUCTION
(EXAMPLE USING ASR A)

BEFORE   AFTER

MEMORY   MEMORY
ADDRESS   CONTENTS   ADDRESS   CONTENTS

200   47   ◄——   200   47

201   201   ◄——

A ACCUMULATOR   A ACCUMULATOR

| 10000001 | | 11000000 |

CONDITION CODE REGISTER   CONDITION CODE REGISTER
          C   C

| 0 | | 1 |

Branch Instructions

All branch instructions, except the "branch always" and the "branch to subroutine" instructions, depend on the status of various bits in the condition code register. The condition code register bits are set or cleared by the last instruction executed by the MPU that affected the condition code register before the branch instruction is encountered. If the conditions for the branch are met, the next instruction executed by the MPU will be specified by the contents of the next byte plus its present address plus 2. If the conditions for the branch are not met, the next instruction executed by the MPU will be at a location equal to its present address plus 2.

The contents of a condition code register are not affected by a branch instruction. For example, the BCC ("branch if carry clear") instruction tells the MPU to check the contents of the C bit in the condition code register. If the C bit is "0" (or clear), the next instruction executed by the MPU will be at a location equal to its present address plus 2 plus the contents of the byte immediately following the BCC instruction. If the C bit is a "1," branching will not take place, that is, the next instruction to be executed by the MPU will be at its present address plus 2.

The various branch instructions are listed in Table 8.1. Notice that all of them are two-byte instructions. (See Sec. 8.4 for examples of conditional branches.)

Table 8.1 Branch Instructions

Mnemonic	Explanation	Execution Time (Cycles)	Instruction Code (Hex)	Conditions for Branch	Source Listing Example (See Note)
BCC	Branch if carry clear	4	24	$C = 0$	BCC
BCS	Branch if carry set	4	25	$C = 1$	BCS
BEQ	Branch if equal to zero	4	27	$Z = 1$	BEQ
BGE	Branch if greater than or equal to zero	4	2C	$(N = 1$ and $V = 1)$ or $(N = 0$ and $V = 0)$	BGE
BGT	Branch if greater than zero	4	2E	$(Z = 0)$ and $[(N = 1$ and $V = 1)$ or $(N = 0$ and $V = 0)]$	BGT
BHI	Branch if higher	4	22	$C = 0$ or $Z = 0$	BHI
BLE	Branch if less than or equal to zero	4	2F	$(Z = 1)$ or $[(N = 1$ and $V = 0)$ or $(N = 0$ and $V = 1)]$	BLE
BLS	Branch if lower or same	4	23	$(C = 1)$ or $(Z = 1)$	BLS
BLT	Branch if less than zero	4	2D	$(N = 1$ and $V = 0)$ or $(N = 0$ and $V = 1)$	BLT
BMI	Branch if minus	4	2B	$N = 1$	BMI
BNE	Branch if not equal to zero	4	26	$Z = 0$	BNE
BPL	Branch if plus	4	2A	$N = 0$	BPL

Mnemonic	Explanation	Execution Time (Cycles)	Instruction Code (Hex)	Conditions for Branch	Source Listing Example (See Note)
BRA	Branch always	4	20	None	BRA $77
BVC	Branch if overflow clear	4	28	V = 0	BVC $4C
BVS	Branch if overflow set	4	29	V = 1	BVS $DF
BSR	See detailed explanation below				

NOTE: All branches should be accomplished using labels (that is, BCC TEMP). The assembler will calculate the offset (second byte of the instruction) referenced from the actual address of the branch instruction plus two (see Sec. 8.2 and Chap. 11 for examples). An alternative method is to use an asterisk (*). In this case, the assembler will calculate the offset (second byte of the instruction) referenced now from the actual address of the branch instruction (that is, BCC * + $20).

"BSR":   Branch to Subroutine

This instruction causes the MPU to branch to a subroutine (another program) at some other location in memory. The location of the subroutine where the MPU is to get its next instruction is determined in the same manner as all other branch instructions. This instruction permits the programmer to use the same subprogram (subroutine) many times during the execution of a larger program rather than repeat that subprogram each time it is needed. At the end of the subroutine will be an RTS instruction that will direct the MPU to return to its original location plus 2.

Execution Time (Cycles)	Instruction Code (Hex)	Source Listing Example
8	8D	BSR $65

BSR $65 causes the MPU to branch to the program located at its present location plus 2 plus hex 65. In the example below, the subroutine is located at hex location 267. Upon detection of an RTS (39) instruction in the subroutine, the MPU will return to its original location plus 2.

BEFORE BRANCHING TO SUBROUTINE   INSTRUCTION TO EXECUTE AFTER RETURNING FROM SUBROUTINE

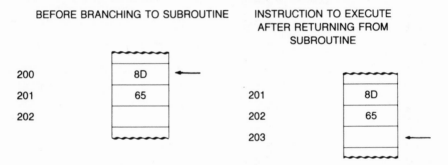

"BIT":   Bit Test

Each bit of the A or B accumulator is logically "ANDed" with each corresponding bit of a memory location for the purpose of setting or clearing the N and Z bits (V is always cleared; other condition codes are not affected) in the condition code register. Neither the A or B accumulators nor the memory location is affected. This instruction is often used before a branch instruction to determine conditions permitting a branch to occur.

Mode	Execution Time (Cycles)	Instruction Code (Hex)	Source Listing Example	Explanation
A IMMEDIATE	2	85	Bit A #$77	Note 33
A DIRECT	3	95	Bit A $77	Note 34
A EXTENDED	4	B5	Bit A $7777	Note 35
A INDEXED	5	A5	Bit A $77,X	Note 36
B IMMEDIATE	2	C5	Bit B #$40	Note 37
B DIRECT	3	D5	Bit B $FD	Note 38
B EXTENDED	4	F5	Bit B $85F6	Note 39
B INDEXED	5	E5	Bit B $20,X	Note 40

The condition code register bits affected are as follows:

N   Set if the most significant bit of the result of the "AND" would be set; cleared otherwise

Z   Set if all bits of the result of the "AND" would be cleared; cleared otherwise

V   cleared

NOTES:

33. (A accumulator) "ANDed" with hex 77
34. (A accumulator) "ANDed" with (memory address hex 77)
35. (A accumulator) "ANDed" with (memory address hex 7777)
36. (A accumulator) "ANDed" with (address specified by index register + hex 77)
37. (B accumulator) "ANDed" with hex 40
38. (B accumulator) "ANDed" with (memory address hex FD)
39. (B accumulator) "ANDed" with (memory address hex 85F6)
40. (B accumulator) "ANDed" with (address specified by index register + hex 20)

"CBA": Compare Accumulators

The contents of the B accumulator are subtracted from the contents of the A accumulator for the purpose of setting or clearing the N, Z, V, and C bits in the condition code register. The contents of the A and B accumulators are not affected.

Execution Time (Cycles)	Instruction Code (Hex)	Source Listing Example
2	11	CBA

The condition code register bits affected are as follows:

N, Z, V   (See Fig. 8.1)

C   Set if the subtraction would require a borrow into the most significant bit of the result; cleared otherwise.

"CLC": Clear Carry

This instruction sets the C bit of the condition code register equal to a "0."

Execution Time (Cycles)	Instruction Code (Hex)	Source Listing Example
2	OC	CLC

The condition code register bits affected are as follows: C is cleared.

"CLI": Clear Interrupt Mask

This instruction sets the I bit in the condition code register to a "0."

Execution Time (Cycles)	Instruction Code (Hex)	Source Listing Example
2	OE	CLI

The condition code register bits affected are as follows: I is cleared.

"CLR": Clear

The contents of the A or B accumulator or some memory location are cleared (replaced with zeros).

Mode	Execution Time (Cycles)	Instruction Code (Hex)	Source Listing Example	Explanation
A ACCUMULATOR	2	4F	CLR A	Note 41
B ACCUMULATOR	2	5F	CLR B	Note 42 (see example)
EXTENDED ADDRESS	6	7F	CLR $76D8	Note 43
INDEXED ADDRESS	7	6F	CLR $52,X	Note 44

The condition code register bits affected are as follows: N, V, and C are cleared; Z is set equal to 1.

NOTES:

41. (A accumulator) is cleared
42. (B accumulator) is cleared
43. (Memory address hex 76D8) is cleared
44. (Address specified by index register + hex 52) is cleared

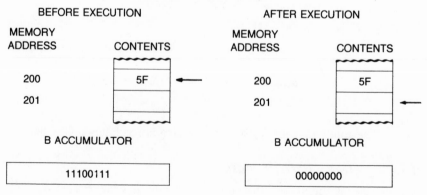

EXECUTION OF CLR INSTRUCTION
(EXAMPLE USING CLR B)

"CLV": Clear Two's Complement Overflow Bit

This instruction sets the V bit in the condition code register equal to a "0."

Execution Time (Cycles)	Instruction Code (Hex)	Source Listing Example
2	OA	CLV

The condition code register bits affected are as follows: V is cleared.

"CMP": Compare

This instruction subtracts the contents of a memory location from either the A accumulator or the B accumulator for the purpose of setting or clearing the N, Z, V, and C bits in the condition code register. Neither the memory location nor the accumulator is changed. This instruction is often used before a branch instruction to determine if a branch should take place.

Mode	Execution Time (Cycles)	Instruction Code (Hex)	Source Listing Example	Explanation
A IMMEDIATE	2	81	CMP A #$52	Note 45
A DIRECT	3	91	CMP A $F3	Note 46
A EXTENDED	4	B1	CMP A $AABC	Note 47
A INDEXED	5	A1	CMP B $12,X	Note 48
B IMMEDIATE	2	C1	CMP B #$43	Note 49
B DIRECT	3	D1	CMP B $75	Note 50
B EXTENDED	4	F1	CMP B $A465	Note 51
B INDEXED	5	E1	CMP B $35,X	Note 52

The condition code register bits affected are as follows: N, Z, V, and C (see Fig. 8.1).

NOTES:

45. (A accumulator) − hex 52
46. (A accumulator) − (memory address hex F3)
47. (A accumulator) − (memory address hex AABC)
48. (A accumulator) − (address specified by index register + hex 12)
49. (B accumulator) − hex 43
50. (B accumulator) − (memory address hex 75)
51. (B accumulator) − (memory address hex A465)
52. (B accumulator) − (address specified by index register + hex 35)

"COM": Complement

This instruction will take each bit of the A accumulator, B accumulator, or a memory location and replace it with its 1's complement. All 1's will be changed to a "0" and all 0's will be changed to a "1."

Mode	Execution Time (Cycles)	Instruction Code (Hex)	Source Listing Example	Explanation
A ACCUMULATOR	2	43	COM A	Note 53
B ACCUMULATOR	2	53	COM B	Note 54
				(see example)
EXTENDED ADDRESS	6	73	COM $723F	Note 55
INDEXED ADDRESS	7	63	COM $35,X	Note 56

The condition code register bits affected are as follows: N, Z (see Fig. 8.1); V is cleared; C is set equal to 1.

NOTES:

53. (A accumulator) replaced with its 1's complement
54. (B accumulator) replaced with its 1's complement
55. (Hex address 723F) replaced with its 1's complement
56. (Hex address specified by index register + hex 35) replaced with its 1's complement.

EXAMPLE OF COM INSTRUCTION
(COM B)

BEFORE   AFTER

MEMORY   MEMORY
ADDRESS   CONTENTS   ADDRESS   CONTENTS

200   53   ◄——   200   53

201   201   ◄——

B ACCUMULATOR   B ACCUMULATOR

| 00001111 | | 11110000 |

"CPX": Compare Index Register

This instruction compares the contents of the index register with two consecutive memory locations since the index register is 16 bits wide (two bytes) and each memory location is eight bits wide (one byte). Neither the contents of the index register nor the contents of the two memory locations are changed by this instruction. The first memory location is subtracted from the most significant byte (bits 8 through 15) of the index register. The second memory location (first memory location + 1) is subtracted from the least significant byte (bits 0 through 7) of the index register.

Mode	Execution Time (Cycles)	Instruction Code (Hex)	Source Listing Example	Explanation
IMMEDIATE ADDRESS	3	8C	CPX #$543F	Note 57
DIRECT ADDRESS	4	9C	CPX $AE	Note 58
EXTENDED ADDRESS	5	BC	CPX $AC52	Note 59 (see example)
INDEXED ADDRESS	6	AC	CPX $71,X	Note 60

The condition code register bits affected are as follows:

N   Set if the most significant bit of the result of the subtraction from the most significant byte of the index register is to be set; cleared otherwise.

Z   Set if all bits of the results of both subtractions are to be cleared; cleared otherwise.

V   Set if the subtraction from the most significant byte of the index register would cause 2's complement overflow; cleared otherwise.

NOTES:

57. (Bits 8 through 15 of index register) − hex 54
    (Bits 0 through 7 of index register)   − hex 3F

58. (Bits 8 through 15 of index register) − (hex address AE)
    (Bits 0 through 7 of index register)   − (hex address AF)

59. (Bits 8 through 15 of index register) − (hex address AC52)
    (Bits 0 through 7 of index register)   − (hex address AC53)

60. (Bits 8 through 15 of index register) − (address specified by index register + hex 71)
    (Bits 0 through 7 of index register)   − (address specified by index register + hex 71 + 1)

N, Z, V bits of condition code register set or cleared as a result

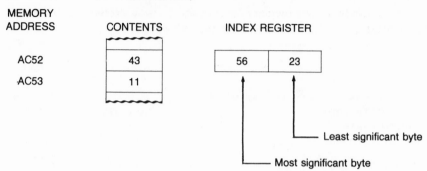

EXAMPLE OF CPX INSTRUCTION
(CPX $AC52)

Upon execution of the CPX $AC52, the following hex operations would take place:

56	(most significant byte	23	(least significant byte
	of index register)		of index register)
−43	(address hex AC52)	−11	(hex address AC52+1)
13		12	

The only action as a result of the above action would be to set or clear bits N, Z, and V of the condition code register. In this example, N = 0, Z = 0, and V = 0.

"DAA": Decimal Adjust the A Accumulator

When doing binary-coded-decimal additions using the ABA, ADD, and ADC instructions, it is possible to obtain invalid results since the A accumulator adds the numbers it has been given (in binary).

To illustrate, when we add add 4_{10} to 99_{10}, the result is 103_{10}. The 99_{10} represented in BCD would be 1001 1001 and 4_{10} would be 0100. Thus,

$$99_{10} \text{ in BCD} = 1001\ 1001$$
$$4_{10} \text{ in BCD} = \underline{0000\ 0100}$$
$$1001\ 1101$$

As can be seen, the result is invalid since 1101 does not exist in BCD. We know that the result must be 12 bits long (103_{10} = 0001 0000 0011). Notice what happens if 66_{10} is added to the result:

$$99_{10} \text{ in BCD} = 1001\ 1001$$
$$4_{10} \text{ in BCD} = \underline{0000\ 0100}$$
$$1001\ 1101$$
$$66_{10} \text{ in BCD} = \underline{0110\ 0110}$$
$$1\ 0000\ 0011$$
$$1\quad 0\quad\quad 3$$

Notice that the decimal adjust of 66_{10} corrects the previously invalid results.

If the DAA instruction is executed immediately following BCD additions with the ABA, ADD, and ADC instructions, it will check all possible situations where invalid results may occur and make the proper adjustment, assuring that the results will be valid for BCD operations.

Execution Time (Cycles)	Instruction Code	Source Listing Example
2	19	DAA

The condition code register bits affected are as follows: N, Z (see Fig. 8.1); C is set or reset according to the same rule applicable if the DAA and an immediately preceding ABA, ADD, or ADC were replaced by a hypothetical binary-coded-decimal addition.

"DEC":   Decrement

The quantity one is subtracted from the contents of the A accumulator, the B accumulator, or a memory address.

Mode	Execution Time (Cycles)	Instruction Code (Hex)	Source Listing Example	Explanation
A ACCUMULATOR	2	4A	DEC A	Note 61
B ACCUMULATOR	2	5A	DEC B	Note 62
EXTENDED ADDRESS	6	7A	DEC $4956	Note 63
INDEXED ADDRESS	7	6A	DEC $19,X	Note 64

The condition code register bits affected are as follows: N, Z (see Fig. 8.1). V is set if the operation resulted in a 2's complement overflow; cleared otherwise. A 2's complement overflow occurs only if (A accumulator), (B accumulator), or (M location) was hex 80 before the operation.

NOTES:

61. (A accumulator) − 1; result will be in A accumulator
62. (B accumulator) − 1; result will be in B accumulator
63. (Hex address 4956) − 1; result will be in hex address 4956
64. (Address specified by index register + hex 19) − 1; result in (address specified by index register + hex 19)

"DES": Decrement Stack Pointer

The quantity one is subtracted from the stack pointer.

Execution Time (Cycles)	Instruction Code (Hex)	Source Listing Example
4	34	DES

The condition code register bits affected are as follows: None.

"DEX": Decrement Index Register

The quantity one is subtracted from the contents of the index register.

Execution Time (Cycles)	Instruction Code (Hex)	Source Listing Example
4	09	DEX

The condition code register bits affected are as follows: Z (see Fig. 8.1).

"EOR": EXCLUSIVE OR (⊕)

This instruction will perform the "EXCLUSIVE OR" between each bit of the A or B accumulator with each corresponding bit of a memory location. The result will go into the A or B accumulator. The memory location will not be changed.

Mode	Execution Time (Cycles)	Instruction Code (Hex)	Source Listing Example	Explanation
A IMMEDIATE	2	88	EOR A #$52	Note 65 (see example)
A DIRECT	3	98	EOR A $C5	Note 66
A EXTENDED	4	B8	EOR A $53F2	Note 67
A INDEXED	5	A8	EOR A $30,X	Note 68
B IMMEDIATE	2	C8	EOR B #$CA	Note 69
B DIRECT	3	D8	EOR B $CA	Note 70
B EXTENDED	4	F8	EOR B $CAF2	Note 71
B INDEXED	5	E8	EOR B $CA,X	Note 72

The condition code register bits affected are as follows: N, Z (see Fig. 8.1); V is cleared.

NOTES:

    65. (A accumulator) ⊕ hex 52; result in A accumulator
    66. (A accumulator) ⊕ (hex address C5); result in A accumulator
    67. (A accumulator) ⊕ (hex address 53F2); result in A accumulator
    68. (A accumulator) ⊕ (address specified by index register + hex 30); result in A accumulator
    69. (B accumulator) ⊕ hex CA; result in B accumulator
    70. (B accumulator) ⊕ (hex address CA); result in B accumulator
    71. (B accumulator) ⊕ (hex address CAF2); result in B accumulator
    72. (B accumulator) ⊕ (address specified by index register + hex CA); result in B accumulator

EXECUTION OF EOR INSTRUCTION
(EXAMPLE USING EOR A #$52)

BEFORE EXECUTION   AFTER EXECUTION

MEMORY ADDRESS	CONTENTS		MEMORY ADDRESS	CONTENTS
200	88 ←		200	88
201	0101 0010		201	0101 0010
202			202	←

A ACCUMULATOR   A ACCUMULATOR

| 1 1 0 0 0 0 0 0 | | 1 0 0 1 0 0 1 0 |

"INC":   Increment

This instruction adds 1 to the contents of the A accumulator, the B accumulator, or a memory location.

Mode	Execution Time (Cycles)	Instruction Code (Hex)	Source Listing Example	Explanation
A ACCUMULATOR	2	4C	INC A	Note 73
B ACCUMULATOR	2	5C	INC B	Note 74
				(see example)
EXTENDED ADDRESS	6	7C	INC $3C51	Note 75
INDEXED ADDRESS	7	6C	INC $26,X	Note 76

The condition code register bits affected are as follows: N, Z, V (see Fig. 8.1).

NOTES:

73. (A accumulator) + 1; result in A accumulator
74. (B accumulator) + 1; result in B accumulator
75. (Hex address 3C51) + 1; result in hex address 3C51
76. (Address specified by index register + hex 26); result in (address specified by index register + hex 26)

EXECUTION OF INC INSTRUCTION (INC B)

B ACCUMULATOR   B ACCUMULATOR
BEFORE EXECUTION   AFTER EXECUTION

| 0 0 0 1 1 1 0 0 | | 0 0 0 1 1 1 0 1 |

"INS":   Increment Stack Pointer

This instruction causes 1 to be added to the stack pointer.

Execution Time (Cycles)	Instruction Code (Hex)	Source Listing Example
4	31	INS

The condition code register bits affected are as follows: None.

"INX":   Increment Index Register

This instruction adds 1 to the contents of the index register.

Execution Time (Cycles)	Instruction Code (Hex)	Source Listing Example
4	08	INX

The condition code register bits affected are as follows: Z set if all 16 bits of the result are cleared; cleared otherwise.

"JMP":   JUMP

Execution of this instruction causes the MPU to execute an instruction at some location other than the sequential one.

Code	Execution Time (Cycles)	Instruction Code (Hex)	Source Listing Example	Explanation
EXTENDED ADDRESS	3	7E	JMP $54F6	Note 77
INDEXED ADDRESS	4	6E	JMP $28,X	Note 78

The condition code register bits affected are as follows: None.

NOTES:

77. The next instruction to be executed by the MPU will be at hex address 54F6
78. The next instruction to be executed by the MPU will be at the address specified by (index register) + hex 28

"JSR":   Jump To Subroutine

This instruction causes the MPU to branch to a subroutine (another program) at some other location in memory. The location of the subroutine where the MPU is to get its next instruction is determined in the same manner as the JMP instruction. This instruction permits the programmer to use the same subprogram (subroutine) many times during the execution of a larger program rather than repeat that same subprogram each time that it is needed. At the end of the subroutine will be an RTS (39) instruction that will direct the MPU to return to its original location plus 3 if it is an extended location, or to its original location plus two if it is an index location.

Mode	Execution Time (Cycles)	Instruction Code (Hex)	Source Listing Example
EXTENDED ADDRESS	9	BD	JSR $F4C5
			(see example)
INDEXED ADDRESS	8	AD	JSR $FF,X

The condition code register bits affected are as follows: None.

EXAMPLE OF JSR INSTRUCTION (JSR $F4C5)

BEFORE			SUBROUTINE LOCATION		AFTER	
MEMORY ADDRESS	CONTENTS	F4C5			MEMORY ADDRESS	CONTENTS
200	BD ←				200	BD
201	F4				201	F4
202	C5				202	C5
203				39	203	

RTS (39) instruction causes MPU to return to its original location plus 3 (203 in this example)

Next instruction after returning from subroutine

"LDA": Load Accumulator

This instruction causes the contents of a memory location to be loaded into the A accumulator or the B accumulator. The memory location is not changed.

Mode	Execution Time (Cycles	Instruction Code (Hex)	Source Listing Example	Explanation
A IMMEDIATE	2	86	LDA A #$25	Note 79
A DIRECT	3	96	LDA A $25	Note 80
A EXTENDED	4	B6	LDA A $2525	Note 81
A INDEXED	5	A6	LDA A $25,X	Note 82
B IMMEDIATE	2	C6	LDA B #$4	Note 83
B DIRECT	3	D6	LDA B $F2	Note 84
B EXTENDED	4	F6	LDA B $FF41	Note 85
B INDEXED	5	E6	LDA B $4,X	Note 86

The condition code register bits affected are as follows: N, Z (see Fig. 8.1); V is cleared.

NOTES:

79. A accumulator is loaded with hex 25
80. A accumulator is loaded with (hex address 25)
81. A accumulator is loaded with (hex address 2525)
82. A accumulator is loaded with (address specified by index register + hex 25)
83. B accumulator is loaded with hex 4
84. B accumulator is loaded with (hex address F2)
85. B accumulator is loaded with (hex address FF41)
86. B accumulator is loaded with (address specified by index register + hex 4)

"LDS": Load Stack Pointer

This instruction causes the stack pointer to be loaded. The most significant byte (bits 8–15) of the stack pointer is loaded from the address specified by the program, and the least significant byte (bits 0–7) of the stack pointer is loaded from the address specified in the program plus 1.

Mode	Execution Code (Cycles)	Instruction Code (Hex)	Source Listing Example	Explanation
IMMEDIATE ADDRESS	3	8E	LDS #$0421	Note 87
DIRECT ADDRESS	4	9E	LDS $F2	Note 88
EXTENDED ADDRESS	5	BE	LDS $A421	Note 89 (see example)
INDEXED ADDRESS	6	AE	LDS $B2,X	Note 90

The condition code register bits affected are as follows:

N   Set if the most significant bit of the stack pointer is set by the operation; cleared otherwise.

Z   Set if all bits of the stack pointer are cleared by the operation; cleared otherwise.

V   Cleared.

NOTES:

87. Stack is loaded with hex 0421
88. Stack is loaded with (hex address F2) and (hex address F3)
89. Stack is loaded with (hex address A421) and (hex address A422)
90. Stack is loaded with (address specified by index register + hex B2) and (address specified by index register + hex B2 + 1)

EXAMPLE OF LDS INSTRUCTION
(USING LDS $A421)

| BEFORE EXECUTION | | AFTER EXECUTION | |

MEMORY
ADDRESS   CONTENTS

200	BE	←
201	A4
202	21
203	

MEMORY
ADDRESS   CONTENTS

200	BE
201	A4
202	21
203		←

| A421 | 10 |
| A422 | 52 |

| A421 | 10 |
| A422 | 52 |

STACK POINTER

| 0 0 0 0 |

STACK POINTER

| 1 0 5 2 |

"LDX": Load Index Register

This instruction loads the index register. The most significant byte of the index register (bits 8–15) is loaded from the address specified by the program, and the least significant byte (bits 0–7) of the index register is loaded from the address specified in the program plus 1.

Mode	Execution Time (Cycles)	Instruction Code (Hex)	Source Listing Example	Explanation
IMMEDIATE ADDRESS	3	CE	LDX #$3245	Note 91
DIRECT ADDRESS	4	DE	LDX $45	Note 92 (see example)
EXTENDED ADDRESS	5	FE	LDX $45FE	Note 93
INDEXED ADDRESS	6	EE	LDX $98,X	Note 94

The condition code register bits affected are as follows:

N   Set if the most significant bit of the index register is set by the operation; cleared otherwise.

Z   Set if all bits of the index register are cleared by the operation; cleared otherwise.

V   Cleared.

NOTES:

91. Index register is loaded with hex 3245
92. Index register is loaded with (hex address 45) and (hex address 46)
93. Index register is loaded with (hex address 45FE) and (hex address 45FF)
94. Index register is loaded with (address specified by index register + hex 98) and (address specified by index register + hex 99)

EXAMPLE OF LDX INSTRUCTION
(USING LDX $45)

BEFORE EXECUTION   AFTER EXECUTION

MEMORY ADDRESS	CONTENTS		MEMORY ADDRESS	CONTENTS
45	F0		45	F0
46	BC		46	BC
200	DE ◄───		200	DE
201	45		201	45
202			202	◄───

INDEX REGISTER   INDEX REGISTER

| 0 0 0 0 |

| F 0 B C |

"LSR":   Logical Shift Right

This instruction results in all bits of the A accumulator, the B accumulator, or a memory location being shifted one place to the right. Bit 7 is loaded with a "0." Bit 0 is shifted into the C bit of the condition code register.

Mode	Execution Time (Cycles)	Instruction Code (Hex)	Source Listing Example	Explanation
A ACCUMULATOR	2	44	LSR A	Note 95
B ACCUMULATOR	2	54	LSR B	Note 96
EXTENDED ADDRESS	6	74	LSR $4521	Note 97
INDEXED ADDRESS	7	64	LSR $78,X	Note 98

The condition code register bits affected are as follows:

Z   Set if all bits of the result are cleared; cleared otherwise
V   Set if, after the completion of the shift operation, either (N = "1"
    and C = "0") or (N = "0" and C = "1"); cleared otherwise
C   Set if, before the operation, the least significant of the accumula-
    tor or memory location being shifted was set ("1"); cleared other-
    wise
N   Cleared

NOTES:

95. (A accumulator) shifted right one place ⎫ Bit 7 is loaded
96. (B accumulator) shifted right one place ⎬ with a "0"; bit 0
97. (Hex address 4521) shifted right one place ⎪ is loaded into
98. (Address specified by index register + hex ⎪ the C bit
                78) shifted right one place ⎭

EXAMPLE OF LOCATION BEING SHIFTED (LSR)

BEFORE EXECUTION   AFTER EXECUTION

| 1 0 0 0 1 1 1 1 | | 0 1 0 0 0 1 1 1 |

                        C   C
                      | 0 | | 1 |

"NEG": Negate

This instruction replaces the contents of the A accumulator, the B
accumulator, or a memory location with its 2's complement.

Mode	Execution Time (Cycles)	Instruction Code (Hex)	Source Listing Example	Explanation
A ACCUMULATOR	2	40	NEG A	Note 99
B ACCUMULATOR	2	50	NEG B	Note 100
EXTENDED ADDRESS	6	70	NEG $2536	Note 101
INDEXED ADDRESS	7	60	NEG $C2,X	Note 102

The condition code register bits affected are as follows:

N, Z   See Fig. 8.1.
V   Set if there would be a 2's complement overflow as a result of
       the implied subtraction from zero; this will occur only if the
       contents of the accumulator or memory location is hex 80.

C   Set if there would be a borrow in the implied subtraction from zero, the C bit will be set in all cases except when the contents of the accumulator or memory location is 00.

NOTES:

99. (A accumulator) is replaced with its 2's complement
100. (B accumulator) is replaced with its 2's complement
101. (Hex address 2536) is replaced with its 2's complement
102. (Address specified by index register + hex C2) is replaced with its 2's complement

EXAMPLE OF NEGATE SOME LOCATION

BEFORE EXECUTION   AFTER EXECUTION

| 1 1 0 0 1 1 1 1 | | 0 0 1 1 0 0 0 1 |

"NOP": No Operation

This instruction just causes the MPU to go on to the next instruction in sequence.

Execution Time (Cycles)	Instruction Code (Hex)	Source Listing Example
2	01	NOP

The condition code register bits affected are as follows: None.

"ORA": INCLUSIVE OR

This instruction performs the logical "OR" between each bit of the A or B accumulator and each corresponding bit of a memory location. The result is placed in that same accumulator.

Mode	Execution Time (Cycles)	Instruction Code (Hex)	Source Listing Example	Explanation
A IMMEDIATE	2	8A	ORA A #$51	Note 103
A DIRECT	3	9A	ORA A $28	Note 104
A EXTENDED	4	BA	ORA A $764A	Note 105
A INDEXED	5	AA	ORA A $B6,X	Note 106
B IMMEDIATE	2	CA	ORA B #$78	Note 107
B DIRECT	3	DA	ORA B $FA	Note 108
B EXTENDED	4	FA	ORA B $C55D	Note 109
B INDEXED	5	EA	ORA B $52,X	Note 110

The condition code register bits affected are as follows: N, Z, V is cleared.

NOTES:

103. (A accumulator) "ORed" with hex 51
104. (A accumulator) "ORed" with (hex address 28)
105. (A accumulator) "ORed" with (hex address 764A)
106. (A accumulator) "ORed" with (address specified by index register + hex B6)

⎫ Result placed in A accumulator

107. (B accumulator) "ORed" with hex 78
108. (B accumulator) "ORed" with (hex address FA)
109. (B accumulator) "ORed" with (hex address C55D)
110. (B accumulator) "ORed" with (address specified by index register + hex 52)

⎫ Result placed in B accumulator

EXAMPLE OF INCLUSIVE "OR"

BEFORE EXECUTION

A ACCUMULATOR

| 1 1 1 1 1 0 0 0 |

MEMORY ADDRESS

| 1 0 1 0 1 0 1 0 |

AFTER EXECUTION

A ACCUMULATOR

| 1 1 1 1 1 0 1 0 |

MEMORY ADDRESS

| 1 0 1 0 1 0 1 0 |

"PSH": Push Data onto Stack

The contents of the A accumulator or the B accumulator are stored in memory at the address contained in the stack pointer. The stack pointer is then decremented by 1. The contents of the accumulator are not changed.

Mode	Execution Time (Cycles)	Instruction Code (Hex)	Source Listing Example	Explanation
A ACCUMULATOR	4	36	PSH A	Note 111
B ACCUMULATOR	4	37	PSH B	Note 112

The condition code register bits affected are as follows: None.

NOTES:

> 111. (A accumulator) contents are stored at address specified by the stack pointer; stack pointer is decremented by 1
> 112. (B accumulator) contents are stored at address specified by the stack pointer; stack pointer is decremented by 1

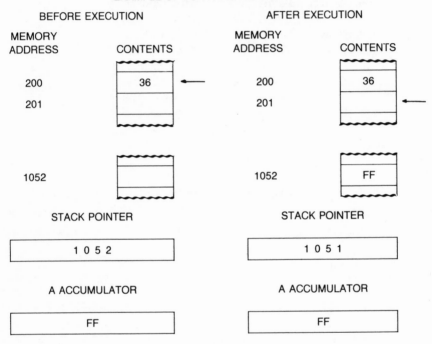

EXAMPLE OF PSH A INSTRUCTION

"PUL": Pull Data from Stack

After the stack pointer is incremented by 1, the A or B accumulator is loaded from the address contained in the stack pointer.

Mode	Execution Time (Cycles)	Instruction Code (Hex)	Source Listing Example	Explanation
A ACCUMULATOR	4	32	PUL A	Note 113
B ACCUMULATOR	4	33	PUL B	Note 114

The condition code register bits affected are as follows: None.

NOTES:

113. (Address specified by stack pointer + 1) is loaded into A accumulator
114. (Address specified by stack pointer + 1) is loaded into B accumulator

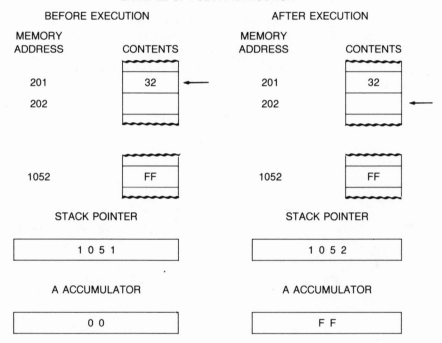

EXAMPLE OF PUL A INSTRUCTION

"ROL": *Rotate Left*

This instruction shifts all bits from the A accumulator, B accumulator, or a memory location one place to the left. The contents of the C bit are loaded into bit 0. The contents of bit 7 are loaded into the C bit.

Mode	Execution Time (Cycles)	Instruction Code (Hex)	Source Listing Example	Explanation
A ACCUMULATOR	2	49	ROL A	Note 115
B ACCUMULATOR	2	59	ROL B	Note 116
EXTENDED ADDRESS	6	79	ROL $2426	Note 117
INDEXED ADDRESS	7	69	ROL $15,X	Note 118

The condition code register bits affected are as follows:

N, Z See Fig. 8.1. *p. 89*
V Set if, after the completion of the operation, either (N = "1" and C = "0") or (N = "0" and C = "1"); cleared otherwise.
C Set if, before the operation, the most significant bit of the location being shifted was set; cleared otherwise.

NOTES:

115. (A accumulator) shifted left one bit
116. (B accumulator) shifted left one bit
117. (Hex address 2426) shifted left one bit
118. (Address specified by index register + hex 15) shifted left one bit.

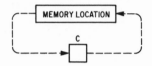

EXAMPLE OF ROL A INSTRUCTION

BEFORE EXECUTION

A ACCUMULATOR

| 0 1 1 1 1 1 1 0 |

C
| 1 |

AFTER EXECUTION

A ACCUMULATOR

| 1 1 1 1 1 1 0 1 |

C
| 0 |

"ROR": Rotate Right

This instruction shifts all bits from the A accumulator, B accumulator, or a memory location one place to the right. The contents of the C bit are loaded into bit 7. The contents of bit 0 are loaded into the C bit.

Mode	Execution Time (Cycles)	Instruction Code (Hex)	Source Listing Example	Explanation
A ACCUMULATOR	2	46	ROR A	Note 119
B ACCUMULATOR	2	56	ROR B	Note 120
EXTENDED ADDRESS	6	76	ROR $4562	Note 121
INDEXED ADDRESS	7	66	ROR $60,X	Note 122

The condition code register bits affected are as follows:

N, Z   See Fig. 8.1.
V   Set if, after the completion of the operation, either (N = "1"
       and C = "0") or (N = "0" and C = "1"); cleared otherwise.
C   Set if, before the operation, the least significant bit of the
       location shifted was set; cleared otherwise.

NOTES:

    119. (A accumulator) shifted right one bit
    120. (B accumulator) shifted right one bit
    121. (Hex address 4562) shifted right one bit
    122. (Address specified by index register + hex 60) shifted right one
         bit

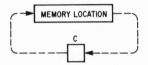

EXAMPLE OF ROR B INSTRUCTION

BEFORE EXECUTION
B ACCUMULATOR

1 0 0 0 0 1 1 1

C
| 0 |

AFTER EXECUTION
B ACCUMULATOR

0 1 0 0 0 0 1 1

C
| 1 |

"RTI": Return from Interrupt

When an interrupt is recognized by the MPU—but before it is serviced—the contents of the condition code register, A accumulator, B accumulator, index register, and the program counter are stored in a memory
area referred to as the stack. During the interrupt program, these registers and
accumulators will be used. If they aren't saved (stored), the MPU will not
know where it was before the interrupt occurred. Therefore, seven memory
locations are required for the stack. The RTI (3B) instruction is included at
the end of the program written to service the interrupt. It tells the MPU that
servicing is complete and that it may restore all registers and accumulators to
the same status as before the interrupt.

Execution Time (Cycles)	Instruction Code (Hex)	Source Listing Example
10	3B	RTI

"RTS": Return from Subroutine

After execution of a BSR or JSR instruction, the MPU will execute instructions at a new location that contains the subprogram or subroutine. When this subroutine is over, an RTS (39) instruction is encountered. This tells the MPU that there are no more instructions in the subroutine and that it should return to its main program at its original address plus 2 if a BSR, or its original address plus 3 if a JSR, instruction.

Execution Time (Cycles)	Instruction Code (Hex)	Source Listing Example
5	39	RTS

The condition code register bits affected are as follows: None.

"SBA": Subtract Accumulators

This instruction subtracts the contents of the B accumulator from the contents of the A accumulator, the result being placed in the A accumulator. The B accumulator is not changed.

Execution Time (Cycles)	Instruction Code (Hex)	Source Listing Example
2	˙10	SBA

The condition code register bits affected are as follows:

C, N, Z, V   See Fig. 8.1.

"SBC": Subtract with Carry

This instruction subtracts the contents of a memory location and the contents of the C bit from the A accumulator or the B accumulator. The result is placed in that same accumulator.

Code	Execution Time (Cycles)	Instruction Code (Hex)	Source Listing Example	Explanation
A IMMEDIATE	2	82	SBC A #$47	Note 123
A DIRECT	3	92	SBC A $F4	Note 124
A EXTENDED	4	B2	SBC A $2588	Note 125
A INDEXED	5	A2	SBC A $27,X	Note 126
B IMMEDIATE	2	C2	SBC B #$FA	Note 127
B DIRECT	3	D2	SBC B $BB	Note 128
B EXTENDED	4	F2	SBC B $8752	Note 129
B INDEXED	5	E2	SBC B $36,X	Note 130

The condition code register bits affected are as follows:

N, Z, V   See Fig. 8.1

C   Carry is set if the absolute value of the contents of memory plus previous carry is larger than the absolute value of the accumulator; cleared otherwise.

NOTES:

123. (A accumulator) − (C) − hex 47
124. (A accumulator) − (C) − (hex address F4)
125. (A accumulator) − (C) − (hex address 2588)
126. (A accumulator) − (C) − (address specified by index register + hex 27)

} Result will be placed in A accumulator

127. (B accumulator) − (C) − hex FA
128. (B accumulator) − (C) − (hex address BB)
129. (B accumulator) − (C) − (hex address 8752)
130. (B accumulator) − (C) − (address specified by index register + hex 36)

} Result will be placed in B accumulator

"SEC": Set Carry

This instruction sets the C bit in the condition code register to a "1".

Execution Time (Cycles)	Instruction Code (Hex)	Source Listing Example
2	OD	SEC

The condition code register bits affected are as follows: C set to a "1".

"SEI": Set Interrupt Mask

This instruction sets the I bit of the condition code register to a "1". The MPU can no longer service an $\overline{\text{IRQ}}$ interrupt until the I bit is cleared. Nonmaskable ($\overline{\text{NMI}}$) interrupts are not affected.

Execution Time (Cycles)	Instruction Code (Hex)	Source Listing Example
2	OF	SEI

The condition code register bits affected are as follows: I bit set to "1".

"SEV": Set 2's Complement Overflow Bit

This instruction sets the 2's complement overflow bit (V bit) of the condition code register to a "1".

Execution Time (Cycles	Instruction Code (Hex)	Source Listing Example
2	OB	SEV

The condition code register bits affected are as follows: V bit set to "1".

"STA": Store Accumulator

This instruction stores the contents of the A accumulator or the B accumulator in a memory location; the contents of the accumulator are not changed.

Mode	Execution Time (Cycles)	Instruction Code (Hex)	Source Listing Example	Explanation
A DIRECT	4	97	STA A $48	Note 131 (see example)
A EXTENDED	5	B7	STA A $A268	Note 132
A INDEXED	6	A7	STA A $28,X	Note 133
B DIRECT	4	D7	STA B $F4	Note 134
B EXTENDED	5	F7	STA B $2652	Note 135
B INDEXED	6	E7	STA B $FF,X	Note 136

The condition code register bits affected are as follows: N, Z (see Fig. 8.1); V is cleared.

NOTES:

131. (A accumulator) is stored in hex address 48
132. (A accumulator) is stored in hex address A268
133. (A accumulator) is stored in address specified by (index register + hex 28)
134. (B accumulator) is stored in hex address F4
135. (B accumulator) is stored in hex address 2652
136. (B accumulator) is stored in address specified by (index register + hex FF).

EXAMPLE OF STA A DIRECT INSTRUCTION (STA A $48)

BEFORE EXECUTION   AFTER EXECUTION

MEMORY ADDRESS	CONTENTS		MEMORY ADDRESS	CONTENTS
48	00		48	BE
200	97 ←		200	97
201	48		201	48 ←
202			202	

A ACCUMULATOR   A ACCUMULATOR

BE

BE

"STS": Store Stack Pointer

This instruction stores the stack pointer in memory. The most significant byte of the stack pointer is stored at the address specified by the program. The least significant byte of the stack pointer is stored at the next consecutive address from the one specified by the program.

Mode	Execution Time (Cycles)	Instruction Code (Hex)	Source Listing Example	Explanation
DIRECT ADDRESS	5	9F	STS $B5	Note 137 (see example)
EXTENDED ADDRESS	6	BF	STS $26F8	Note 138
INDEXED ADDRESS	7	AF	STS $25,X	Note 139

The condition code register bits affected are as follows:

Z   See Fig. 8.1
V   Cleared
N   Set if the most significant bit of the stack pointer (bit 15) is set; cleared otherwise

NOTES:

137. (Stack pointer) is stored at hex address B5 and hex address B6
138. (Stack pointer) is stored at hex addresses 26F8 and 26F9
139. (Stack pointer) is stored at address specified by(index register + hex 25) and address specified by(index register + hex 25 + 1)

EXAMPLE OF STS DIRECT INSTRUCTION (STS $B5)

BEFORE EXECUTION

MEMORY ADDRESS	CONTENTS
B5	00
B6	00

MEMORY ADDRESS	CONTENTS
200	9F	←
201	B5
202	

STACK POINTER

2 0 4 6

AFTER EXECUTION

MEMORY ADDRESS	CONTENTS
B5	20
B6	46

MEMORY ADDRESS	CONTENTS
200	9F
201	B5
202		←

STACK POINTER

2 0 4 6

"STX": Store Index Register

This instruction stores the index register in memory. The most significant byte of the index register is stored at the address specified by the program. The least significant byte of the index register is stored at the next consecutive address from the one specified by the program.

Mode	Execution Time (Cycles)	Instruction Code (Hex)	Source Listing Example	Explanation
DIRECT ADDRESS	5	DF	STX $55	Note 140
EXTENDED ADDRESS	6	FF	STX $326B	Note 141 (see example)
INDEXED ADDRESS	7	EF	STX $BE,X	Note 142

The condition code register bits affected are as follows:

Z   See Fig. 8.1
V   Cleared
N   Set if the most significant bit of the index register (bit 15) is set; cleared otherwise

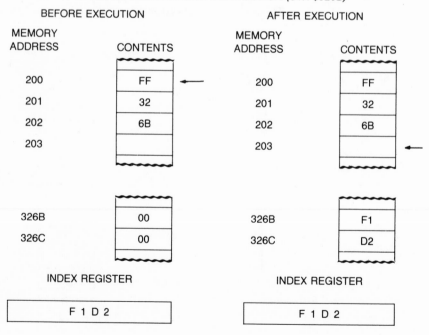

EXAMPLE OF STX EXTENDED INSTRUCTION (STX $326B)

NOTES:

> 140. (Index register) is stored at hex address 55 and hex address 56
> 141. (Index register) is stored at hex address 326B and hex address 326C
> 142. (Index register) is stored at address specified by(index register + hex BE) and address specified by(index register + hex BE + 1)

"SUB": Subtract

This instruction subtracts the contents of a memory location from the A or B accumulator and places the result in that same accumulator.

Mode	Execution Time (Cycles)	Instruction Code (Hex)	Source Listing Example	Explanation
A IMMEDIATE	2	80	SUB A #$20	Note 143
A DIRECT	3	90	SUB A $FB	Note 144*
A EXTENDED	4	B0	SUB A $1158	Note 145
A INDEXED	5	A0	SUB A $15,X	Note 146
B IMMEDIATE	2	C0	SUB B #$59	Note 147
B DIRECT	3	D0	SUB B $CB	Note 148
B EXTENDED	4	F0	SUB B $AAC2	Note 149
B INDEXED	5	E0	SUB B $FF,X	Note 150

*See example.

The condition code register bits affected are as follows:

N, Z, V   See Fig. 8.1.
C   Set if the absolute value of the contents of memory are larger than the absolute value of the accumulator; cleared otherwise.

NOTES:

> 143. (A accumulator) − hex 20
> 144. (A accumulator) − (hex address FB)   Result is placed
> 145. (A accumulator) − (hex address 1158)   in A
> 146. (A accumulator) − (address specified by   accumulator
>   index register + hex 15)
> 147. (B accumulator) − hex 59
> 148. (B accumulator) − (hex address CB)   Result is placed
> 149. (B accumulator) − (hex address AAC2)   in B
> 150. (B accumulator) − (address specified by   accumulator
>   index register + hex FF)

EXAMPLE OF SUB A ACCUMULATOR DIRECT INSTRUCTION (SUB A $FB)

BEFORE EXECUTION   AFTER EXECUTION

MEMORY ADDRESS	CONTENTS	MEMORY ADDRESS	CONTENTS
FB	00000011	FB	00000011

200	90 ←	200	90
201	FB	201	FB
202		202	←

A ACCUMULATOR   A ACCUMULATOR

01111111	01111100

"SWI": Software Interrupt

This instruction is used when it is desired for the MPU to execute some special program. The condition code register, the program counter, the A and B accumulators, and the index register will be stored in memory (stack) when this instruction is encountered. The interrupt mask (I bit) will be set to a "1". The program counter is then loaded from the memory locations that respond to the addresses FFFA and FFFB, which contain the address of the software interrupt pointer. The MPU will then proceed to execute instructions starting at the address defined by the software interrupt pointer until the RTI instruction is encountered. At this time, all registers and accumulators will be restored to their original contents, and the program will proceed from where it was before the SWI instruction.

Execution Time (cycles)	Instruction Code (Hex)	Source Listing Example
12	3F	SWI

The condition code register bits affected are as follows: I is set.

"TAB": Transfer from Accumulator A to Accumulator B

This instruction transfers the contents of accumulator A to accumulator B. The contents of accumulator A are not changed, but those of accumulator B are lost.

Execution Time (Cycles)	Instruction Code (Hex)	Source Listing Example
2	16	TAB

The condition code register bits affected are as follows: N, Z (see Fig. 8.1); V is cleared.

"TAP": Transfer from Accumulator A to Condition Code Register

This instruction transfers the contents of bit 0 through bit 5 of the A accumulator to bit 0 through bit 5 of the condition code register.

Execution Time (Cycles)	Instruction Code (Hex)	Source Listing Example
2	06	TAP

The condition code register bits affected are as follows: Set or cleared according to contents bit 0–5 of A accumulator:

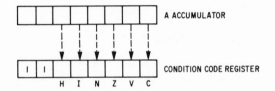

C   Carry–borrow
V   Overflow (2's complement)
Z   Zero
N   Negative
I   Interrupt mask
H   Half carry

"TBA": Transfer from B Accumulator to A Accumulator

This instruction transfers the contents of the B accumulator to the A accumulator. The contents of accumulator B are not changed, but those of accumulator A are lost.

Execution Time (Cycles)	Instruction Code (Hex)	Source Listing Example
2	17	TBA

The condition code register bits affected are as follows: N, Z (see Fig. 8.1); V is cleared.

"TPA": Transfer from Condition Code Register to A Accumulator

This instruction transfers the contents of the condition code register to bit 0 through bit 7 of the A accumulator.

Execution Time (Cycles)	Instruction Code (Hex)	Source Listing Example
2	07	TPA

The condition code register bits affected are as follows: None.

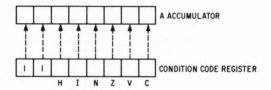

C   Carry–borrow
V   Overflow (2's complement)
Z   Zero
N   Negative
I   Interrupt mask
H   Half carry

"TST":   Test (Zero or Minus)

This instruction sets the N and Z bits of the condition code register according to the contents of the A accumulator, B accumulator, or a memory location.

Mode	Execution Time (Cycles)	Instruction Code (Hex)	Source Listing Example	Explanation
A ACCUMULATOR	2	4D	TST A	Note 151
B ACCUMULATOR	2	5D	TST B	Note 152
EXTENDED ADDRESS	6	7D	TST $372D	Note 153
INDEXED ADDRESS	7	6D	TST $BD,X	Note 154

The condition code register bits affected are as follows: N, Z (see Fig. 8.1); C and V are cleared.

NOTES:

151. (A accumulator) determines status of N and Z bits
152. (B accumulator) determines status of N and Z bits
153. (Hex address 372D) determines status of N and Z bits
154. (Address specified by index register + hex BD) determines status of N and Z bits

"TSX":   Transfer from Stack Pointer to Index Register

This instruction loads the index register with the contents of the stack pointer plus 1. The stack pointer contents remain the same.

Execution Time (Cycles)	Instruction Code (Hex)	Source Listing Example
4	30	TSX

The condition code register bits affected are as follows: None.

"TXS": Transfer from Index Register to Stack Pointer

This instruction loads the contents of the index register minus 1 into the stack pointer. The contents of the index register remain the same.

Execution Time (Cycles)	Instruction Code (Hex)	Source Listing Example
4	35	TXS

The condition code register bits affected are as follows: None.

"WAI": Wait for Interrupt

This instruction is used when it is desired for the MPU to wait for some external event to happen. The condition code register, the program counter, the A and B accumulators, and the index register will be stored in memory (stack) when this instruction is encountered. Program execution will then be suspended until an external interrupt occurs (providing the I bit is clear). If it is an $\overline{IRQ}$ interrupt, the I bit is first set and the program counter will then be loaded with the contents of memory locations that respond to FFF8 and FFF9. If it is an $\overline{NMI}$ interrupt, the I bit is first set and the program counter will then be loaded with the memory locations that respond to addresses FFFC and FFFD. These addresses contain the "interrupt vector pointer," which is the address where the servicing routine is located. The highest memory address occurs when all address lines are high (FFFF).

Normally an RTI instruction will be encountered at some point in the servicing routine. This directs the MPU to restore all registers and accumulators to their original contents. Program execution will now continue from the instruction immediately following the "WAI" instruction.

Execution Time (Cycles)	Instruction Code (Hex)	Source Listing Example
9	3E	WAI

The condition code register bits affected are as follows: I bit will be set to a "1" when interrupt occurs. If previously set, an $\overline{NMI}$ is required to exit the wait state.

8.2 M6800 Assembler

In Chap. 6, the basic principles of an assembler were discussed. We will now look at the M6800 assembler in much greater detail. The previous section described each instruction in the M6800 instruction set for all addressing modes. The mnemonic and the hex operation code were shown for each instruction. The M6800 assembler program translates these *source programs,* written in mnemonics, into *object programs,* that is, programs in machine language. There are many rules that you must observe when writing a source program if the assembler is to understand what you wish to accomplish. Remember that the assembler is nothing more than a program in itself—a program that has been written to make life easier for the programmer. Source programs using mnemonics are much easier to write than programs in machine language. This section will illustrate how to write source programs that are to be assembled on one of the several time-sharing networks available to the M6800 assembler. Slightly different rules apply if other systems are used to assemble source programs.

Line Numbers

In Sec. 8.1, a source listing example of each instruction was shown. For example, LDA A #42 is a source statement. The source program must contain only *one* source statement per line. Each line must start with a *line number* (often called a sequence number). Each line number must be higher than the previous line number. The line numbers may be from 1 to 5 digits long. It doesn't really matter what your first line number is, and the line numbers do not have to be consecutive. The following example shows acceptable line numbers:

> 100   Source statement No. 1
> 102   Source statement No. 2
> 110   Source statement No. 3
> 130   Source statement No. 4

As you can see, the only requirements are that each line number be higher than the previous one and that it be between one and five digits long. It must be emphasized that the line numbers are for the assembler's use only. They are *not* part of the program.

Label Field

In the discussion on relative addressing in Chap. 7, it was shown how to calculate a branch instruction, that is, how to transfer to a location other than the next one. When writing programs in source language, the assembler will do this for you by placing a group of *alphanumeric characters,* referred to as a "label," starting at the second space following the line number (the first space following must be blank). When this same label—for example, "TEMP" —is included as part of a source statement elsewhere in the program—as "BRA TEMP," say—the assembler will calculate the second byte of the instruction. The following is an example of the proper use of a label:

100   TEMP LDA A #41
101   .
   .   .
   .   .
   .   .
   .   .
125   BRA TEMP

Labels are often assigned characters that have meaning to the programmer, but there are rules that must be observed:

1. The label must consist of one to six alphanumeric characters.
2. The first character must be alphabetic.
3. The label must begin in the second space after the line number.
4. A particular label may be used only once following a line number.
They may be used in more than one source statement (for example, BRA
TEMP, JMP TEMP, etc.).
5. A label may not be one of the single characters A, B, or X.

Some examples of labels are TEMP1, TEMP2, COINA, HLP21,
HLP22, STP5A, TBL1, TOM1, DICKA, and so forth.

Source Statements

Source statements may begin in the third space (or any space after the
third space) following a line number, or in the second space (or any space after
the second space) following a label:

100 TEMP STA A $52
   └─ one space with label
or
100 STA A $52
   └─ two spaces without label

As source statements are written, the assembler must be informed about the
addressing mode you are using and what base system your numbers are in. The
sign indicates the immediate mode, that is, that data will be found in the
next byte. Lack of a # sign indicates one of the other modes. The assembler
will determine the mode by analyzing the instruction and the operand of the
source instruction:

# indicates the immediate addressing mode.
$ indicates that the number following is in hex.
@ indicates that the number following is in octal
% indicates that the number following is in binary.
' (apostrophe) indicates an ASCII literal character.

NOTE: If a number is listed in the source statement, and is not preceded by a $, @, or %, the assembler will assume it to be a decimal number. Examples of source statements are shown below:

1. If the contents of the A accumulator are to be stored in hex address 52:

$$100 \text{ TEMP STA A \$52}$$
single space

2. If the contents of the A accumulator are to be stored in an address that has been assigned the label TEMP:

$$100 \text{ STA A TEMP}$$
single space
double space

3. If the binary number 11000111 is to be loaded into the A accumulator:

$$100 \text{ LDA A } \#\%11000111$$
single space
double space

Each of the above statements would be converted to a machine language equivalent and assigned to consecutive memory locations.

Comment Field

Many times in the course of writing a program, it is desirable to insert comments to clarify what is being done. If an asterisk is placed in the second space after a line number, the assembler will ignore the remainder of the line, yet will list that line when the assembled program is printed:

$$100 \text{ * THIS ROUTINE CALCULATES SPEED}$$
one space

Selective comments of this sort can be of considerable help to the programmer (or someone else) when he is looking at the assembled output. Comments may also follow the source statement if separated with one or more spaces.

Assembler Directives

Just as the assembler is given a directive specifying the base system the number is in, it must also be given other directions:

1. *ORG (Origin)*   The *ORG statement* tells the assembler at what address you would like your program to begin. The ORG statement must start in the third space from the line number. If no ORG statement is given, the

assembler will put your first instruction at address 0. For example, when given the statements,

                    100   ORG $425
                    105   LDA A #$63
                        └─2 spaces

the assembler will assign the LDA A immediate operation code of hex 86 to memory location hex 425 and will assign the hex number 63 to memory location hex 426. Any time an ORG statement is encountered in the program, the assembler will assign addresses thereafter, starting with the address specified in the ORG statement.

        2. *EQU (Equate Symbol Value)*   Very often it is convenient to assign a value to a symbol (label) in a program. For example, if we wish to assign the symbol PIA1AC the value of hex 4005, an *EQU statement* would be written prior to the ORG statement as follows:

                    100 PIA1AC EQU $4005
                    105   ORG $500
                    110   LDA A PIA1AC

This would allow you to use the symbol (label) PIA1AC anywhere in the source listing, although the output from the assembler would show the actual value. For example, given the source statement LDA A PIA1AC shown in line 110 above, the assembled output would be:

Memory Address	*Contents*		*Explanation*
500	10110110	(B6)	LDA A (Extended mode)
501	01000000	(40)	($4005)
502	00000101	(05)	

        3. *RMB (Reserve Memory Byte)*   The *RMB assembler directive* is used to reserve memory space for labels. It is placed *after* the ORG statement since the assembler must assign the memory space an address that is determined by the ORG statement. Labels are generally used with the RMB assembler directive. For example:

                    100   ORG $200
                    101   TEMP RMB 1

This will cause the assembler to assign the label TEMP to hex address 200. If line 101 read 101 TEMP RMB 3, hex address 200 would be assigned to the label TEMP, hex address 201 would be assigned to the label TEMP+1, and hex address 202 would be assigned to the label TEMP+2. These bytes in memory are reserved for the label TEMP, TEMP+1, and TEMP+2. This allows the programmer to refer to these addresses by their labels only rather than having to keep track of their actual numeric value. Examples of source statements using the above labels are as follows:

                    150   LDA B TEMP
                    155   STA A TEMP+2
                    160   STA B TEMP+1

4. *NAM (Name)*   The NAM directive just assigns a name to your program. It must start in the third space after the line number and must be followed by a program name of up to eight characters. For example:

100   NAM RONBI
      Ⳑ—double space

The NAM directive is generally the first statement in the source program.

5. *SPC (Space)*   This assembler directive causes vertical spaces to be left when the assembled output is listed. For example:

190   LDA A #52
200   SPC 2
210   STA A $FF

This will result in two spaces being placed between the output machine code of line 190 and the output machine code of line 210 on the assembled listing.

6. *FCB (Form Constant Byte)*   This directive will assign constant values to consecutive memory locations. For example:

200   ORG $400
205 TABLE FCB 0, $25, $FE, $40

In the assembled output, the following memory locations would be assigned values as shown:

Memory Location	Contents (in hex)
400	00
401	25
402	FE
403	40

7. *FDB (Form Constant Double Byte)*   This assembler directive is similar to FCB except that constant double bytes are formed, that is, constants that require two bytes of memory. For example:

200   ORG $400
206 TABLE FDB 0, $BF51, $55C1

The assembled output listing would assign the double byte numbers to memory as follows:

Memory Location	Contents (in hex)
400	00
401	00
402	BF
403	51
404	55
405	C1

8. *FCC (Form Constant Character)*   This assembler directive is used to store the binary ASCII equivalent characters in consecutive memory locations. For example, the ASCII code for the letter P is 1010000 (50_{16}). This would be stored in memory as 01010000. The FCC assembler directives permit the programmer to list the ASCII characters in his source program. The assembler will then convert these characters to their ASCII binary equivalent and assign the binary number to the proper memory location in accordance with the ORG statements. For example:

200 ORG $500
210 TABLE FCC *ALL GREAT!*

The assembler would assign the ASCII binary equivalent of ALL GREAT!, as follows:

Character	Address	Contents
A	500	01000001
L	501	01001100
L	502	01001100
space	503	00100000
G	504	01000111
R	505	01010010
E	506	01000101
A	507	01000001
T	508	01010100
!	509	00100001

NOTE: The delimiter (*   * in this example) must be a nonnumeric character. The delimiter must consist of only one character, that is, [ ] is not legal since it consists of two *different* nonnumeric characters. However, [[is legal.

9. *MON (Monitor)*   This assembler directive is used to signal the assembler that the end of a particular source program has been reached. Control is then returned to the monitor (terminal) after assembly of the source program. For example:

200 MON
  ᒻ—2 spaces

NOTE: A label should-*not* be used with the MON assembler directive.

10. *END (End)*   This assembler directive is used when more than one source program must be assembled. After assembling a program terminated by an END directive, the assembler is prepared to assemble another source program. Only when a MON directive is encountered will control be returned to the monitor. Labels must not be used with the END directive. For example:

201 END
  ᒻ—2 spaces

A label cannot be used with this directive.

11. *PAGE (Page)*   This assembler directive directs the assembler to advance the paper to the top of the next page. The listing after the PAGE directive will start at the top of the next page. For example:

205   PAGE
    └─2 spaces

A label cannot be used with this assembler directive.

12. *OPT (Output Option)*   This assembler directive provides optional formats for the assembler output. Several options may be shown on one line, but each option must be separated with a comma. Available options are as follows:

Description	Listed in Source Program As
(a) Assembler will generate an object tape. If no option is selected, this option will be assumed.	OPT O
(b) No object tape will be generated.	OPT NOO
(c) Assembler will store machine language code into memory.	OPT M
(d) Assembler does not save the assembled (object) program.	OPT NOM
(e) Assembler will print all symbols (labels) at the completion.	OPT S
(f) Assembler will not print symbols.	OPT NOS
(g) Assembler will print list of assembled output.	OPT L
(h) Assembler will not print list of assembled output.	OPT NOL
(i) Assembler will not print a heading at the top of each page. A heading will be printed if this directive is not used.	OPT NOP
(j) Assembler will print all data generated by the FCC, FCB, and FDB directives. OPT G will be selected by default unless OPT NOG is selected.	OPT G
(k) Assembler will list only one line of data from the FCC, FCB, and FDB directives. For example:	OPT NOG

200   OPT M,S
    └── 2 spaces

8.3 Sample Source Program

Let us now summarize the way to write a source program that an assembler will translate into machine language. The following partial program is presented to illustrate as many of the rules just discussed as possible:

```
100  NAM RONB
105  OPT M, S, L
110  PIA1AC EQU $4005
115  TEMP EQU $251
120  ORG $10
125 COIN RMB 5
130  ORG $20
135  TAB FCB $10,$20,$30
140  ORG $30
145  TAB1 FDB $1000,$2000,$3000
150  PAGE
155  ORG $60
160  TYPE FCC *HELP*
165  SPC 6
170  *THIS IS START OF MAIN PROGRAM
175  ORG $300
180  NEW LDA A PIA1AC
185  STA A COIN
190  AGAIN LDA B TAB1+1
195  STA B COIN+1
     •        •
     •        •
     •        •
220  BRA NEW
     •        •
     •        •
     •        •
300  END
305  MON
```

Notice that all source statements, except for label and comment statements, have two spaces between the line number and the source statement. Label and comment statements only require one space after the line number.

Let us now review this example program, line by line, and define what is accomplished by each line:

100 NAM RONB: Assigns name of RONB to the program. This will be printed on the header of the assembled output listing.

105 OPT M,S,L: These options will cause the assembler to store machine code in memory (M), to print the symbol table (S), and to print the assembled program (L).

110 PIA1AC EQU $4005:   The label PIA1AC will be set equal to hex 4005.

115 TEMP EQU $251:   The label TEMP will be set equal to hex 251.

120 ORG $10 and *125 COIN RMB 5:*   These two lines will

direct the assembler to assign the label COIN to hex address 10, label COIN + 1 to hex address 11, etc. These labels are used only in the source program.

130   ORG $20 and *135   TAB FCB $10,$20,$30:*   These two lines will direct the assembler to assign the label TAB to hex address 20. Hex 10 will be loaded in address 20, hex 20 will be loaded in hex address 21, and hex 30 will be loaded in hex address 22.

140   ORG $30 and *145   TAB1 FDB $1000,$2000,$3000:*   These two lines will direct the assembler to assign the label TAB1 to hex address 30 and cause the following hex numbers to be loaded in the following memory locations:

Address	Hex # Stored
30	10
31	00
32	20
33	00
34	30
35	00

150   PAGE: Assembler skips rest of page and starts printing at top of next page.

155   ORG $60 and *160   TYPR FCC *HELP*:*   These two lines will direct the assembler to assign the label TYPR to hex address 60 and to store the ASCII binary equivalent of HELP in consecutive memory locations starting at hex address 60 as follows:

Address	Hex # Stored (ASCII)	
60	48	H
61	45	E
62	4C	L
63	50	P

165   SPC 6:   Assembler leaves the next six spaces blank.

*170   *THIS IS START OF MAIN PROGRAM*:*   Directs the assembler to print this line on the output listing.

175   ORG $300 and *180   NEW LDA A PIA1AC:*   Directs the assembler to assign the label NEW to hex address 300 and the LDA A PIA1AC source code to hex addresses 300, 301, and 302, as follows:

Address	Contents
300	B6
301	40
302	05

(PIA1AC was assigned value of 4005 in line 110)

185 STA A COIN: Directs the assembler to assign the STA A COIN (direct addressing mode) to hex addresses 303 and 304, as follows:

Address	Contents
303	97
304	10

(COIN was assigned address of 10 in line 125)

190 AGAIN LDA B TAB1+1: Directs the assembler to assign the label AGAIN to hex address 305 and LDA B TAB1 + 1 machine code to hex addresses 305 and 306, as follows:

Address	Contents
305	D6
306	31

(TAB1 was assigned address of 30, TAB1+1 address of 31, etc., in line 145)

195 STA B COIN+1: Directs the assembler to assign the STA B COIN + 1 machine code to hex addresses 307 and 308, as follows:

Address	Contents
307	D7
308	11

(COIN+1 was assigned address of 11 in line 125)

220 BRA NEW: Directs the assembler to calculate the number of instructions over which the MPU is to branch. The assembled output is as follows:

Address	Contents
309	20
30A	F5

NOTE: F5 is 2's complement of hex 0B (present address + 2 [30B] minus address of label NEW [300]).

300 END: Tells assembler that this is the end of this particular program.

305 MON: Returns control to monitor.

Refer to Chap. 11 for several examples of machine generated results of assembled programs.

8.4 Branch Instruction Examples

A program going through memory executing one instruction at a time, frequently encounters "BRANCH" instructions. This section will explain how the MPU determines whether to branch out of the sequence at such times or to continue with the next instruction. Remember that, unless a "BRANCH TO SUBROUTINE" or "BRANCH ALWAYS" instruction is involved, it is the status of certain bits in the condition code register that determines whether a branch is to take place. (Such branches are referred to as "conditional branches.") These bits were set or reset by some previous instruction executed by the MPU that affected them. For a branch to take place, their status must be favorable. If the branch is taken, refer to Sec. 7.8 to determine its destination. If it is not taken, the MPU will execute the *next instruction in sequence* (present location plus 2). Following are some examples:

Instructions	Status of Condition Code Register Bits After Execution						Will Conditional Branch Occur?
	H	I	N	Z	V	C	
1. LDA B #$FF	NA	NA	1	0	0	NA	
TST B	NA	NA	1	0	0	0	
BCC	NA	NA	1	0	0	0	Yes
2. LDA B #$FF	NA	NA	1	0	0	NA	
COM B	NA	NA	0	1	0	1	
BCC	NA	NA	0	1	0	1	No
3. LDA A #0	NA	NA	0	1	0	NA	
ADD A #$80	0	NA	1	0	0	0	
BHI	0	NA	1	0	0	0	Yes
4. LDA A #01	NA	NA	0	0	0	NA	
ASR A	NA	NA	0	1	1	1	
BLE	NA	NA	0	1	1	1	Yes
5. LDA A #$85	NA	NA	1	0	0	NA	
LDA B #$05	NA	NA	0	0	0	NA	
SBA	NA	NA	1	0	0	0	
BMI	NA	NA	1	0	0	0	Yes
6. LDX #$01	NA	NA	0	0	0	NA	
DEX	NA	NA	0	1	0	NA	
BEQ	NA	NA	0	1	0	NA	Yes
7. LDA A #7F	NA	NA	0	0	0	NA	
ROR A	NA	NA	0	0	1	1	
BVS	NA	NA	0	0	1	1	Yes

	Status of Condition Code Register Bits After Execution						Will Conditional Branch Occur?
Instructions	H	I	N	Z	V	C	
8. LDA A #7F	NA	NA	0	0	0	NA	
ADD A #1	NA	NA	1	0	1	0	
COM A	NA	NA	0	0	0	1	
BGE	NA	NA	0	0	0	1	Yes
9. LDA A #7F	NA	NA	0	0	0	NA	
LDA B #7E	NA	NA	0	0	0	NA	
SBA	NA	NA	0	0	0	0	
LSR A	NA	NA	0	1	1	1	
BCS	NA	NA	0	1	1	1	Yes

\#   Indicates Immediate Mode
$ Indicates Hex Number
NA Not Affected

Problems

1. Write instructions in M6800 source language to accomplish the following:
   - (a) Store contents of B accumulator in hex location 2452.
   - (b) Store contents of B accumulator in hex location 24.
   - (c) Store contents of B accumulator in address formed by adding hex 24 to contents of index register.
   - (d) Decrement the A accumulator.
   - (e) Read the contents of hex location 24 into the A accumulator.
   - (f) Add 16 to the contents of the B accumulator.
   - (g) Compare the contents of the index register with hex memory location ABFD.
   - (h) Store hex CD52 in the index register.
2. What is the status of each bit in the condition code register after execution of the instructions in problem 1?
3. Show how each source statement in problem 1 would appear in the machine language stored in memory.
4. Calculate the offset (number to be added to the contents of present memory location plus 2) for the following branches:

	Address	Instruction	
(a)	500	20	(Branch Always to
	501	—	location 520)
(b)	500	20	(Branch Always to
	501	—	location 491)

5. Examine the following program, starting at address 00F9. Upon *completion* of the instruction ending at address 0106, show the contents of each of the MPU registers:

		Hex Address	Hex Contents
A	_____	00F9	D6
B	_____	00FA	FE
PC	_____	00FB	86
X	_____	00FC	AB
SP	_____	00FD	FE
		00FE	01
	H I N Z V C	00FF	02
		0100	20
CC	1 1 _ X _ _ _	0101	02
		0102	00
		0103	FA
		0104	AE
		0105	02
		0106	1B

6. Write the instruction LDA A in four addressing modes (make up your own data, addresses, and offsets):

Immediate	LDA A	_____
Direct	_____	_____
Extended	_____	_____
Indexed	_____	_____

7. Study each of the following programs, starting at the first address shown. Show the contents of each register upon completion of the program.

(a)

		Memory Location	Contents
A	_____	FA	CE
B	_____	FB	01
PC	_____	FC	03
X	_____	FD	E6
SP	_____	FE	00
		FF	20
		100	03
		101	01
		102	3F
		103	B2
		104	B6
		105	01
		106	01
		107	9E
		108	FB

A [   ]

B [   ]

PC [   ]

X [   ]

SP [   ]

(b) *Memory*
     Location   *Contents*

Location	Contents
F9	FE
FA	01
FB	00
FC	AE
FD	00
FE	20
FF	02
100	01
101	03
102	D6
103	FC
104	86
105	13

A [   ]

B [   ]

PC [   ]

X [   ]

SP [   ]

X is initially 00FB

(c) *Memory*
     Location   *Contents*

Location	Contents
F8	EE
F9	02
FA	F6
FB	01
FC	03
FD	96
FE	F9
FF	8E
100	20
101	A1
102	4A
103	26
104	FD

9

M6800 Microcomputer Family

In the last chapter, the complete M6800 instruction set was discussed. Before any of these instructions can be of any use, however, there must be some type of hardware to implement and execute them. This chapter will therefore take a look at the complete M6800 family of integrated circuits (chips). Each device and component will be described, including all internal registers, all pin numbers, and all signals applied to these external pins.

9.1 System Overview

The M6800 family of LSI (Large Scale Integration) devices permits the design of a system with a minimum amount of time and effort. The heart of the M6800 family is the *MC6800 Microprocessor Unit (MPU)*. Basic supporting chips are as follows:

1. MCM6810 *Random Access Memory (RAM)*
2. MC6821 *Peripheral Interface Adapter (PIA)*
3. MCM6830 *Read Only Memory (ROM)*
4. MC6850 *Asynchronous Communications Interface Adapter (ACIA)*

The MPU addresses these devices through a 16-bit "address bus," and the transfer of data is accomplished over an 8-bit "data bus."

LARGE SCALE INTEGRATION (LSI): This is a term applied to single chips (integrated circuits) that contain many circuits. The actual number of circuits on a chip to qualify it to be called LSI varies with the discussion; however, a number in excess of 1000 gets few arguments.

The MPU generates all addresses placed on the address bus. Since this is a 16-bit address bus, addresses from 0000 0000 0000 0000 (0000_{16}) to 1111

1111 1111 1111 (FFFF$_{16}$) can be generated. Such a bus is often referred to as a "64K address bus," but, in reality, there are 65536 distinct addresses. When the MPU generates an address, only the device with that address will communicate with the MPU. The 16 bits are usually designated A0 through A15—bit 1 (the least significant) being designated A0, bit 2 being designated A1, and so forth, through bit 16 (the most significant) designated A15.

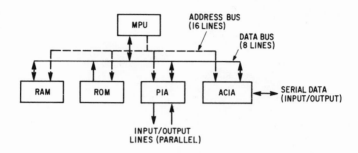

Fig. 9.1 M6800 system

The 8-bit data bus is common to all devices shown in Fig. 9.1. Notice the direction of the data flow between each device and the MPU as indicated by the arrows. The ROM can send instructions to the MPU, but the MPU *cannot* send data to the ROM. However, RAMs, PIAs, and ACIAs all have the capability of sending data to and receiving data from the MPU. The individual lines of the data bus are designated D0 through D7—bit 1 (the least significant) being designated D0, bit 2 being designated D1, and so forth, through bit 8 (the most significant), designated D7. All common data line pins of each device are tied together. For example, all D0 pins are tied together, all D1 pins are tied together, and so on.

Once a device has been addressed, how does it know whether it is supposed to receive data or send data? This is the purpose of another line between the MPU and all devices called the *Read/Write (R/W)* line. This line allows the MPU to control the flow of data between devices. If the R/W line is high, the addressed device is to send data to the MPU. If the R/W line is low, the MPU is to send data to the addressed device.

The M6800 system is capable of operating at clock rates from 100,000 Hz (100 kHz) to 2,000,000 Hz (2 MHz), depending upon the model. The system will operate from a *single* +5 volt power supply.

9.2 Microprocessor Unit (MPU)

The nucleus of the M6800 microcomputer family is the M6800 microprocessing unit. The MPU is enclosed in a 40-pin package as shown in Fig.

9.2. It features six internal registers (see Fig. 9.3), that users must be concerned with, as follows:

1. A Accumulator (A)
2. B Accumulator (B)
3. Index Register (X)
4. Program Counter (PC)
5. Stack Pointer Register (SP)
6. Condition Code Register (CC)

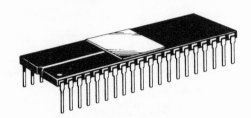

Fig. 9.2 Forty-pin package of the MPU

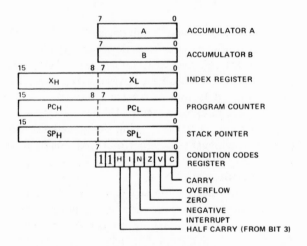

Fig. 9.3 M6800 registers

Internal M6800 Registers

1. *A Accumulator (A)*   The A accumulator is an eight-bit (one-byte) register within the MPU that is used as a temporary holding register for MPU operations performed by the arithmetic logic unit.

2. *B Accumulator (B)*   The B accumulator is also an eight-bit (one-byte) register within the MPU that is also used as a temporary holding register for MPU operations performed by the arithmetic logic unit.

3. *Index Register (X)*   The index register, often indicated by X, is a 16-bit (two-byte) register that is primarily used to modify addresses when the indexed mode of addressing is employed. This register may be decremented, incremented, loaded, stored, or compared.

4. *Program Counter (PC)*   The program counter is a 16-bit (two-byte) register that contains the address of the next byte of the instruction to be fetched from memory. When the current value of the program counter is placed on the address bus, the program counter will be incremented automatically.

5. *Stack Pointer (SP)*   The stack pointer is a 16-bit (two-byte) register that contains a beginning address, normally in RAM, where the status of the MPU registers may be stored when the MPU has other functions to perform, such as during an interrupt or during a branch to subroutine (BSR). The address in the stack pointer is the starting address of sequential memory locations in RAM, where MPU contents of the registers will be stored. The status of the MPU will be stored in the RAM as follows:

Stack Point Address   ← contents of PCL
Stack Pointer Address −1   ← contents of PCH
Stack Pointer Address −2   ← contents of XL
Stack Pointer Address −3   ← contents of XH
Stack Pointer Address −4   ← contents of A
Stack Pointer Address −5   ← contents of B
Stack Pointer Address −6   ← contents of CC

After the status of each register is stored on the stack, the stack pointer will be decremented. When the stack is unloaded (status of registers restored), the status of the last register on the stack will be the first register that is restored.

6. *Condition Code Register*   The condition code register is an eight-bit (one-byte) register that is used by branch instructions to determine whether the MPU should execute an instruction located at some address other than the next in sequence. Branches will occur according to the status of specific bits in this register. It must be emphasized that different instructions affect the various bits of this register in different ways. To determine how a particular instruction affects each bit, refer to the M6800 instruction set in

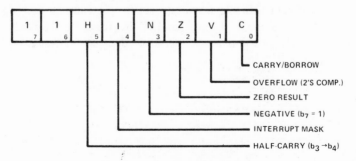

Fig. 9.4 Condition code register

Chap. 8. Bits 6 and 7 of this register are always set to a "1", that is, they are not really used as conditions for a branch to occur. The remaining bits, bits 0 through 5, are designated the H, I, N, Z, V, and C bits, as shown in Fig. 9.4.

6(a). *Carry–Borrow (C Bit)*   This bit (bit 0) of the condition code register will be set to a "1" if, after the execution of certain instructions, there was a carry or borrow from the most significant bit of the results of the operation being performed. Otherwise, it will be cleared.

EXAMPLE USING ABA INSTRUCTION

BEFORE EXECUTION   AFTER EXECUTION

A   1000 0000   A   0000 0000

B   1000 0000   B   1000 0000

                       C   C
CC   0 or 1   CC   1

6(b). *Overflow (V Bit)*   This bit (bit 1) of the condition code register will be set to a "1" when a 2's complement overflow results from an arithmetic operation and will be set to a "0" if a 2's complement overflow does not occur at that time. Two's complement overflow ordinarily occurs if the last operation resulted in a number larger than the $\pm$ 127 range of an eight-bit register.

EXAMPLE USING DEC A INSTRUCTION

BEFORE EXECUTION   AFTER EXECUTION

A   1000 0000   A   0111 1111

                       V   V
CC   0 or 1   CC   1

Remember that subtraction is accomplished by the addition of 2's complement. Therefore, to subtract the number 1 (DEC) from the A register, it must be converted to its 2's complement and then added to the contents of the A register:

$$
\begin{array}{rcl}
\text{Number} & \rightarrow & 0000\ 0001 \\
\text{1's complement} & \rightarrow & 1111\ 1110 \\
\text{2's complement} & = & 1111\ 1111 \\
\text{Contents of A Register} & = & +\ \underline{1000\ 0000} \\
\text{2's complement of 1} & = & 1\ 0111\ 1111
\end{array}
$$

Since there is an overflow, the V bit is set to "1".

6(c). *Zero (Z Bit)*   This bit (bit 2) of the condition code register is set to a "1" if the result of an arithmetic operation is zero; otherwise, it is reset to a "0".

EXAMPLE USING DEC A INSTRUCTION

BEFORE EXECUTION   AFTER EXECUTION

A | 0000 0001 | A | 0000 0000 |

                    Z   Z
CC | 0 or 1 | CC | 1 |

                              Or . . .

A | 0000 0010 | A | 0000 0001 |

                    Z   Z
CC | 0 or 1 | CC | 0 |

6(d). *Negative (N Bit)*   This bit (bit 3) of the condition code register is set to a "1" if bit 7 of an arithmetic operation is set to a "1". If the arithmetic operation results in bit 7 being reset to a "0", then this bit will also be reset to a "0".

EXAMPLE USING LDA A #$80 INSTRUCTION

BEFORE EXECUTION   AFTER EXECUTION

A | 0000 0000 | A | 1000 0000 |

                    N   N
CC | 0 or 1 | CC | 1 |

6(e). *Interrupt Mask (I Bit)*   This bit (bit 4) of the condition code register inhibits all $\overline{IRQ}$ interrupts if set to a "1". If this bit is reset to a "0", the processor may be interrupted by $\overline{IRQ}$ in the low state. This I bit can be set to a "1" with the SEI instruction; it will be set to a "1" by the MPU if an interrupt occurs or the SWI instruction is encountered. This bit will be cleared (I = "0") when the MPU encounters an RTI if the interrupt was caused by the $\overline{IRQ}$ input line or CLI instruction.

6(f). *Half–Carry (H Bit)*   This bit (bit 5) of the condition code register is set to a "1" if, during an arithmetic operation involving the ABA,

ADC, and ADD instructions, there is a carry from bit 3 to bit 4 of the results. If there was no carry to bit 4, this bit will be reset to "0".

EXAMPLE USING ABA INSTRUCTION

BEFORE EXECUTION		AFTER EXECUTION	
A	0000 1000	A	0001 0000
B	0000 1000	B	0000 1000
	H		H
CC	0 or 1	CC	1

6(g). *Bit 6 and Bit 7*   Always equal to a "1".

M6800 Input/Output Signals

As mentioned previously, the M6800 microprocessor is a 40-pin device. Figure 9.5 shows the pin-out of the MPU and the direction, via the arrows, of the signal flow. Notice that pins 38 and 35 are not used.

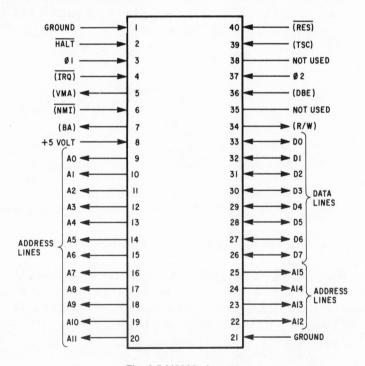

Fig. 9.5 M6800 pin outs

1. *Ground (Pins 1 and 21)*   These pins must be tied to the system ground, which is the negative side of the 5-volt power supply.

2. $\overline{\text{HALT}}$ *(Pin 2)*   When the input on this pin is in the high state ("1"), the MPU will fetch and execute instructions. When the HALT line goes low, the MPU will finish execution of the instruction it is processing before halting. When the MPU is in the halt mode, the Bus Available (BA) line will be high, the Valid Memory Address (VMA) line will be low, and the Read/-Write (R/W) line, the address bus, and the data bus will be in the high-impedance state. If an interrupt ($\overline{\text{IRQ}}$ or $\overline{\text{NMI}}$) should occur while the MPU is in the halt state, it will be latched into the MPU until the latter is taken out of the halt mode, at which time it will service the interrupt. The $\overline{\text{HALT}}$ line permits an external source to control program execution by executing one instruction at a time. This capability is particularly useful during program debugging. During normal operation of a system, this pin would be tied to $+5$ V.

3. *Phase 1 Clock (Pin 3)*   The NMOS ϕ1 output of the system clock will be inputted on this pin.

4. *Interrupt Request Line ($\overline{\text{IRQ}}$) (Pin 4)*   When the $\overline{\text{IRQ}}$ line from the PIAs (or some other external device) goes low, the MPU will complete the instruction it is executing and then go into an interrupt sequence, providing the interrupt mask has not been previously set to inhibit interrupts. During the first step in this sequence, the contents of the index register, the program counter, the A and B accumulators, and the condition code register will be stored on the stack (in RAM) for later use. Next, the I bit in the condition code register will be set to a "1" so that no further interrupts may occur. The MPU will now load the contents of the highest ROM address minus 6 and the contents of the highest ROM address minus 7 into the program counter. This vectoring address will occur when the MPU puts the addresses FFF8 and FFF9 on the address bus. The contents of these locations contain the address of the program that is to service the interrupt by prescribing the action the MPU is to take because of the interrupt. At some point in the servicing program, an RTI instruction will be encountered that will cause the MPU and its internal registers to be restored to the condition they were in before the interrupt. See Fig. 9.6 for a detailed flowchart of the interrupt sequence.

The $\overline{\text{IRQ}}$ sequence is as follows:

(1) If the I bit in the condition code register is not set ($I = 0$) and the $\overline{\text{IRQ}}$ goes low for at least one ϕ2 cycle, the $\overline{\text{IRQ}}$ sequence will be entered.

(2) After completion of the current instruction, internal registers PC, X, A, B, and CC will be stored in RAM at the address indicated by the stack pointer in descending locations (seven bytes in all).

(3) The $\overline{\text{IRQ}}$ mask (I bit $= 1$) is set.

(4) Data at FFF8 gets loaded into PCH.

(5) Data at FFF9 gets loaded into PCL.

(6) PC contents go out on address bus during $\phi 1$.

(7) Contents of the location addressed enter instruction register during $\phi 2$ and are decoded as first instruction of interrupt routine.

(8) If it is a more than 1-byte instruction, additional bytes enter MPU for execution. If not, go to next step.

(9) After execution, step 7 is repeated for subsequent instructions. The loop is repeated until the instruction "RTI" is executed.

The SWI sequence is as follows:

(1) Contents of MPU registers PC, X, A, B, and CC are stored in RAM at the address indicated by the stack pointer in descending location (seven bytes in all).

(2) The $\overline{\text{IRQ}}$ mask (I bit = 1) is set.

(3) Data at FFFA gets loaded into PCH.

(4) Data at FFFB gets loaded into PCL.

(5) PC contents go out on address bus during $\phi 1$.

(6) Contents of the byte addressed enter instruction register during $\phi 2$ and are decoded as first instruction of SWI subroutine.

(7) If it is more than a one-byte instruction, additional bytes enter MPU for execution. If not, go to next step.

(8) After execution, step 6 is repeated for subsequent instructions. The loop is repeated until the instruction RTI is executed.

5. *Valid Memory Address (VMA) (Pin 5)*   When this line is in the high state, it is a signal from the MPU to all devices tied to the address bus that there is a valid address in the address bus. This line will be either a "1" or a "0". The signal is not three-state.

6. *Nonmaskable Interrupt* $(\overline{\text{NMI}})$*(Pin 6)*   This input pin is similar to the $\overline{\text{IRQ}}$ input, except that the interrupt is *nonmaskable.* As with the $\overline{\text{IRQ}}$, the MPU will complete the instruction being executed before it recognizes the $\overline{\text{NMI}}$ interrupt. After the contents of the program counter, index register, A and B accumulators, and the condition code register have been stored on the stack (RAM) for later use, the I bit will be set to a "1". The contents of ROM locations FFFC and FFFD will next be loaded into the program counter. These locations contain the address of the program that services the nonmaskable interrupt. Again, when the MPU comes to an RTI instruction in the servicing program, it, along with its registers, will be restored to the condition it was in before the nonmaskable interrupt. See Fig. 9.6 for a detailed flowchart of the interrupt sequence.

The $\overline{\text{NMI}}$ sequence is as follows:

(1) If the $\overline{\text{NMI}}$ goes low for at least one $\phi 2$ cycle, the MPU will wait for completion of the current instruction.

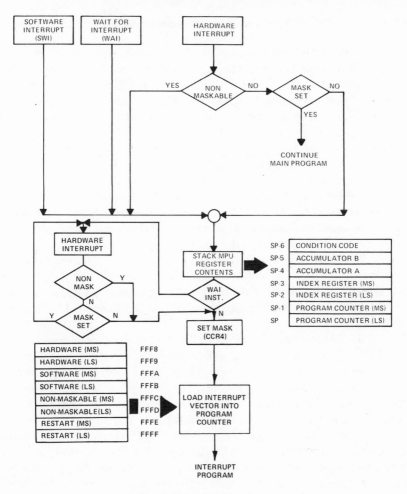

Fig. 9.6 Interrupt flow chart

(2) The internal registers PC, X, A, B, and CC will then be stored in RAM at the address indicated by the stack pointer in descending locations (seven bytes in all).

(3) The $\overline{\text{IRQ}}$ (bit I = 1) mask is set.

(4) Data at FFFC is loaded into PCH.

(5) Data at FFFD is loaded into PCL.

(6) PC contents go out on address bus during $\phi 1$.

(7) Contents of the location addressed enter instruction register during $\phi 2$ and are decoded as first instruction of NMI subroutine.

(8) If it is a more than one-byte instruction, additional bytes enter MPU for execution. If not, go to next step.

(9) After execution, step 7 is repeated for subsequent instructions. This loop is repeated until the instruction RTI is executed.

7. *Bus Available (BA) (Pin 7)*   Normally, this line will be in the low state, indicating that the address bus and the data bus are under MPU control. When it is in the high state, the address bus and the data bus are available, that is, they are in a high-impedance state. This condition will occur if the $\overline{\text{HALT}}$ line is in the halt (low) mode or the MPU is in a wait condition as the result of the WAI instruction.

8. *+5-Volt Power (Pin 8)*   This pin must be tied to the positive side of the 5-volt system power supply.

9. *Address Lines (A0–A15) (Pins 9 through 20 and 22 through 25)* These 16 output lines are used to address devices external to the MPU. The addresses are generated by the MPU. The outputs of the 16 lines are three-state bus drivers capable of driving one standard TTL load and 130pF at 1 MHz. When the output is turned off, the circuit is essentially open.

10. *Data Lines (D0–D7) (Pins 26 through 33)*   These eight bidirectional lines are used to transfer data to a peripheral device from the MPU and vice versa. They can be put in the three-state condition (high impedance) and have three-state output buffers capable of driving one standard TTL load and 130 Pf at 1 MHz.

11. *Read/Write Line (R/W) (Pin 34)*   This signal generated by the MPU tells all devices external to itself that it is in a Read state if the line is high ("1") or in a Write state (send) if the line is low ("0"). The normal stand-by state is the high, or Read, state. The line is put in the high-impedance state when the three-state line goes high. Also, when the processor is halted, it will be in the OFF state (high impedance).

12. *Data Bus Enable (DBE) (Pin 36)*   This input signal will enable the data bus output drivers when in the high state. It is normally from the phase 2 (ϕ2) clock. When in the high state, it will permit data to be output in the data bus during the MPU write cycle. During the MPU read cycle, the data bus drivers will be disabled internally.

13. *Phase Two Clock (Pin 37)*   The ϕ2 output of the system clock is inputted on this pin.

14. *Three-State Control (TSC) (Pin 39)*   This high input causes all address lines and the read/write line to go into the high-impedance state. The VMA (Valid Memory Address) and BA (Bus Available) signals will be forced low, thereby preventing a false read or write to or from a device enabled by the VMA line. The data bus is not affected by TSC and has its own enable code. When the TSC line is held high, the ϕ1 and ϕ2 clock inputs must be held high and low, respectively, in order to delay program execution and free the address bus for use by other devices. Since the MPU is a dynamic device, caution must be taken not to hold the system in the three-state condition for longer than 9.5 μsec or the data in the MPU will be destroyed.

15. *Reset $(\overline{RES})$ (Pin 40)*   This input signal is used to start the MPU from a power-down condition. After the power is turned on and reaches 4.75 V, the $\overline{\text{RES}}$ input *must* be held low for at least eight clock cycles, during which time the address bus contains the address FFFE. After a minimum of

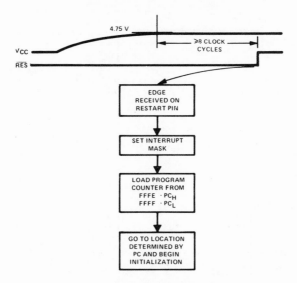

Fig. 9.7 Restart sequence

Table 9.1   M6800 Pin Summary

Pin No.	Signal Description	Signal Name	Signal Type	Three State
1	Ground	GND	Input	No
2	Halt	$\overline{\text{HALT}}$	Input	No
3	Phase 1	$\phi 1$	Input	No
4	Interrupt Request	$\overline{\text{IRQ}}$	Input	No
5	Valid Memory Address	VMA	Output	No
6	Nonmaskable Interrupt	$\overline{\text{NMI}}$	Input	No
7	Bus Available	BA	Output	No
8	Power	+5	Input	No
9–20 22–25	Address Lines	A0–A15	Output	Yes
21	Ground	GND	Input	No
26–33	Data Lines	D0–D7	Input/Output	Yes
34	Read/Write	R/W	Output	Yes
35,38	Not Used			
36	Data Bus Enable	DBE	Input	No
37	Phase 2	$\phi 2$	Input	No
39	Three-State Control	TSC	Input	No
40	Reset	$\overline{\text{RES}}$	Input	No

eight clock cycles, the $\overline{\text{RES}}$ line may be allowed to go high to signal the MPU to begin the restart sequence. The contents of the ROM location addressed by FFFE will be placed in the most significant byte of the program counter, and the contents of the ROM location addressed by FFFF will be placed in its least significant byte. The program counter now contains the address of the initializing routine. During the restart sequence (Fig. 9.7), the interrupt mask bit (I)

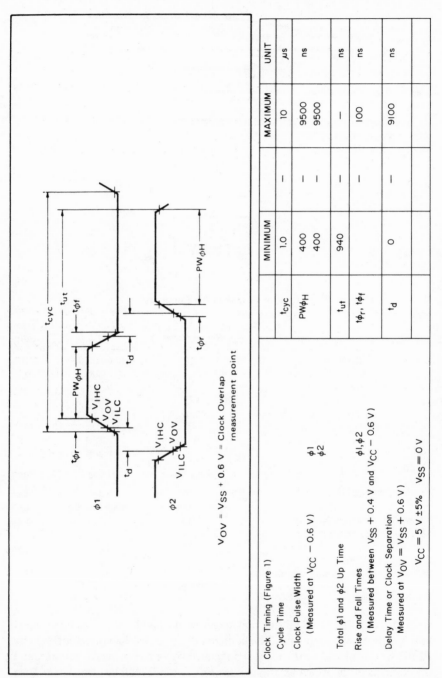

Clock Timing (Figure 1)		MINIMUM	MAXIMUM	UNIT
Cycle Time	t_{cyc}	1.0	10	μs
Clock Pulse Width (Measured at $V_{CC} - 0.6$ V)	$PW_{\phi H}$ $\phi 1$ $\phi 2$	400 400	9500 9500	ns ns
Total $\phi 1$ and $\phi 2$ Up Time	t_{ut}	940	—	ns
Rise and Fall Times (Measured between $V_{SS} + 0.4$ V and $V_{CC} - 0.6$ V)	$t_{\phi r}, t_{\phi f}$ $\phi 1, \phi 2$		100	ns
Delay Time or Clock Separation Measured at $V_{OV} = V_{SS} + 0.6$ V)	t_d	0	9100	ns

$V_{CC} = 5$ V ±5% $V_{SS} = 0$ V

Fig. 9.8 Waveform and clock specifications

of the condition code register is set. Part of the initialization procedure in the start-up program might use the CLI instruction that resets the I bit to "0".

The reset sequence is as follows:

1. While $\overline{\text{HALT}}$ is high, $\overline{\text{RESET}}$ goes low for at least eight cycles of $\phi1$ and $\phi2$, during which time the interrupt bit (I) is set.

2. Contents of FFFE are loaded into the program counter (most significant byte).

3. Contents of FFFF are loaded into the PCL program counter (least significant byte).

4. PC contents go out on address bus during $\phi1$.

Table 9.1 gives a M6800 pin summary.

System Clock

As mentioned in Chap. 5, all digital systems must have a clock signal so that functions may be accomplished in a timed, orderly manner. The M6800 Microcomputer System is no different. It requires a two-phase nonoverlapping clock capable of operating from the 5-V system power. The waveform and clock specifications are shown in Fig. 9.8.

It will be the purpose of this section to describe the operation of the system clock and to show how all operations in the MPU are based around it. Inside the MPU is a register called an *instruction register* (IR), whose purpose is to decode instructions so that the MPU knows which one is current and which of the various addressing modes is to be used.

When the phase 1 ($\phi1$) clock signal goes high, the contents of the program counter are transferred to the address bus. While this is taking place, VMA will go high ("1"), indicating a valid address. On the falling edge of $\phi1$, the program counter will be incremented by one. When $\phi2$ goes high (assuming that the $\phi2$ clock signal is used as a chip select or an enable), data from the memory location addressed is placed on the address bus, and during

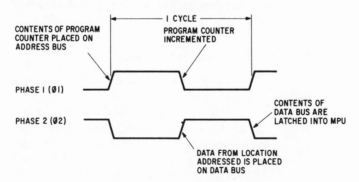

Fig. 9.9 Instruction register sequence

the falling edge of $\phi2$, the data is latched into the MPU. This general sequence (Fig. 9.9) occurs every time the MPU addresses a memory location and data is transferred.

To illustrate the role of the system clock in the execution of instructions by the MPU, let us investigate several instructions from a simple program and see what happens during each clock cycle:

Address	Contents	Description
100	86	Load A Immediate
101	25	Data
102	D6	Load B Direct
103	35	Address
104	B7	STA A Extended
105	40	Address
106	02	

1. Addresses 100 and 101 (two cycles):

Cycle 1: (a) The contents of the P counter (100) are placed on the address bus.
  (b) The P counter is then incremented by 1 (to 101).
  (c) The contents of address 100 (86) are placed on the data bus, latched into the MPU instruction register (IR), and decoded as a load A Immediate instruction (R/W and VMA are "1").

Cycle 2: (a) The contents of the P counter (101) are placed on the address bus.
  (b) The P counter is then incremented by 1 (to 102).
  (c) The contents of address 101 (25) are placed on the data bus and then latched into the A accumulator (R/W and VMA are "1").

2. Addresses 102 and 103 (three cycles):

Cycle 1: (a) The contents of the P counter (102) are placed in the address bus.
  (b) The P counter is then incremented by 1 (to 103).
  (c) The contents of address 102 (D6) are placed on the data bus, latched into the MPU instruction register, and decoded as a load B direct instruction (VMA and R/W are "1")

Cycle 2: (a) The contents of the P counter (103) are placed on the address bus.
   (b) The P counter is then incremented by 1 (to 104).
   (c) The contents of address 103 (35) are placed in the data bus and then latched into the MPU address bus register (VMA and R/W are "1").

Cycle 3: (a) The contents of the address bus register (35) are placed on the address bus.
   (b) The contents of address 35 are placed in the data bus and then latched into the B accumulator (VMA and R/W are "1").

3. Addresses 104–106 (five cycles):

Cycle 1: (a) The contents of the P counter (104) are placed on the address bus.
   (b) The P counter is then incremented by 1 (to 105).
   (c) The contents of address 104 (B7) are placed on the data bus, latched into the MPU instruction register, and decoded as a store A Extended instruction (VMA and R/W are "1").

Cycle 2: (a) The contents of the P counter (105) are placed in the address bus.
   (b) The P counter is then incremented by 1 (to 106).
   (c) The contents of address 105 (40) are placed in the data bus and then latched into the MPU temporary register (most significant byte) (VMA and R/W are "1").

Cycle 3: (a) The contents of the P counter (106) are placed on the address bus.
   (b) The P counter is then incremented by 1 (to 107).
   (c) The contents of address 106 (02) are placed on the data bus and then latched into the MPU address bus register (least significant byte) (VMA and R/W are "1").

Cycle 4: (a) The contents of the address bus register (4002) are placed on the address bus.
   (b) The contents of the A accumulator (25) are readied for transfer to the data bus (VMA is "0" and R/W is "1").

Cycle 5: (a) Address 4002 is accessed, the R/W line is put in a low state (write), VMA is "1", and the contents of the A accumulator are gated to the data bus and then stored in the address accessed (4002).

9.3 Random Access Memory (RAM)

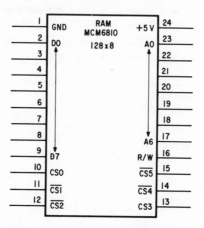

Fig. 9.10 RAM package

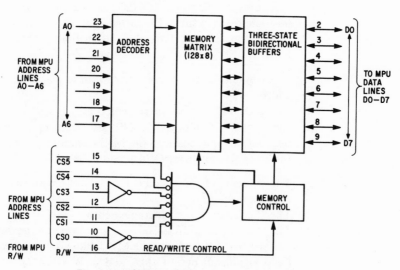

Fig. 9.11 MCM6810 RAM functional block diagram

The MCM6810 is a TTL compatible, static Random Access Memory (RAM). It is a three-state N-MOS chip containing 128 eight-bit words (128 bytes) housed in a 24-pin package (Fig. 9.10). The eight RAM data bus pins, D0 through D7, are tied to the MPU data bus pins, D0 through D7. The seven address pins from the RAM (A0 through A6) must be tied to MPU address lines A0 through A6. These seven address lines are used by the MPU to select an eight-bit word on the particular chip addressed. If there is more than one MCM6810 RAM in the system, all A0's are tied to the A0 address line from the MPU, all A1's are tied to the A1 address line from the MPU, and so forth. The MCM6810 RAM also has six chip select pins. These chip selects will be tied to the address bus from the MPU in such a manner that only one RAM chip is addressed at a time. To address an MCM 6810 RAM requires a low level on four of the chip selects and a high level on two of the chip selects. The addressing scheme for connecting the chip selects to the address bus will be covered in greater detail in Chap. 10. The read/write (R/W) line is the same R/W from the MPU discussed in Sec. 9.2. To read data from a RAM location, the R/W line must be in a high state; to store data in a RAM location, the R/W line must be in a low state. When a RAM is not addressed, the RAM data bus goes to the three-state condition (high impedance).

A functional diagram of the MCM6810 RAM is shown in Fig. 9.11.

9.4 Read Only Memory (ROM)

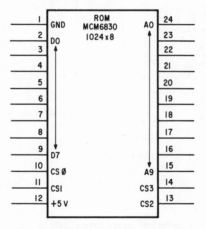

Fig. 9.12 ROM package

The MCM6830 is a TTL compatible, mask-programmable Read Only Memory (ROM). It is a three-state N-MOS chip containing 1024 eight-bit words (bytes) housed in a 24-pin package (Fig. 9.12). The eight ROM data bus pins, D0 through D7, are tied to the MPU data bus pins, D0 through D7. The ten address pins from the ROM (A0 through A9) must be tied to the MPU address bus pins, A0 through A9. These ten address lines are used by the MPU to select an eight-bit word on the particular chip addressed. If there is more than one MCM6830 ROM in the system, the A0 of each ROM is tied to the A0 line in the MPU, the A1 of each ROM is tied to the A1 line in the MPU, and so forth. The MCM6830 ROM has four chip selects available. These four chip selects must be defined by the user as to how many will be positive (CS) and how many negative ($\overline{CS}$). Since this device is mask-programmable, the chip selects will be manufactured into the device. They will be tied to the address bus from the MPU in such a manner that only one ROM is addressed at a time. To select a ROM, a +2-V (or greater) signal must be applied to each positive chip select (CS) and a 0-V level to each negative one ($\overline{CS}$). The addressing scheme for connecting the chip selects to the address bus will be covered in great detail in Chap. 10. When a ROM is not addressed, the ROM data bus goes into the three-state condition (high impedance).

A functional diagram of the MCM6830 ROM is shown in Fig. 9.13.

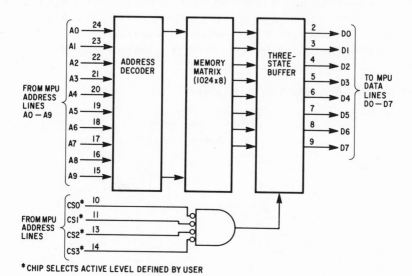

*CHIP SELECTS ACTIVE LEVEL DEFINED BY USER

Fig. 9.13 MCM6830 ROM functional block diagram

9.5 Peripheral Interface Adapter (PIA)

The MC6821 Peripheral Interface Adapter (PIA) is an N-MOS device housed in a 40-pin package and used as a means of interfacing peripheral equipment and external signals with the MPU (Fig. 9.14). The PIA communicates with the MPU through the same eight-bit bidirectional data bus that the RAMs and ROMs share. The PIA has two separate eight-bit bidirectional peripheral data busses for interfacing to the outside world. The 16 bidirectional input/output lines may be programmed to act as either input or output lines (Fig. 9.15).

In addition to the 24 lines shown in Fig. 9.15, there are three chip select pins (CS0, CS1, and $\overline{CS2}$), a reset pin ($\overline{RES}$), two interrupt pins ($\overline{IRQA}$ and $\overline{IRQB}$), a read/write Pin (R/W), four control line pins (CA1, CA2, CB1, and CB2), an enable pin (E), two register select pins (RS0 and RS1), and two input power pins (+5 and ground), as shown in Fig. 9.16.

The MC6821 PIA has two sides, an A side and a B side. Each side has a *peripheral data register,* a *data direction register,* and a *control register.*

Each peripheral data register is the interface register between the PIA chip and the outside world. This register is eight bits (one byte) wide.

The data direction register is used by the programmer to define each peripheral line as an input or an output line. When each bit in this eight-bit

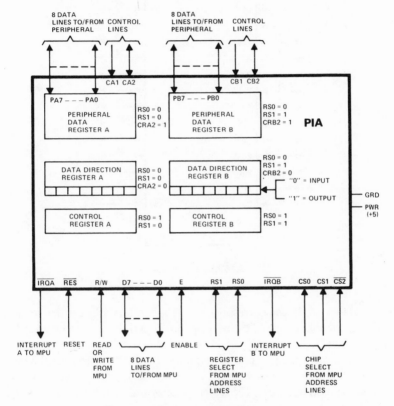

Fig. 9.14 MC6821 PIA

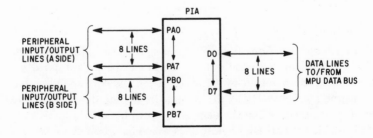

Fig. 9.15 MC6821 PIA input/output lines

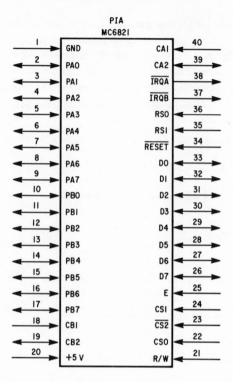

Fig. 9.16 MC6821 package

register is set to a "1", the corresponding peripheral data line is defined as an output line; when set to a "0", the corresponding peripheral data line is defined as an input line.

The control register is used to permit the MPU to control the operation of the four peripheral control lines CA1, CA2, CB1, and CB2. This register is also used to control the interrupt lines and monitor the status of the interrupt flags. Bit 2 of this register is used, in conjunction with the register selects, to determine whether the peripheral data register or the data direction register is to be addressed.

PIA Interface Lines

1. *Peripheral Data Lines PA0 through PA7*   Each of these eight data lines interfacing with the outside world can be programmed to act as either an input or an output by setting a "1" in the corresponding bit in the data direction register (DDR) if the line is to be an output or a "0" in the DDR if it is to be an input. When the data in the peripheral data lines is read into the MPU by a load instruction, those lines which have been designated as input lines (0 in DDR) will be gated directly to the data bus and into the register

selected in the MPU. In the input mode, each line represents a maximum of 1.5 standard TTL load.

On the other hand, when an output data instruction (STA A PIA) is executed, data will be transferred via the data bus to the peripheral data register. A "1" output will cause a "high" on the corresponding data line, and a "0" output will cause a "low." Data in peripheral register A that has been programmed as output may be read by an MPU "LDA A from PIA" instruction. If the voltage is above 2 V for a logic "1" or below 0.8 V for a logic "0", the data will agree with the data outputted. However, if these output lines have been loaded so that they do not meet the levels for logic "1", the data read back into the MPU may differ from data stored in PIA peripheral register A.

2. *Peripheral Data Lines PB0 through PB7*   The eight data lines interfacing with the outside world on the B side may also be programmed to act either as an input or output by setting a "1" in the corresponding bit in the data direction register (DDR) if the line is to be an output or a "0" in the DDR if it is to be an input. The output buffers driving these lines have three-state capability, allowing them to enter a high-impedance state when the peripheral data line is used as an input. Data in peripheral register B that has been programmed as output may be read by an MPU "LDA A from PIA" instruction even though the lines have been programmed as outputs. If a line is first programmed as an output line by storing a "1" in data direction register B and then storing a "1" in that same bit position in peripheral data register B, reading the bit status back will indicate a "1" even though excess loading (possibly due to a short) may have occurred at the pin. This is because of the buffering between the register and the output pin.

3. *Data Lines (D0 through D7)*   The eight bidirectional data lines permit transfer of data to/from the PIA and the MPU. The MPU both sends and receives data to and from the outside world through the PIA via these eight data lines. The data bus output drivers are three-state devices that remain in the high-impedance (off) state except when the MPU performs a PIA Read operation.

4. *Chip Select Lines (CS0, CS1, $\overline{CS2}$)*   These lines are tied to the address lines of the MPU. It is through them that a particular PIA is selected (addressed). For selection of a PIA, the CS0 and CS1 lines must be high and the $\overline{CS2}$ must be low. After the chip selects have been addressed, they must be held in that state for the duration of the E (Enable) pulse, which is the only timing signal supplied by the MPU to the PIA. This enable pulse (E) is normally the $\phi2$ clock. One of the address lines should be ANDed with the VMA line, with the output of the AND gate tied to a chip select.

5. *Enable Line (E)*   The enable pulse (E) is the only timing signal supplied to the PIA by the MPU. Timing on all other signals is referenced to the leading or trailing edges of the E pulse.

6. *Reset Line ($\overline{RES}$)*   This line, which resets all registers in the PIA to a logical zero, is primarily used during a reset or power-on operation.

It is normally in the high state. The transition of high-to-low-to-high resets all registers in the PIA, causing the PA0–PA7, PB0–PB7, CA2 and CB2 to be inputs and disabling all interrupts.

7. *Read/Write Line (R/W)*   This signal generated by the MPU controls the direction of the data transfers on the data bus. A low state on the PIA Read/Write line enables the input buffers, and data is transferred from the MPU to the PIA (MPU Write) on the falling edge of the E ($\phi2$) signal if the device has been selected. A high on the Read/Write line sets up the PIA for a transfer of data to the data bus (MPU Read). The PIA output buffers are enabled when the proper address and the enable pulse are present, thus transferring data to the MPU.

8. *Interrupt Request Lines ($\overline{IRQA}$ and $\overline{IRQB}$)*   These lines, which interrupt the MPU either directly or indirectly through interrupt priority circuitry, are "open source" (no load device on the chip). They are capable of sinking a current of 3.2 mA from an external source, thereby permitting all interrupt request lines to be tied together in a "wired OR" configuration. Interrupts are serviced by a software routine that sequentially reads and tests, on a priority basis, the two control registers in each PIA for the interrupt flag bits (bits 6 and 7) that are set. (These control registers and the way in which the flag bits get set will be discussed shortly.) When the MPU reads the peripheral data register, the interrupt flags (bits 6 and 7) are cleared and the interrupt request is cleared.

These request lines ($\overline{IRQA}$ and $\overline{IRQB}$) are active when low.

9. *Interrupt Input Lines (CA1 and CB1)*   These lines are input only to the PIA and set the interrupt flag (bit 7) of the control registers in the PIA. Discussion of these lines in conjunction with the control register will follow.

10. *Peripheral Control Line (CA2)*   This line can be programmed to act either as an interrupt input or peripheral output. As an output, it is compatible with standard TTL, and as an input, represents 1.5 standard TTL load. The function of this line is programmed with control register A (bits 3, 4, and 5).

11. *Peripheral Control Line (CB2)*   This line may also be programmed to act as an interrupt input or peripheral output. As an input, it has greater than 1-megohm input impedance and is compatible with standard TTL. As an output, it is compatible with standard TTL and may also be used as a source of up to 1 mA at 1.5 V and thus to drive the base of a transistor switch directly. The function of this line is programmed with control register B (bits 3, 4, and 5).

Addressing

To access a PIA, a high state ("1") must be applied to CS0 and CS1 while a low state ("0") is applied to $\overline{CS2}$. The RS0 and RS1 pins are tied to

MPU address lines A0 and A1, respectively. Once the PIA has been accessed, the RS0 and RS1 input pins are used to select one of the six internal registers in the PIA. How is it possible to select one of six registers with only two input lines? This is the only purpose of bit 2 of the control registers. If bit 2 of control register A (CRA) is a "0", and RS0 and RS1 (from A0 and A1) are also "0", then data direction register A (DDRA) is addressed. The level of each bit in data direction register A (DDRA) defines whether each corresponding line of peripheral data register A is an input (if a "0") or an output (if a "1"). The following sequence of instructions will define bits 0 through 4 of peripheral data register A (PDRA) as inputs, and bits 5, 6, and 7 of this same register as outputs (address of the PIA is 4004 through 4007).

Address	Contents	Description
100	86	LDA A #% 11100000
101	11100000	
102	B7	STA A $4004
103	40	
104	04	

The above series of instructions would be *part* of the initialization program that would be run after applying power since the control register has selected the DDR as opposed to the output register.

The next step after defining the individual peripheral lines on the A side of this PIA as inputs or outputs is to load a "1" into bit 2 of control register A (CRA). Normally, the remaining bits of this register would have data loaded into them during this same operation, but this matter will be discussed later. Since bit 2 is the only bit of control register A (CRA) that affects addressing, we will look at bit 2 only rather than complicate the issue at this time. If the previous example were continued, it might look as follows:

Address	Contents	Description
105	86	LDA A #% 00000100
106	00000100	
107	B7	STA A $4005
108	40	
109	05	

This will store a "1" in bit 2 of control register A (CRA). Once it has been loaded, addressing hex location 4004, as we did initially, will access peripheral data register A (PDRA).

To summarize, using the above example, addressing hex location 4004 allows the MPU to communicate with data direction register A (DDRA) if bit 2 of control register A (CRA) is a "0". After this bit is put at a "1", addressing hex location 4004 allows the MPU to communicate with peripheral data register A (PDRA):

Summary of A Side Addressing

RS1	RS0	CRA (Bit 2)	Register Selected
0	0	0	Data direction register A
0	1	Doesn't matter	Control register A
0	0	1	Peripheral data register A

NOTE: CS0 and CS1 must be high while $\overline{CS2}$ is low.

Addressing on the B side is handled in much the same way as on the A side. To address data direction register B (DDR B), RS0 is set equal to a "0" and RS1 is set to a "1" while bit 1 of central register B (CRB) is held at a "0" level. After the individual bits in data direction register B (DDRB) are loaded with "1s" or "0s" to define the individual peripheral data register B lines as inputs and outputs, a "1" is stored in bit 2 of control register B by setting RS0 to a "1" and RS1 to a "1". After the "1" has been stored in bit 2 of CRB, peripheral data register B will be addressed whenever RS0 is a "0" and RS1 is a "1".

Summary of B Side Addressing

RS1	RS0	CRA (Bit 2)	Register Selected
1	0	0	Data direction register B
1	1	Doesn't matter	Control register B
1	0	1	Peripheral data register B

To summarize, one of the functions of the initialization program that will be run immediately after powering up is to configure the PIAs. The following program would define lines 0–3 of the A side as inputs and lines 4–7 of the B side as inputs; the remaining lines on both sides would be outputs:

PIA Address:	Hex 4004–4007
Output Lines:	A Side: lines 4–7
	B Side: lines 0–3
Input Lines:	A Side: lines 0–3
	B Side: lines 4–7

Address	Contents	Description
Address	*Contents*	*Description*
100	C6	LDA B IMMED
101	11110000	
102	F7	STA B EXTENDED
103	40	LOADS 11110000 IN
104	04	DDR A
105	C6	LDA B IMMED
106	00001111	
107	F7	STA B EXTENDED
108	40	LOADS 00001111
109	06	IN DDR B
10A	C6	LDA B IMMED
10B	00000100	
10C	F7	STA B EXTENDED
10D	40	SETS BIT 2
10E	05	IN CRA TO A "1"
10F	F7	STA B EXTENDED
110	40	SETS BIT 2 IN
111	07	CRB TO A "1"

CONTROL REGISTER A (CRA)

7	6	5	4	3	2	1	0
IRQA1	IRQA2	CA2 Control			DDRA	CA1 Control	

CA1 Control (Bits 0 and 1)

Peripheral control line CA1 is an *input only* line. It may be used to cause an interrupt by setting the interrupt flag IRQA1 (bit 7) of control register A. Bits 0 and 1 of CRA are used to determine how the interrupt is to be handled. The IRQA1 flag (bit 7) of CRA will get set to a "1" *only* under one of the following conditions:

1. A negative transition on the CA1 line is detected *and* bit 1 of CRA is a "0".

2. A rising transition on the CA1 is detected *and* bit 1 of CRA is a "1".

(All other combinations will be ignored.)

Whether the IRQA1 flag is permitted to pull the $\overline{\text{IRQA}}$ line low, thus interrupting the MPU, depends upon the status of bit 0 of CRA. If this bit is a "0", the interrupt will be masked (disallowed).

Peripheral control line CA1 is summarized in Table 9.2.

Table 9.2   Summary of CA1 Control

Transition of interrupt input line CA1	Status of bit 1 in CRA (edge)	Status of bit 0 in CRA (mask)	IRQA1 (interrupt flag) Bit 7 of CRA	Status of $\overline{IRQA}$ line (MPU interrupt request)
‾‾|___	0	0	1	Masked (remains high)
‾‾|___	0	1	1	Goes low (processor interrupted)
___|‾‾	1	0	1	Masked (remains high)
___|‾‾	1	1	1	Goes low (processor interrupted)
‾‾|___	1	—	0	Remains high
___|‾‾	0	—	0	Remains High

As seen in Table 9.2, bit 0 of DRA is the IRQA1 interrupt "mask programming bit." If bit 0 is a "0", setting the interrupt flag IRQA1 will not cause the interrupt line $\overline{IRQA}$ to go low. If bit 0 contains a "1", the $\overline{IRQA}$ line will be permitted to go low when IRQA1 gets set to a "1".

Bit 1 of CRA is the "edge programming bit." A "0" in bit 1 programs the interrupt flag IRQA1 (bit 7) to get set to a "1" in a *negative* transition of the CA1 line, and a "1" in bit 1 programs the flag to get set to a "1" in a *positive* transition. (NOTE: If the IRQA1 flag was set to a "1" during a period when bit 0 had masked all interrupts, the interrupt will be allowed when bit 0 of CRA is changed to a "1" by the MPU.)

Data Direction Register (DDR A) (Bit 2)

This bit, in conjunction with register select lines RS0 and RS1, is used to select either the peripheral data register or the data direction register, as follows:

RS1	RS0	CRA (Bit 2)	Register Selected
0	0	0	Data Direction Register A
0	1	Doesn't matter	Control Register A
0	0	1	Peripheral Data Register A

CA2 Control (Bits 3, 4, and 5)

As mentioned earlier, this line can be programmed to function as an interrupt input line or a peripheral output line. The status of bits 3, 4, and 5 of control register A determine how it is to function. Bit 5 determines whether the CA2 line is to be an interrupt input line or a peripheral output line. If bit 5 contains a "0", it will be used as an interrupt line; if bit 5 contains a "1", it will be used as an output line.

CA2 As an Interrupt Input Line (Bit 5 = "0") Bits 3 and 4 determine how the interrupt is to be handled. The IRQA2 flag (bit 6) of CRA will be set to a "1" only under one of the following conditions:

1. A negative transition on the CA2 line is detected *and* bit 4 is a "0".
2. A rising transition on the CA2 line is detected *and* bit 4 is a "1".

(All other combinations are ignored.)

The CA2 control is summarized in Table 9.3.

Table 9.3 Summary of CA2 Control

Transition of input CA2	Status of bit 5 in CRA (I/O control)	Status of bit 4 in CRA (edge)	Status of bit 3 in CRA (Mask)	IRQA2 (interrupt flag) Bit 6 of CRA	Status of IRQA line (MPU interrupt request)
‾|_	0	0	0	1	Masked (remains high)
‾|_	0	0	1	1	Goes low (processor interrupted)
_|‾	0	1	0	1	Masked (remains high)
_|‾	0	1	1	1	Goes low (processor interrupted)
‾|_	0	1	—	0	Remains high
_|‾	0	0	—	0	Remains high

As seen in Table 9.3, bit 3 of CRA is the interrupt "mask programming bit." If it is a "0", setting the interrupt flag IRQA2 will not cause interrupt line $\overline{IRQA}$ to go low. If it is a "1", the $\overline{IRQA}$ line will be permitted to go low when IRQA2 gets set to a "1".

Bit 4 of CRA is the "edge programming bit." A "0" in bit 4 programs interrupt flag IRQA2 (bit 6) to get set to a "1" on a *negative* transition of the

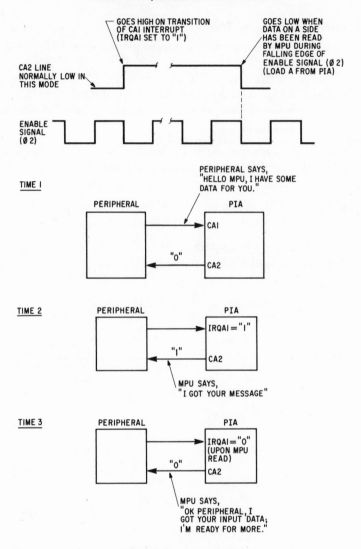

Fig. 9.17 Handshake mode

CA2 line. A "1" in bit 4 programs the flag to get set to a "1" on a *rising* transition. NOTE: If the IRQA2 flag was set to a "1" during a period when bit 4 had masked all interrupts, the interrupt will be allowed when bit 4 of CRA is changed to a "1" by the MPU.

CA2 As an Output Line (Bit 5 = "1")   If bit 5 of CRA is set to a "1", the CA2 line is designated as an output line. Whenever it is used as an output, the IRQA2 flag (bit 6 of CRA) remains a "0" and the $\overline{\text{IRQA}}$ remains high. As an output, it has four options:

1. *Bits 5, 4, and 3 of CRA = 100 (Handshake Mode)*   The handshake mode is used when a peripheral is transmitting data to the MPU. The peripheral must tell the MPU when it has some data, and the MPU must tell the peripheral when it has taken the data (see Fig. 9-17). The typical sequence is as follows:

    (1) Peripheral sends signal via interrupt line CA1 to set IRQA1 flag (bit 7) of control register A, which tells the MPU it has data to give to the MPU.

    (2) When the IRQA1 flag gets set to a "1", the CA2 line goes high.

    (3) After the MPU reads the contents of peripheral register A (load A from PIA), the CA2 line will go low. This signals the peripheral that the MPU took the data and is now ready for more.

2. *Bits 5, 4, and 3 of CRA = 101 (Pulse Mode)*   This mode, which tells the peripheral that the data on peripheral data register A has been read by the MPU, is used when a complete handshake is not required. The peripheral may make data available to the MPU on a continuing basis but needs to know when the MPU takes the data (see Fig. 9.18).

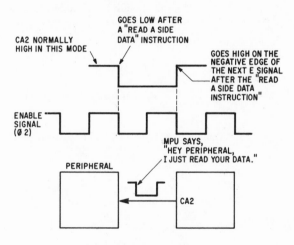

Fig. 9.18 Pulse mode

3. *Bits 5, 4, and 3 of CRA = 110*   In this mode, the CA2 output line will always be in the low state.

4. *Bits 5, 4, and 3 of CRA = 111*   In this mode, the CA2 output line will always be in the high state.

Interrupt Flag Bits (IRQA1 and IRQA2)

As already seen, bits 6 and 7 of control register A get set when an interrupt occurs. Flag bit IRQA1 (bit 7) is the interrupt bit for the CA1 input line. Flag bit IRQA2 (bit 6) is the interrupt bit for the CA2 input line. The *only* way that these bits can get set is via the CA1 and CA2 interrupt input lines. The MPU *cannot* store a "1" in these two locations, but it can read their status. When the MPU reads the status of peripheral data register A, bits 6 and 7 of the control register will be cleared ("0").

Control Register B (CRB)

7	6	5	4	3	2	1	0
IRQB1	IRQB2	CB2 Control			DDRB	CB1 Control	

CB1 Control (Bits 0 and 1)

Peripheral control line CB1 is an *input only* line that may be used to cause an interrupt by setting interrupt flag IRQB1 (bit 7) of control register B. Bits 0 and 1 of CRB are used to determine how the interrupt is to be handled. The IRQB1 flag (bit 7) of CRB wil get set to a "1" *only* under one of the following conditions:

1. A negative transition on the CB1 line is detected *and* bit 1 of CRB is a "0".

2. A rising transition on the CB1 is detected *and* bit 1 of CRB is a "1".

(All other combinations will be ignored.)

Whether the IRQB1 flag is permitted to pull the $\overline{IRQB}$ line low, thus

Table 9.4   Summary of CB1 Control

Transition of interrupt input line CB1	Status of bit 1 in CRB (edge)	Status of bit 0 in CRB (mask)	IRQB1 (interrupt flag) Bit 7 of CRB	Status of $\overline{IRQB}$ Line (MPU interrupt request)
⌐L	0	0	1	Masked (remains high)
⌐L	0	1	1	Goes low (processor interrupted)
⌐⌐	1	0	1	Masked (remains high)
⌐⌐	1	1	1	Goes low (processor interrupted)
⌐L	1	—	0	Remains high
⌐⌐	0	—	0	Remains high

interrupting the MPU, depends on the status of bit 0 of CRB. If the bit is a "1", the $\overline{IRQB}$ line will go low, causing the interrupt. If it is a "0", the interrupt will be masked (disallowed).

The CB1 control is summarized in Table 9.4.

As seen in Table 9.4, bit 0 of CRB is the IRQB1 interrupt "mask programming bit." If bit 0 is a "0", setting the interrupt flag IRQB1 will not cause the interrupt line $\overline{IRQB}$ to go low. If bit 0 contains a "1", the $\overline{IRQA}$ line will be permitted to go low when IRQB1 gets set to a "1".

Bit 1 of CRB is the "edge programming bit." A "0" in bit 1 programs the interrupt flag IRQB1 (bit 7) to get set to a "1" on a *negative* transition of the CB1 line. A "1" in bit 1 programs the flag to get set to a "1" on a *positive* transition. (NOTE: If the IRQB1 flag was set to a "1" during a period when bit 0 had masked all interrupts, the interrupt will be allowed when bit 0 of CRB is changed to a "1" by the MPU.)

Data Direction Register B (DDRB) (Bit 2)

This bit, in conjunction with register select lines RS0 and RS1, is used to select either the peripheral data register or the data direction register.

RS1	RS0	CRB (Bit 2)	Register Selected
1	0	0	Data direction register B
1	1	Doesn't matter	Control register B
1	0	1	Peripheral data register B

CB2 Control (Bits 3, 4, and 5)

As mentioned earlier, this line can be programmed to function as an interrupt input line or a peripheral output line. The status of bits 3, 4, and 5 of control register B determine how the CB2 line is to function. Bit 5 determines whether it will be an interrupt input line or an output line. If bit 5 contains a "0", it will be an interrupt line. If bit 5 contains a "1", it will be an output line.

CB2 As an Interrupt Input Line (Bit 5 = "0")   Bits 3 and 4 of CRB are used to determine how the interrupt is to be handled. The IRQB2 flag (bit 6) of CRB will get set to a "1" only under one of the following conditions:

1. A negative transition in the CB2 line is detected *and* bit 4 is a "0".
2. A rising transition in the CB2 line is detected *and* bit 4 is a "1".

All other combinations are ignored.

The CB2 control is summarized in Table 9.5.

As seen in Table 9.5, bit 3 of CRB is the interrupt "mask program-

Table 9.5   Summary of CB2 Control

Transition of input CB2	Status of bit 5 in CRB (I/O control)	Status of bit 4 in CRB (edge)	Status of bit 3 in CRB (mask)	IRQB2 (interrupt flag) Bit 6 of CRB	Status of IRQB line (MPU interrupt request)
‾‾_	0	0	0	1	Masked (remains high)
‾‾_	0	0	1	1	Goes low (processor interrupted)
_/‾‾	0	1	0	1	Masked (remains high)
_/‾‾	0	1	1	1	Goes low (processor interrupted)
‾‾_	0	1	—	0	Remains high
_/‾‾	0	0	—	0	Remains high

ming bit". If bit 3 is a "0", setting the interrupt flag IRQB2 will not cause the interrupt line IRQB to go low. If it contains a "1", the IRQB line will be permitted to go low when IRQB2 gets set to a "1".

Bit 4 of CRB is the "edge programming bit". A "0" in bit 4 programs the interrupt flag IRQB2 (bit 6) to get set to a "1" on a *negative* transition of the CB2 line. A "1" in bit 4 programs it to get set to a "1" on a *rising* transition. (NOTE: If the IRQB2 flag was set to a "1" during a period when bit 3 had masked all interrupts, the interrupt will be allowed when bit 3 of CRB is changed to a "1" by the MPU.

CB2 As an Output Line (Bit 5 = "1")   If bit 5 of CRB is set to a "1", the CB2 line is designated as an output line. Whenever it is used as an output, the IRQB2 flag (bit 6 of CRB) remains a "0" and the IRQB remains high. As an output, it has four options:

1. *Bits 5, 4, and 3 of CRB = 100 (Handshake Mode)*   This mode is used when the MPU sends data to a peripheral device. The peripheral must tell the MPU it is ready for the data. After the MPU sends the data to peripheral data register B, it sends a signal to the peripheral telling it that the data is available at that register. After the peripheral takes the data, it can request more data, and the sequence is repeated. The typical sequence (see Fig. 9.19) is as follows:
   (1) In order to tell the MPU that it wants some data, the peripheral sends a signal via interrupt line CB1 to set the IRQB1 flag (bit 7) of central register B.

(2) When the IRQB1 flag gets set to a "1", the CB2 line goes high.
(3) After the MPU sends the data to peripheral data register B, the CB2 line will go low, thereby signaling the peripheral that the data is there for the taking.

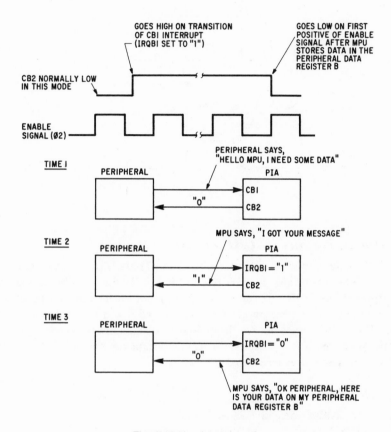

Fig. 9.19 Handshake mode

2. *Bit 5,3 of CRB = 101 (Pulse Mode)*   This mode is used to tell the peripheral that data is available in PIA peripheral data register B (see Fig. 9.20).

3. *Bits 5, 4, and 3 of CRB = 110*   In this mode, the CB2 output line will always be in the low state.

4. *Bits 5, 4, and 3 of CRB = 111*   In this mode, the CB2 output line will always be in the high state.

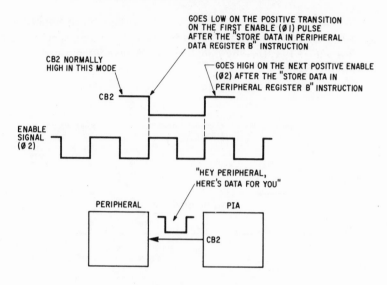

Fig. 9.20 Pulse mode

Interrupt Flag Bits (IRQB1 and IRQB2)

As already seen, these two bits (6 and 7) of control register A get set when an interrupt occurs. Flag bit IRQB (bit 7) is the interrupt bit for the CB1 input line. Flag bit IRQB2 (bit 6) is the interrupt bit for the CB2 input line. The *only* way these bits can get set is via the CB1 and CB2 interrupt input lines. The MPU *cannot* store a "1" in these two locations, but it *can* read their status. When it reads the status of peripheral data register B, bits 6 and 7 of control register B will be cleared ("0").

PIA Summary

1. *Register Selects RS1 and RS0*
(a) If RS1 is set to a "0", then the A side of the PIA is selected.
(b) If RS1 is set to a "1", then the B side of the PIA is selected.
(c) If RS0 is set to a "0" and CRA (or CRB) bit 2 is a "1", then the peripheral data register is selected.
(d) If RS0 is set to a "0" and CRA (or CRB) is a "0", then the data direction register is selected.
(e) If RS0 is set to a "1", then the control register is selected.

2. *CA1 or CB1 Interrupt Lines*   If bit 0 of CRA (or CRB) is set to a "0", all interrupts caused by CA1 (or CB1) are masked by the PIA. However, the interrupts flags will still get set if the proper transition occurs on CA1 (CB1). If bit 0 of CRA (or CRB) is set to a "1", all interrupts caused by CA1 (or CB1) will be allowed to interrupt the MPU.

3. *CA2 or CB2 Interrupt Line*   If bit 3 of CRA (or CRB) is set to a "0", and bit 5 = "0", all interrupts caused by CA2 (or CB2) are masked by the PIA. However, the interrupt flags will still get set if the proper transition occurs on CA2 (or CB2). If bit 3 of CRA (CRB) is set to a "1", all interrupts by CA2 (or CB2) will be allowed to interrupt the MPU.

If bit 5 = "1", then the CA2 (or CB2) lines are used as outputs.

4. *IRQA1, IRQA2, IRQB1, IRQB2 Flag Bits*   These bits (bits 6 and 7 of CRA & CRB) are read only bits. The MPU *cannot* write into them, and *only* interrupts from the outside world can set them. They will be cleared only when the peripheral data register is read or there is a hardware reset.

5. *Control Registers CRA and CRB*   Control registers CRA and CRB have total control of CA1, CA2, CB1, and CB2 lines. The status of all eight bits may be read into the MPU, although it can only write into bits 0 through 5.

6. *Addressing*   Before addressing PIAs, the Data Direction Register (DDR) must first be loaded with the bit pattern that defines how each line is to function, that is, as an input or output. A logic "1" in the register defines the corresponding line as an output, and a logic "0" defines it as an input. Since the DDR and the peripheral data register have the same address, control register bit 2 determines which is being addressed. If bit 2 is a logic "0", then the DDR is addressed; if it is a logic "1", the peripheral data register is addressed. Therefore, it is essential that the DDR be loaded before setting bit 2 of the control register.

The above sequence of setting up the PIA assumes that the data outputs of the PIA are active high (True   2.4 V).

7. *PIA—After Reset*   When the $\overline{RES}$ (Reset Line) has been held low for a minimum of eight machine cycles, all registers in the PIA will have been cleared. Because of the reset conditions, the PIA has been defined as follows:

(1) All I/O lines to the "outside world" are defined as inputs.
(2) CA1, CA2, CB1, and CB2 are defined as interrupt input lines that are negative-edge sensitive.
(3) All interrupts on the control lines are masked. Setting of interrupt flag bits will not cause $\overline{IRQA}$ or $\overline{IRQB}$ to go low.

Active Low Outputs

When all the outputs of a given PIA port are to be active low (True ≤ 0.4V), then the following procedure should be used:

1. Set bit 2 in the control register.
2. Store all 1's ($FF) in the peripheral data register.
3. Clear bit 2 in the control register.
4. Store all 1's ($FF) in the data direction register.
5. Store control word (bit 2 = 1) in the control register.

Example   The B side of PIA1 is set up to have all active low outputs. CB1 and CB2 are set up to allow interrupts in the handshake mode and CB1 will respond to positive edges (low-to-high transitions). Assume reset conditions. Addresses are set up and equated to the same labels as in the previous example.

1. LDA A #4	
2. STA A PIA1BC	Set bit 2 in PIA1BC (control register)
3. LDA B #$FF	
4. STA B PIA1BD	All 1's in peripheral data register
5. CLR PIA1BC	Clear bit 2
6. STA B PIA1BD	All 1's in data direction register
7. LDA A #$27	
8. STA A PIA1BC	00100111 Control register

The above procedure is required in order to prevent outputs from going low—to the active low True state—when all 1's are stored in the data direction register, as would be the case if the normal configuration procedure were followed.

PIA Polling Routine

This routine is one of the various techniques for determining which PIA has generated an interrupt. Recall that every PIA has an A side and a B side that may cause the $\overline{IRQ}$ line to go low, thus generating an interrupt. All PIA interrupt lines are tied together and connected to the one interrupt input pin ($\overline{IRQ}$) of the MPU. Consequently, when an interrupt is generated, a bit 6 or 7 of a PIA is set. The only way to determine where the interrupt came from is to poll bits 6 and 7 of every PIA control register to see which one is a "1" (and thus an interrupt).

This routine (see Fig. 9.21 for its flowchart) polls the control registers of two PIAs. It reads the contents of each control register and executes the BMI instruction that effectively checks on whether bit 7 is set. If it is not set, a ROL A instruction is executed that shifts bit 6 into bit 7, thus permitting use of the BMI instruction again. Once a set control bit is detected, the processor branches to a subroutine to service that particular interrupt. After the interrupt has been serviced, an RTI instruction is executed that causes the processor to return to whatever it was doing before the interrupt.

The source program for the PIA polling routine is as follows:

```
100   NAM POLL
110   OPT MEM
120 PIA1AC EQU $4005
130 PIA1BC EQU $4007
140 PIA2AC EQU $4009
150 PIA2BC EQU $400B
200   ORG $100
210 POLL LDA A PIA1AC
220   BMI POUT1
```

```
230   ROL A
240   BMI POUT2
250   LDA A PIA1BC
260   BMI POUT3
270   ROL A
280   BMI POUT4
290   LDA A PIA2AC
300   BMI POUT5
310   ROL A
320   BMI POUT6
330   LDA A PIA2BC
340   BMI POUT7
350   ROL A
360   BMI POUT8
370   RTI
380 ROUT1 NOP     *THIS IS PIA1AC CA1 SERVICE ROUTINE
390   RTI
400 POUT2 NOP     *THIS IS PIA1AC CA2 SERVICE ROUTINE
410   RTI
420 POUT3 NOP     *THIS IS PIA1BC CB1 SERVICE ROUTINE
430   RTI
440 POUT4 NOP     *THIS IS PIA1BC CB2 SERVICE ROUTINE
450   RTI
460 POUT5 NOP     *THIS IS PIA2AC CA1 SERVICE ROUTINE
470   RTI
480 POUT6 NOP     *THIS IS PIA2AC CA2 SERVICE ROUTINE
490   RTI
500 POUT7 NOP     *THIS IS PIA2BC CB1 SERVICE ROUTINE
510   RTI
520 POUT8 NOP     *THIS IS PIA2BC CB2 SERVICE ROUTINE
530   RTI
540   MON
```

The assembled program for the routine is as follows:

```
00100                   NAM    POLL
00110                   OPT    MEM
00120     4005  PIA1AC  EQU    $4005
00130     4007  PIA1BC  EQU    $4007
00140     4009  PIA2AC  EQU    $4009
00150     400B  PIA2BC  EQU    $400B
00200 0100              ORG    $100
00210 0100 B6 4005 POLL LDA A  PIA1AC
00220 0103 2B 1C        BMI    ROUT1
00230 0105 49           ROL A
00240 0106 2B 1B        BMI    ROUT2
00250 0108 B6 4007      LDA A  PIA1BC
00260 010B 2B 18        BMI    ROUT3
00270 010D 49           ROL A
00280 010E 2B 17        BMI    ROUT4
00290 0110 B6 4009      LDA A  PIA2AC
00300 0113 2B 14        BMI    ROUT5
00310 0115 49           ROL A
00320 0116 2B 13        BMI    ROUT6
00330 0118 B6 400B      LDA A  PIA2BC
00340 011B 2B 10        BMI    ROUT7
00350 011D 49           ROL A
00360 011E 2B 0F        BMI    ROUT8
00370 0120 3B           RTI
00380 0121 01    ROUT1  NOP           *THIS IS PIA1AC CA1 SERVICE
00390 0122 3B           RTI
00400 0123 01    ROUT2  NOP           *THIS IS PIA1AC CA2 SERVICE
00410 0124 3B           RTI
00420 0125 01    ROUT3  NOP           *THIS IS PIA1BC CB1 SERVICE
00430 0126 3B           RTI
00440 0127 01    ROUT4  NOP           *THIS IS PIA1BC CB2 SERVICE
```

```
00450 0128 3B              RTI
00460 0129 01       ROUT5  NOP        •THIS IS PIA2AC CA1 SERVICE
00470 012A 3B              RTI
00480 012B 01       ROUT6  NOP        •THIS IS PIA2AC CA2 SERVICE
00490 012C 3B              RTI
00500 012D 01       ROUT7  NOP        •THIS IS PIA2BC CB1 SERVICE
00510 012E 3B              RTI
00520 012F 01       ROUT8  NOP        •THIS IS PIA2BC CB2 SERVICE
00530 0130 3B              RTI
00540                      MON
```

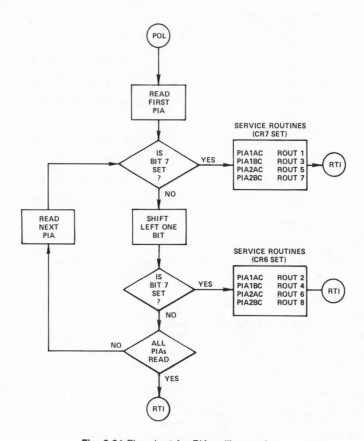

Fig. 9.21 Flowchart for PIA polling routine

9.6 Asynchronous Communications Interface Adapter

In the previous section, it was shown how the MPU communicates with the outside world via the PIA, through which data can be sent to or received from the MPU eight bits at a time in parallel. For this purpose, eight lines are needed between the PIA and the peripheral (data).

When it is necessary to send or receive data over very long distances, eight separate lines must be run from the data service to the PIA. The Asynchronous Communications Interface Adapter (ACIA) permits data to be transmitted in a serial format with only one line, not the eight lines a PIA requires. The ACIA can function either as a serial-to-parallel converter or as a parallel-to-serial converter (Fig. 9.22). Data can be sent to the ACIA over the D0-through-D7 data lines; it is then converted to a series of 1's and 0's in the ACIA and sent out over a single line to a receiver. Likewise, data in the form of 1's and 0's can be received by the ACIA from an external source, converted to a parallel format in the ACIA and sent to the MPU over the D0-through-D7 data lines. As one can well imagine, a great deal of bookkeeping must be done when data bits are transmitted or received in a serial format to resolve such questions as: (1) Where does each group of bits stop and the next group start? (2) How does the ACIA know when it is to receive or send data? (3) How does the ACIA detect if a bit is lost? These questions, and many others, will be answered in this section.

General

In any type of data communications, two terms are encountered— *synchronous* and *asynchronous*—that refer to the type of clocking used to transfer the data. In *synchronous transmission,* the data rate is locked into the system clocking. The receiver and the transmitter must be synchronized with each other since there is no two-way communication. Usually, one device will

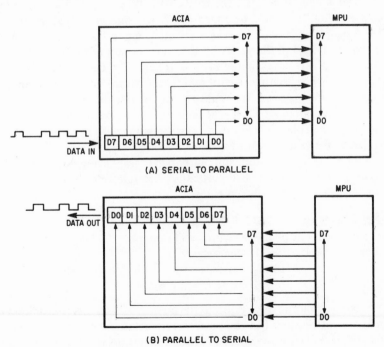

Fig. 9.22 Conversion functions of the ACIA

request some data from the other device, wait a fixed period, and then read the data (assuming that the data was placed on the bus during the waiting period). In *asynchronous transmission,* "start" and "stop" bits are added to the data word to let the receiver know where each word ends and begins. After the receiver detects the stop bit (end of data word), it will then wait for the next data word. The data words are not locked into the system timing.

Baud rate is a term used frequently in serial data communications but often is misunderstood. A *baud* is defined as the reciprocal of the shortest pulse duration in a data word (signal), including start, stop, and parity bits. This is often taken to mean the same as "bits per second," a term that expresses only the number of *data* bits transferred per second. Very often, the parity bit is included as an information or data bit. Definitions of various bits follow.

Start Bit   The first bit of a serial data word that signals the start of transmission of a series of data bits. This bit is usually detected as a transition from a "1" to "0," referred to as a "mark-to-space" transition.

Stop Bit   The last bit of a serial data word that signals the end of that word. This bit is usually a high ("1") signal.

Parity Bit   When transmitting a series of bits, it is common for the transmitter to add what is known as a "parity bit" to the regular data bits transmitted. Two types of parity are used. If *odd* parity is used, the sum of the "1s" transmitted, including the parity bit, will be odd. For example, if the data word contains three "1s", the parity bit will be zero. If four "1s" are in the data word, a "1" would be added by the transmitter so that the number of "1s" transmitted is odd. The same principle applies to *even* parity. A "1" or "0" will be added in the parity bit to make the sum of bits transmitted an even number. The receiver, in both cases, will check to make sure that an odd number of "1"s has been received if odd parity is used or an even number of "1"s if even parity is used. It should be pointed out that if two bits change within the transmitted word, it will not be detected by the parity detection circuit. Only when one bit is lost during transmission will the error be detected and an error message presented.

The role of start, stop, and parity bits is graphically displayed in Fig. 9.23. The relationship of the baud rate, the word rate, and the number of bits transmitted per second is shown below:

Baud rate = 1/bit time = 1/9.09 msec = 110 baud
Time to transmit one character word = (11 bits) $\times$ (9.09 msec/bit) = .1 sec
Word rate = 1/.1 sec = 10 characters/sec
Baud rate of 110 = (10 characters/sec) $\times$ (8 bits/character)
                 = 80 bits/sec (including parity)

Notice that the baud rate and the number of data bits transmitted per second are not the same. The baud rate of 110 includes the start and stop bits, whereas the rate of 80 bits per second includes only information bits (including parity). In Fig. 9.23, a seven-bit ASCII word was transmitted. With the ACIA,

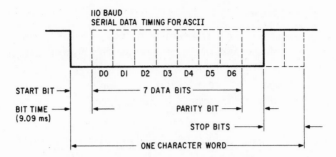

Fig. 9.23 Role of stop, start, and parity bits

several options are available as to the number of data bits (seven or eight), odd or even parity, and the number of stop bits (one or two). Table 9.6 gives bit time, character time, characters/sec, and data bits/sec for various baud rates.

Table 9.6 Baud Rate Data

Baud rate	110	150	300	1200
Bit time(msec)	9.09	6.66	3.33	.833
*Character time	.1 sec	0.73 sec	.0366 sec	.0092 sec
Characters/sec	10	13.7	27.32	108.7
Data bits/sec	80	110	218.6	870

*Assume one start bit, eight data bits (including parity), and two stop bits, or eleven bits per character.

Bit time = 1/baud rate
Character time = (total number of bits in word) × (bit time)
Characters/sec = 1/character time = $\frac{BAUD\ RATE}{NO.\ BITS}$
Data bits/sec = 8 × characters/sec

To send the ASCII character X (58_{16}) with one start bit, even parity, and two stop bits, the pulse train would be as shown in Fig. 9.24.

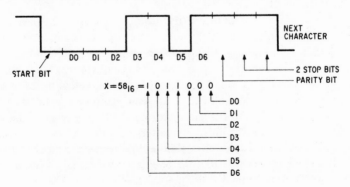

Fig. 9.24 Pulse train

Bit Synchronization

As digital signals are transmitted over a single line, it is possible to read erroneous results because of the noise on the line. To minimize the chance of such error, a sampling technique is used to determine whether the start bit is valid. After it has been proved valid, *each* bit in the character word is sampled at approximately the center of the bit.

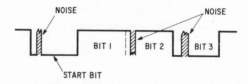

Fig. 9.25 Reading start bit in presence of noise pulse

If the receiving circuit were to read the value of the start bit while a noise pulse is present (Fig. 9.25), it would determine that the start bit is invalid. Likewise, if a reading of bits 2 and 3 were taken during a noise pulse, it would read a "0" for bit 2 and a "1" for bit 3, neither of which would be correct. The erroneous reading of bits 2 and 3 would not be detected by the parity detection circuit since the total number of "1s" remains the same.

A method of minimizing the chance for an erroneous reading is to sample the start bit several times to determine if it is valid and then to sample each bit thereafter with a short pulse at approximately the center of the bit. Sampling at approximately the center of the bit minimizes the chance of error since the noise pulse would have to be present at *precisely* the point where the sampling occurs. This sampling is accomplished by adding an external clock signal. Clock frequencies of 16, 32, and 64 times the baud rate are often used. The higher the clock frequency, the less the chance for a false reading. The MC6850 ACIA, which will be discussed shortly, can accommodate a clock frequency of 1, 16, and 64 times the baud rate. These frequencies are referred to as the ÷ 1, ÷ 16, and ÷ 64 modes.

To illustrate what all this really means, assume that the partial character being received is preceded by the normal start bit. If a clock rate of 16 times the baud rate (÷ 16 mode) is being used, as shown in Fig. 9.26, the receiver, upon detection of the mark-to-space transition, will start its sampling on the rising edge of the external clock. If the signal remains low for nine separate samplings (in the ÷ 16 mode), the bit is assumed to be a valid start bit and is shifted into the ACIA shift register during the falling edge of the internal clock. After every sixteenth pulse thereafter from the center of the start bit, a reading will be made to determine whether that respective bit is a "1" or "0".

If a clock rate of 64 times the baud rate were used (÷ 64 mode), the start bit would be determined valid after a sampling of 33 readings. The data bits would be sampled every 64 pulses from the center of the start bit.

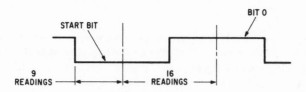

Fig. 9.26 ÷ 16 mode sampling

If the start bit in Fig. 9.26 is expanded, the sampling would appear as shown in Fig. 9.27. Notice the noise pulse on the start bit. Since it did not occur during the sampling period, it goes by undetected, and the start bit is determined to be valid.

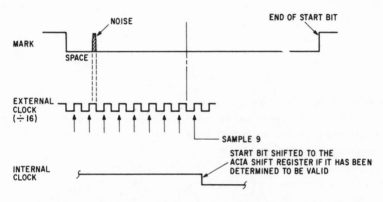

Fig. 9.27 Sampling with expanded start bit

The same argument applies to each data bit. Notice in Fig. 9.28 that on the sixteenth pulse from the center of the start bit, a sampling takes place, yet, despite the noise on the line, the correct data is shifted into the ACIA since the noise does not occur during the sampling period.

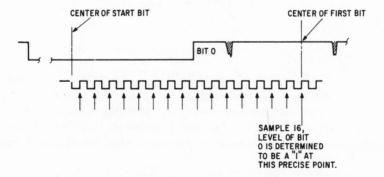

Fig. 9.28 Sampling at sixteenth pulse

Description of the ACIA

The MC6850 Asynchronous Communications Interface Adapter (ACIA) is an N-MOS device housed in a 24-pin package that is used as a means of receiving and transmitting as many as eight bits of data in a serial format (Fig. 9.29). The ACIA communicates (transmits/receives data) with the MPU via an eight-bit bidirectional data just as RAMs, ROMs, and PIAs do.

The ACIA has four registers that may be addressed by the MPU. The Status Register (SR) and the Receiver Data Register (RDR) are "read only" registers, meaning that the MPU cannot *write* into them. The Transmit Data Register (TDR) and the Control Register (CR) are "write only" registers, meaning that the MPU cannot *read* them.

In addition to these four registers, the ACIA has three chip select lines (CS0, CS1, $\overline{CS2}$), one register select line (RS), one interrupt request line ($\overline{IRQ}$), one enable line (E), one read/write line (R/W), and seven data and data control lines (RXC, TXC, $\overline{DCD}$, $\overline{RTS}$, RXD, TXD, and $\overline{CTS}$).

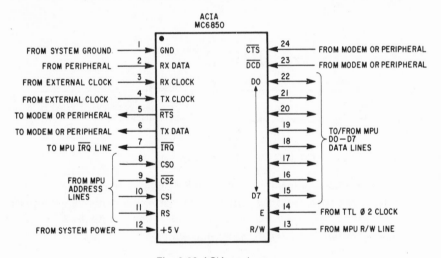

Fig. 9.29 ACIA package

MPU Interface Lines

Bidirectional Data Lines (D0–D7)　　　The eight bidirectional data lines permit transfer of data to and from the ACIA and the MPU. The MPU receives and sends data from and to the outside world through the ACIA via these eight data lines. The data bus output drivers are three-state devices that remain in the high impedance (off) state except when the MPU performs an ACIA read operation.

Chip Select Lines (CS0, CS1, and $\overline{CS2}$)　　　It is through these lines, which are tied to the address lines of the MPU, that a particular ACIA is selected (addressed). For this selection, the CS0 and CS1 lines must be high and the CS2 must be low. After the chip selects have been addressed, they must be held in that state for the duration of the E enable pulse, which is the only timing signal supplied by the MPU to the ACIA.

Enable Line (E)   The enable pulse is a high-impedance, TTL-compatible input from the MPU that enables the ACIA input or output buffers and that clocks data to and from the ACIA. This input is usually the TTL $\phi2$ signal from the clock.

Read/Write Line (R/W)   The read/write line is a high-impedance, TTL-compatible input that is used to control the direction of data flow between the ACIA's eight-bit parallel data bus and the MPU. When read/write is high (MPU read), the ACIA output driver is turned on, and a selected register is read by the MPU. When the read/write line is low (MPU write), the ACIA output driver is turned off, and the MPU writes into a selected register.

Register Select (RS)   The register select line is a high-impedance, TTL-compatible input from the MPU that is used to select, in conjunction with the read/write line, either the transmit/receiver data register or the control/status register in the ACIA (Fig. 9.30). It must be tied to an address line from the MPU. A high or RS selects transmit/receive data registers; a low selects control/status registers.

Modem Control Lines

Serial data to be transmitted over telephone lines must be sent to a modem that prepares the signal for transmission (Fig. 9.31). Three signals between the ACIA and the Modem permit a limited control of the latter.

Clear to Send ($\overline{CTS}$)   This high-impedance TTL-compatible *input* provides automatic control of the transmitting end of the communications link via the modem $\overline{CTS}$-signal active-low output by inhibiting the Transmit Data Register Empty (TDRE) status bit. If this line is not used, it should be tied to system ground.

Request to Send ($\overline{RTS}$)   This ACIA *output* enables the MPU to control a peripheral or modem via the data bus. The $\overline{RTS}$ output corresponds to the state of control register bits 5 and 6. When CR6 equals "0" or both CR5 and CR6 equal "1", the $\overline{RTS}$ output is low (the active state). This output can also be used for the Data Terminal Ready ($\overline{DTR}$) on the 6860 modem.

Data Carrier Detect ($\overline{DCD}$)   This high-impedance, TTL-compatible *input* provides automatic control of the receiving end of a communication link by means of the modem Data Carrier Detect ($\overline{DCD}$) output. The $\overline{DCD}$ *input* inhibits and initializes the receiver section of the ACIA when high. A low-to-high transition of the $\overline{DCD}$ line initiates an interrupt to the MPU to indicate that a loss carrier has occurred when the Receiver Interrupt Enable (RIE) bit is set. If this line is not used, it should be tied to system ground.

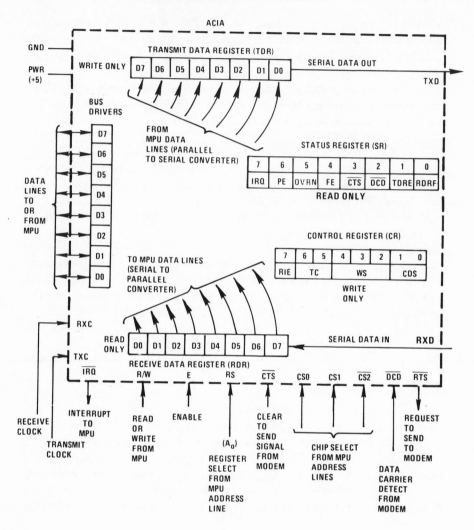

Fig. 9.30 Register select line

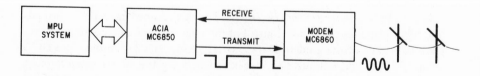

Fig. 9.31 Modem control line

Serial Data Lines

The ACIA has two lines for transfer of data. The Transmit Data (TX DATA) line is used to send, and the Receive Data (RX DATA) line to receive, data from a peripheral. Before transferring data, the ACIA will add the start bit automatically. The number of stop bits and odd or even parity will also be specified in the data word per instructions via bits 2, 3, and 4 of the control register. As data is received over the receive data line, the ACIA will use the parity bit to check the accuracy of the number of "1"s received, and it will strip the start, stop, and parity bits from the data word before converting the data bits to a parallel format for transfer to the MPU over the data bus.

Receive Data (RX DATA)   The receive data line is a high-imped- ance TTL-compatible *input* through which data is received in a serial format. Internal synchronization for detection of data is possible with clock rates of 16 or 64 times the bit rate. Data rates in the range of 0 to 500,000 bits per second are possible with external synchronization (in the ÷ 1 mode).

Transmit Data (TX DATA)   The transmit data *output* line is used to transfer data in a serial format to a modem or peripheral. Data rates in the range of 0 to 500,000 bits per second are possible with external synchronization (in the ÷ 1 mode).

External Clock Inputs

Separate high-impedance, TTL-compatible inputs are provided for clocking of transmitted and received data. Clock frequencies of 1, 16, or 64 times the data rate may be selected.

Transmit Clock (TXC)   The transmit clock input is used for clock- ing transmitted data. The transmitter initiates data on the negative transition of the clock.

Receive Clock (RXC)   The receive clock input is used for syn- chronization of received data. The receiver strobes the data on the positive transition of the clock. (In the ÷ 1 mode, the clock and data must be synchro- nized externally.)

Transmit Data Register (TDR)

The transmit data register, an eight-bit register within the ACIA, is used to hold the data from the MPU (converted from parallel format to serial format) until it is transferred. The data is written into the transmit data register on the negative transition of the enable (E) signal after the ACIA has been addressed through the CS0, CS1, and $\overline{\text{CS2}}$ lines and the RS line is a "1" and the R/W line is a "0". Writing data into the transmit data register causes the Transmit Data Register Empty (TDRE) bit in the status register to go low ("0"). After the TDRE bit goes low, data will be transmitted. If the transmitter is idling (no character being transmitted), then the transmission will occur within one bit time of the trailing edge of the write command. If previous data is being transmitted, it will be transferred upon completion of the previous transmission. After the data has been transferred, the TDRE will be changed to a "1", indicating that TDR is empty.

Receive Data Register (RDR)

The receive data register, an eight-bit register within the ACIA, holds the data that is transferred from the modem or peripheral to the ACIA. After the receive data register is full, the data is ready for transfer to the MPU over the parallel data bus, and the Receive Data Register Full (RDRF) bit in the status register will go high ("1"), indicating that the register is full. The RDRF bit's going high may cause the IRQ bit of the status register to go high as well (if enabled) and to remain high until the data is read into the MPU by addressing the ACIA through the CSO, CS1, and $\overline{CS2}$ lines and by setting the RS and R/W lines to a "1". After the data is read by the MPU, the RDRF and IRQ bits will be reset to a "0", but the data will remain in the RDR.

Status Register (SR)

The Status Register (SR) is an eight-bit register within the ACIA that maintains the current condition of internal ACIA activities (Fig. 9.32). A *read only* register in that the MPU cannot store any data in it, it is used by the MPU to check the status of certain events. To read its contents, the ACIA must be selected through the CS0, CS1, and the $\overline{CS2}$ lines, with the register select (RS) line being held low ("0") and the R/W line high ("1").

STATUS REGISTERS (SR)

7	6	5	4	3	2	1	ϕ
IRQ	PE	OVRN	FE	$\overline{CTS}$	$\overline{DCD}$	TDRE	RDRF

Fig. 9.32 Status register

Bit 0—Receiver Data Register Full (RDRF)

"1": (a) Indicates that the receiver data register is full.
      (b) The IRQ bit, if enabled, also gets set to a "1" and remains set until the data is read by the MPU (see pg. 198).

"0": (a) Indicates that the contents of the receiver data register have been read into the MPU. The data is retained in the register.
      (b) If there is a loss of carrier, the $\overline{DCD}$ line goes high, and the RDRF bit is clamped at "0", indicating that the contents of the RDR are not current.
      (c) A master reset condition also forces the RDRF bit to a "0".

Bit 1—Transmit Data Register Empty (TDRE)

"1": (a) Indicates that the contents of the transmit data register have been transferred and the register is ready for more data.

(b) The IRQ bit, if enabled, also gets set to a "1" and remains set until a write operation to the transmit data register (see pg. 198).

"0": (a) Indicates that the transmit data register is full.

(b) When a "1" is present on the $\overline{CTS}$ pin and causes the $\overline{CTS}$ (bit 3) of the SR to get set to a "1" to indicate that it is not clear to send, bit 0 of the TDRE will be clamped to a "0".

Bit 2—Data Carrier Detect ($\overline{DCD}$)

"1": (a) Indicates that there is no carrier from the modem.

(b) The IRQ bit, if enabled, also gets set and remains set until the MPU reads the status register and the receiver data register or until a master reset occurs (see pg. 198).

(c) This causes the RDRF bit to be clamped at a "0", inhibiting further interrupts from RDRF.

"0": (a) The carrier from the modem is present.

Bit 3—Clear to Send ($\overline{CTS}$)

"1": Indicates, via the high clear-to-send line from the modem, that the latter is not ready for data.

"0": Indicates, via the low clear-to-send line from the modem, that the modem is ready for data.

Bit 4—Framing Error (FE)

"1": Indicates that the received character is improperly framed by the start and stop bit. This error is detected by the absence of the first stop bit and indicates a synchronization error, faulty transmission, or a break condition. The error flag is set or reset during the receiver data transfer time and is therefore present throughout the time that the associated character is available.

"0": Indicates that the received character is properly framed.

Bit 5—Receiver Overrun (OVRN)

"1": Indicates that one or more characters in the data stream has been lost, that is, a character or a number of characters has been received, but not read, from the Receiver Data Register

(RDR) prior to subsequent characters being received. The overrun condition begins at the midpoint of the last bit of the second character received in succession without a read of the RDR having occurred. The overrun does not occur in the status register until the valid character prior to overrun has been read. Character synchronization is maintained during the overrun condition. The overrun error flag is reset after the reading of data from the RDR. Overrun is also reset by the master reset.

"0": No receiver overruns have occurred.

Bit 6—Parity Error (PE)

"1": Indicates that the number of highs ("1"s) in the character does not agree with the preselected odd or even parity. By definition, odd parity occurs when the total number of "1"s, including the parity bit, is odd. The parity error indication will be present as long as the data character is in the RDR. If no parity is selected, then both the transmitter parity generator output and the receiver parity check results are inhibited.

"0": No parity error occurred.

Bit 7—Interrupt Request (IRQ)

"1": Indicates that there is an interrupt present that has caused the $\overline{IRQ}$ output line to go low. The interrupt will be cleared by a read operation to the RDR, a write operation to the TDR, or a read of the SR, followed by a read of the RDR if caused by $\overline{DCD}$. A master reset always clears this bit.

"0": Indicates no interrupt present.

Control Register (CR)

The Control Register (CR), an eight-bit register within the ACIA, is used by the MPU to control the transmitting and receiving of serial data (Fig. 9.33). It is a write only register since the MPU cannot read it. To write into it, the ACIA must be selected via CS0, CS1, and $\overline{CS2}$, and both the RS line and the R/W line must be low ("0").

CONTROL REGISTER (CR)

7	6	5	4	3	2	1	φ
R I E	Transmitter Control		Word Select			Counter Divide	

Receiver Interrupt Enable

Fig. 9.33 Control register

Bits 0 and 1—Counter Divide Select Bits (CDS)

These two bits determine the divide ratios utilized in both the transmitter and receiver sections of the ACIA. They are also used for master reset of the ACIA, which clears the status register (except for external conditions on $\overline{CTS}$ and $\overline{DCD}$) and initializes both the receiver and the transmitter. Master reset does not affect other control register bits. After a power failure or restart, the ACIA must be reset before setting the clock divide ratio. Bit patterns for the various functions are shown below.

CR1	CR0	Function
0	0	÷ 1
0	1	÷ 16
1	0	÷ 64
1	1	Master reset

Bits 2, 3, 4—Word Select Bits (WS)

The programmer has the option of selecting the word length, number of stop bits, and type of parity by using the proper bit pattern from the chart below.

B4	B3	B2	Word Length	+	Parity	+	Stop Bits
0	0	0	7		Even		2
0	0	1	7		Odd		2
0	1	0	7		Even		1
0	1	1	7		Odd		1
1	0	0	8		None		2
1	0	1	8		None		1
1	1	0	8		Even		1
1	1	1	8		Odd		1

Bits 5 and 6—Transmitter Control Bits (TC)

The status of bits 5 and 6 of the control register provide for control of the interrupt from the Transmit Data Register Empty (TDRE) condition, the Request To Send ($\overline{RTS}$) output, and the transmission of a break level (space), as shown below.

CR6	CR5	Function
0	0	The $\overline{RTS}$ pin is *low* and Transmit Interrupts are inhibited. This is the code used when requesting that the communications channel be set up. It is not clear to send data yet.
0	1	The $\overline{RTS}$ pin is *low* and the communications channel has been set up. Therefore, this code is used to generate IRQs via the TRDE bit in the Status Register.
1	0	The $\overline{RTS}$ pin is *high* and transmit interrupts are inhibited. This code can be used to "knock down" the communications channel.
1	1	The $\overline{RTS}$ pin is *low* (keep up communications channel) and a break signal (low level on transmit data out line) is transmitted. This is used to interrupt the remote system.

Bit 7—Receiver Interrupt Enable (RIE)

"1":   Enables interrupts caused by:
(a) Receiver Data Register Full (RDRF) going high.
(b) A low-to-high transition on the Data Carrier Detect ($\overline{DCD}$) signal line.
"0":   Inhibits interrupts caused by RDRF or by the loss of receive data carrier.

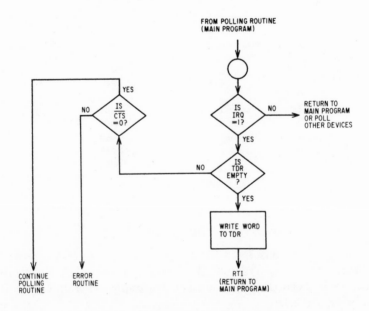

Fig. 9.34 Flowchart of transmit sequence

Power On

After the system power is applied, the ACIA master reset should be set by the initialization program, which stores a "1" in CR0 and CR1 of the ACIA control register. After master reset, the variable clock divide ratio bits, the transmitter interrupt bits, and the receiver interrupt bit of the ACIA control register should be set by the initialization program.

Transmit Sequence

The flowchart in Fig. 9.34 illustrates a typical sequence followed in transmission of serial data (for an example of ACIA programs, see Chap. 11).

Receive Sequence

The flowchart in Fig. 9.35 illustrates a typical sequence followed in

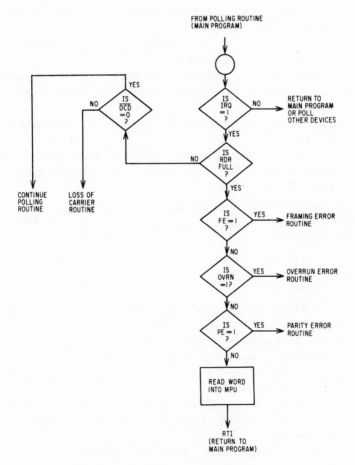

Fig. 9.35 Flowchart of receive sequence

the receiving of serial data by the ACIA (for an example of an ACIA program, see Chap. 11).

Problems

Microprocessor

1. How many bits does each of the following registers contain?

    (a) A _____   (d) X _____

    (b) B _____   (e) PC _____

    (c) CC _____   (f) SP _____

2. How many bits wide is the data bus? The address bus?
3. Running at the maximum rated clock frequency, what is the time required to execute the shortest instructions on the 6800?
4. Where does the MPU get the program starting address upon first starting up?

    (a) It clears the program counter (sets to zero) and therefore always starts a program at 0000.

    (b) It goes to the program starting address set up by the front panel switches of the microcomputer.

    (c) It fetches an address for the program start from the two highest bytes in memory corresponding to FFFE and FFFF on the address bus.

    (d) It always starts executing a program at addresses FFFE and FFFF.

    (e) The MPU inherently knows where to start a program and will automatically set the program counter to the proper address without being directed.

5. What is the state (0 or 1) of each of the following condition code register bits after instruction LDA A #$FF (load accumulator A with hexadecimal number FF) is executed?

    (a) Bit N

    (b) Bit Z

    (c) Bit V

6. If the interrupt bit (I bit) is set to a "1" and a WAI instruction is encountered, how can the MPU exit from this situation?
7. Assume the address of the stack pointer is hex 8B. What address will each of the MPU registers be stored in if an interrupt occurs?
8. If a system has two PIAs and two ACIAs, how does the MPU know which device causes an interrupt?
9. How many locations can be addressed by the MPU in hex? In decimal?
10. Which pin can halt the processor for an indefinite amount of time?
11. Which interrupt pin can be masked?
12. Which pin indicates that a number on the address bus is an arithmetic operand?

13. Which pin can halt the microprocessor for a maximum of 9.5 μsec?
14. Which pin refreshes the data bus drivers?
15. Which pin indicates that the address bus and the data bus have gone three-state during a halt?
16. Which output pins cannot be three-stated?
17. Determine the state of the condition code bits after the following operations:

(a) ABA

A = 1111 1111   A + B= _____   H = ___ N = ___
B = 0000 0001   Z = ___ V = ___ C = ___

(b) DECA

A = 0000 0000   A= _____   H = ___ N = ___
                       Z = ___ V = ___ C = ___

(c) LDA A #01

                 A= _____   H = ___ N = ___
                       Z = ___ V = ___ C = ___

(d) INC A

A = 0111 1111   A= _____   H = ___ N = ___
                       Z = ___ V = ___ C = ___

18. What is the value of the program counter (PC) after completion of the following interrupt sequences:

(a) After an $\overline{\text{IRQ}}$
(b) After an $\overline{\text{NMI}}$
(c) After an SWI
(d) After restart

Address		
FFFF	0	0
FFFE	F	E
FFFD	8	0
FFFC	F	C
FFFB	0	0
FFFA	F	D
FFF9	8	0
FFF8	F	D

Memories

19. How many bytes in a MCM6830 ROM?

(a) 128   (d) 1024
(b) 256   (e) 4096
(c) 512

20. Which pin(s) on the MCM6810 and MCM6830 is (are) three-state?

(a) Data bus   (d) Chip selects
(b) Read/Write   (e) All of the above
(c) Address bus

21. Why doesn't the MCM6830 ROM have a R/W pin?
22. What are the purposes of the positive and negative chip selects on the ROMs and RAMs?
23. What are the contents of the last eight ROM locations in any system?
24. What power supply voltages are required for the MCM6810 RAM and MCM6830 ROM?

  (a) +5, −12   (d) +5, −5
  (b) +5   (e) None of the above
  (c) +15, +5, −15

25. What is the organization of the MCM6810 RAM?

  (a) 1024 × 1   (d) 128 bytes (128 × 8)
  (b) 512 × 4   (e) 1024 bytes (1024 × 8)
  (c) 4K bytes (4096 × 8)

PIA

26. How many registers are in the PIA?
27. How many register select pins are in the PIA?
28. How many total lines can we have to the "outside world" on a PIA?
29. Although the A side and B side of the PIA are identical in most respects, there are two differences. One difference is in the internal I/O construction; the other difference is that

  (a) The A side can be either input or output on the eight data lines, whereas the B side can only be output.
  (b) The B side has no control register.
  (c) The A side does not have the "bit following" mode capability.
  (d) Both A and B side interrupts are reset as a result of a read of the A side data register, whereas only the B side interrupts are reset as a result of a read of the B side data register.
  (e) Reading from the A side or writing to the B side causes the handshake or pulse modes on the respective side if it is programmed for one of those modes.

30. Can we have three inputs and five outputs on the PIA A side?
31. How does the microprocessor know whether it is the A side or the B side which causes an interrupt? (Recall that both the IRQ lines from both sides are normally tied together.)
32. How can six registers be addressed with only two register selects?
33. After restart, what steps must be taken before the PIAs can be used?
34. In each of the following diagrams, fill in the bits of the data direction registers that match the I/O lines.

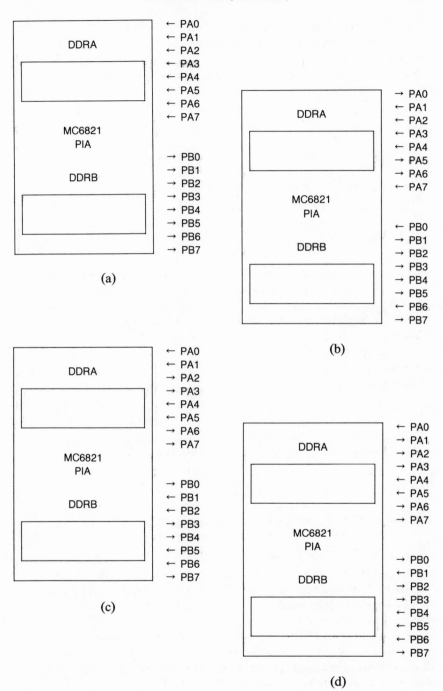

(a)

(b)

(c)

(d)

35. In the following diagrams, fill in the bits required to program the interrupt control lines as specified.

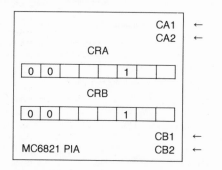

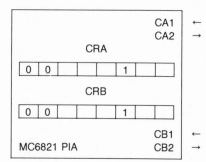

(a) CA1—Negative edge, masked
     CA2—Positive edge, unmasked
     CB1—Positive edge, masked
     CB2—Negative edge, unmasked

(b) CA1—Positive edge, masked
     CA2—Pulse mode
     CB1—Positive edge, unmasked
     CB2—Zero

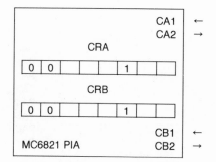

(c) CA1—Positive edge, unmasked
     CA2—One
     CB1—Negative edge, masked
     CB2—Handshake mode

(d) CA1—Negative edge, unmasked
     CA2—Handshake mode
     CB1—Negative edge, unmasked
     CB2—Pulse mode

36. In the following diagrams, determine the data that would be read from the A and B sides with the logic levels shown on the I/O lines and with the data shown in the registers.

L = Low logic level   H = High logic level

(a)

	PA0 — L
	PA1 — L
	PA2 — L
	PA3 — L
	PA4 — L
	PA5 — L
	PA6 — L
	PA7 — L
00000000	PDRA
11111111	DDRA
00000000	PDRB
00000000	DDRB
	PB0 — H
	PB1 — H
	PB2 — H
	PB3 — H
	PB4 — H
	PB5 — H
	PB6 — H
	PB7 — H

(a) A side data = _____
     B side data = _____

(b)

	PA0 — L
	PA1 — L
	PA2 — L
	PA3 — L
	PA4 — H
	PA5 — H
	PA6 — H
	PA7 — H
00001111	PDRA
00000000	DDRA
01110111	PDRB
00001111	DDRB
	PB0 — H
	PB1 — L
	PB2 — H
	PB3 — L
	PB4 — H
	PB5 — L
	PB6 — H
	PB7 — L

(b) A side data = _____
     B side data = _____

(c)

	PA0 — L
	PA1 — H
	PA2 — H
	PA3 — L
	PA4 — L
	PA5 — H
	PA6 — H
	PA7 — L
00000001	PDRA
11101101	DDRA
11111010	PDRB
01010011	DDRB
	PB0 — L
	PB1 — H
	PB2 — H
	PB3 — H
	PB4 — L
	PB5 — H
	PB6 — H
	PB7 — H

(c) A side data = _____
     B side data = _____

(d)

	PA0 — H
	PA1 — H
	PA2 — L
	PA3 — H
	PA4 — L
	PA5 — L
	PA6 — H
	PA7 — H
11011010	PDRA
00110010	DDRA
10000001	PDRB
01100110	DDRB
	PB0 — H
	PB1 — L
	PB2 — L
	PB3 — H
	PB4 — H
	PB5 — L
	PB6 — L
	PB7 — H

(d) A side data = _____
     B side data = _____

37. Each PIA shown in the following diagrams has interrupted the processor. Determine the control line that caused the interrupt in each case.

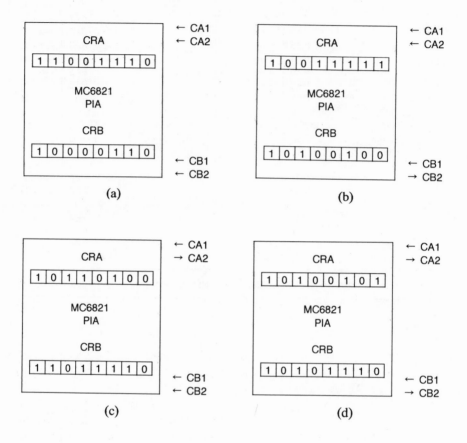

(a)   (b)

(c)   (d)

ACIA

38. During serial transmission at 300 baud, how many information bits are transmitted each second if each character has seven information bits with no parity bit?

39. If the ACIA control register word select bits contain a hex 5, how many external clock pulses are needed in the 16 mode to transfer both the start bit and the information bits?

40. What does ASCII stand for?
  - (a) American Standard Code for Information Interchange
  - (b) A Standard Communication—Version 2
  - (c) Asynchronous Standard Code—Version 2
  - (d) Asynchronous Serial Code in Industry

41. Can the MC6850 ACIA be used to transmit eight-bit data other than ASCII code serially?
42. How many registers in the ACIA are accessible from the data bus?
43. How are these registers selected with only one register select line?
44. What is the first thing that must be done to initialize the ACIA?
45. Which of the following bits in the status register could cause an interrupt? (Choose all that apply.)
    (a) RDRF (Receive Data Register Full)
    (b) TDRE (Transmit Data Register Empty)
    (c) $\overline{DCD}$ (Data Carrier Detect)
    (d) $\overline{CTS}$ (Clear To Send)
    (e) FE (Framing Error)
    (f) OVRN (Receiver OverRuN)
    (g) PE (Parity Error)
46. If we were using odd parity, give the parity bit (0 or 1) for the following data bits:
    (a) 1101100
    (b) 0000000
    (c) 1100001
47. What bit pattern (for bits 4, 3, and 2 only) should we write into the control register to send/receive from a standard 10-character/sec. model 33 Teletype machine? (Assume even parity.)

System

48. Assume, as part of your system, that you have two MCM6810 RAMs that start at the very bottom of memory. Your program is to check the first five bytes of the second RAM. If the contents of that RAM location is an odd number, invert each bit and store this result back in that RAM location; if an even number, clear that RAM location. Generate a flowchart and write a program to accomplish the above task. The program is to start at hex location 2000.

10

System Configuration

In Chap. 9, each of the basic devices in the M6800 family was discussed. How do we wire all these devices together to form a system? How are addresses determined? Such questions will be answered in this chapter. The connection of each pin on each device will be shown.

To illustrate as many principles as possible, a system consisting of three MCM6810 RAMs, three MCM6830 ROMs, three MC6821 PIAs, one MC6850 ACIA, and one-MC6800 MPU will be configured. This is the maximum possible number of devices which may be tied to the data bus without additional buffering.

The RAMs will be located at consecutive addresses starting at address 0000. Since the RAMs are used for reading and storing data frequently, the first 256 bytes of the RAMs can be addressed in the direct mode, that is, with two rather than three bytes of memory. (STA A $75 takes two bytes of memory whereas STA A $7505 takes three bytes of memory.) In our sample system, the RAM addresses will be 0000 to 017F.

The ROMs will be located in consecutive addresses with the highest address in the system assigned to ROM. This arrangement is necessary because the contents of the last eight addresses in the last ROM contain the addresses of the IRQ, SWI, NMI, and RESTART programs. During restart, the MPU places addresses FFFE and FFFF on the address bus sequentially, thus causing the contents of these locations to be placed in the program counter. Since the program counter now contains the address of the restart program, the MPU is ready to start program execution. In the example we will be showing, the ROMs will be located at address 8400 to 8FFF.

The PIAs and ACIAs will be located at addresses between the highest RAM address and the lowest ROM address in the system. PIA #1 will be at addresses 4004 through 4007, PIA #2 at addresses 4008 through 400B, and PIA #3 at addresses 4010 through 4013. As you have probably noticed, these addresses are not consecutive. There is no reason why they need be. However, because of the chip selects available, it is not possible, normally, to have all three PIAs at consecutive addresses. This fact will become obvious when we review the system layout worksheet later on.

The ACIA will be at addresses 4020 and 4021.

ALL LIKE DATA LINES ARE TIED TOGETHER

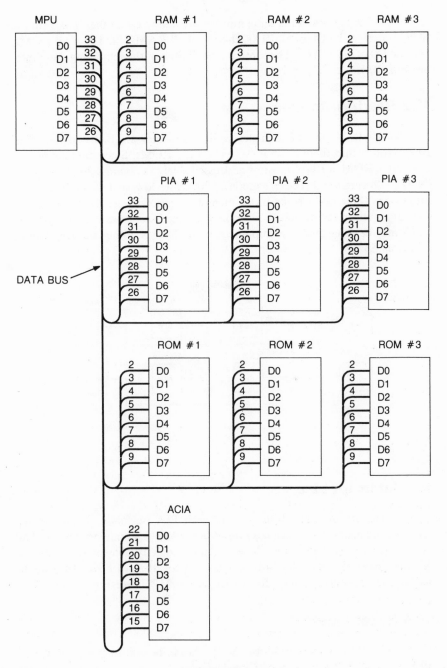

Fig. 10.1 Data bus

10.1 Data Bus

All data lines of the same number are tied to each other. D0 from the MPU is tied to the D0 of all PIAs, the D0 of all RAMs, the D0 of all ROMs, and the D0 of all ACIAs. The same is true of each of the remaining data lines. See Fig. 10.1.

10.2 Read/Write Line

All R/W pins of each device in the system are tied together (Fig. 10.2). Notice that there is no R/W pin on the ROMs. Since data cannot be stored in a ROM, a ROM must be addressed solely to obtain data (read only). (NOTE: During the three-state modes, VMA goes low, and we have to make sure that nothing gets written into a memory location by accident. We can do so with a pull-up resistor on R/W to insure a read state, or, in some systems, VMA may be connected to a chip select on the RAMs. Either way, protection is adequate.)

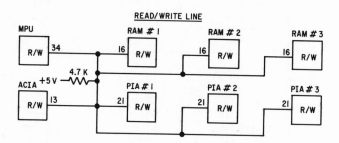

Fig. 10.2 Read/write line

10.3 Interrupt Line

The $\overline{\text{IRQA}}$ and $\overline{\text{IRQB}}$ lines of each PIA normally should be tied together and connected to the $\overline{\text{IRQ}}$ input of the MPU. In our system, we shall assume that $\overline{\text{IRQB}}$ of PIA#3 will be used for a nonmaskable interrupt ($\overline{\text{NMI}}$). All remaining $\overline{\text{IRQA}}$ and $\overline{\text{IRQB}}$ will be tied together with the $\overline{\text{IRQ}}$ of the ACIA and connected to the $\overline{\text{IRQ}}$ input on the MPU. See Fig. 10.3.

10.4 Reset Line

The $\overline{\text{RES}}$ input pin on the MPU should be tied to the $\overline{\text{RES}}$ pins on all PIAs. The signal applied to the reset line will be from an external circuit. See Fig. 10.4.

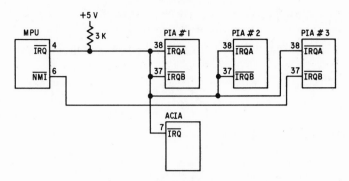

Fig. 10.3 Interrupt line

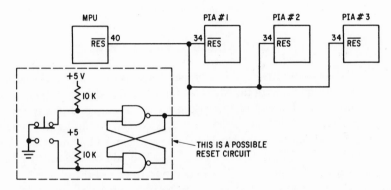

Fig. 10.4 Reset line

10.5 Valid Memory Address

The VMA signal, when high, indicates that a valid address is being applied to the bus by the MPU. There are two times when the address on the address bus is invalid (thus producing a low signal):

1. During some internal operations, the MPU allows invalid addresses to appear on the bus because they are not used.

2. Anytime the bus is three-stated (TSC high), it is floating and therefore invalid.

VMA is used to prevent destruction of data in the system caused by writing into a location inadvertently, or, in the case of a PIA or ACIA, by reading a register and accidently erasing some interrupt flags.

During condition 1 above, the MPU holds the R/W line in the read state so that nothing can be written into any location. By ANDing VMA and an address line that is tied to a chip select input on the PIAs and ACIAs, the PIAs and ACIAs are protected from an accidental read that would clear possible interrupt flags (Fig. 10.5). (NOTE: VMA may be connected to ROM if desired. The connection is not absolutely necessary since data in ROM cannot be destroyed, but no harm will come from doing so.)

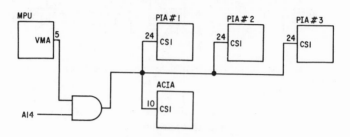

Fig. 10.5 Valid memory address

10.6 Phase 1 (φ1) and Phase 2 (φ2) Clock

The φ2 clock-driver NMOS output signal must be tied to the φ2 and data bus enable input pins of the MPU, and the φ1 clock-driver NMOS output to its φ1 input pin. Phase 2 (φ2) is also used as a sync signal to any part of the system that the MPU can write into. This φ2 should not be the same as the NMOS φ2 signal from the clock, for this is a non-TTL-compatible clock signal, but rather a TTL type φ2. This TTL φ2 should be tied to the enable pins (E) of the PIAs and the ACIA in addition to one of the chip selects on each RAM. In our sample system, it will be tied to the CS0 inputs of each RAM (Fig. 10.6). Notice that the TTL φ2 is not required in the ROMs, although it may be gated into a positive chip select if desired. In most clock chips, there is usually a separate φ2 TTL output signal. The Motorola MC6871A clock chip has these outputs available.

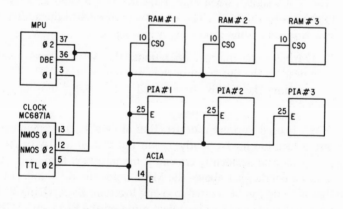

Fig. 10.6 Phase 1 and phase 2 clock signals

10.7 Unused Inputs

$\overline{HALT}$ Since the $\overline{HALT}$ input is usually used for external control of the MPU (for debugging purposes), this input pin for the general system should be tied to the $+5$-V input power through a 3.3-k resistor to permit normal execution (Fig. 10.7).

BA   Since this is an output line, it should be left alone unless it is to be used as a signal to some external device.

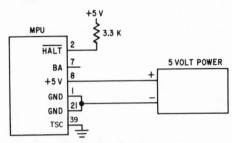

Fig. 10.7 Unused inputs

10.8 Address Lines

When the address lines are assigned, we must remember that each device is to have its own unique address.

Recall that the four chip selects (CS) in the ROMs are mask-programmable, that is, defined by the customer and manufactured into the device. In our sample system (Fig. 10.8), we will assume the presence of three positive chip selects and one negative chip select in the ROMs. A positive chip select (CS) requires a $+2$-V signal to activate the input. A negative chip select $(\overline{CS})$ requires a 0-V level to activate. Recall that a ROM has ten address lines to address 1,024 different locations in the ROM. Since the chip selects determine which ROM is addressed, our goal is to select a ROM while making sure that the other ROMs in the system are not activated, and then, with MPU address lines A0 through A9, which are connected to ROM address lines A0 through A9, to select an address in that ROM.

In assigning address lines to the RAMs, the same basic philosophy is applied as for the ROMs. Since the RAMS have 128 separate locations, however, seven address lines are required. Therefore, MPU address lines A0 through A6 will be tied to RAM address lines A0 through A6. The RAM chip selects (two positive and four negative) are then tied to the MPU address lines to produce the desired address. Also recall that the TTL phase 2 (ϕ2) signal is applied to a positive chip select (CS0).

The PIAs have only two register selects available, and these must be tied to MPU address lines A0 and A1. Remember that there are six registers to be addressed with only two register selects, an action accomplished with the aid of control register bit 2, as shown in Chap. 9. The remaining chip selects of the PIA (two positive and one negative) are tied to the proper MPU address line to achieve the desired address.

The ACIA has only one register select tied to MPU address line A0. The remaining chip selects (two positive and one negative) are tied to the proper MPU address line to achieve the desired address.

In our sample system, the RAMs will be at addresses 0000 through 017F; the ROMs, at addresses 8400 through 8FFF; the PIAs, at addresses 4004 through 4007, 4008 through 400B, and 4010 through 4013; and the ACIA, at addresses 4020 and 4021.

The procedure for wiring up a complete system using these addresses is as follows:

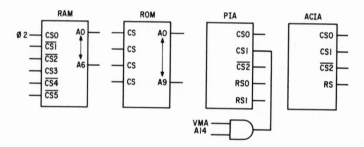

Fig. 10.8 Sample system

Step 1   With the use of a system layout work sheet such as that shown in Fig. 10.9, list all devices and place an X in the columns that represent the MPU address lines to which the devices must be tied. The A0 through A6 pins of all RAMs must be tied to MPU address lines A0 through A6. All A0 through A9 pins of the ROMs must be tied to MPU address lines A0 through A9. RS0 pins of all PIAs must be tied to MPU address line A0. The RS1 pins of all PIAs must be tied to MPU address line A1. The RS pin of the ACIA must be tied to MPU address line A0.

Device	\multicolumn{16}{c}{MPU Address Lines (A0–A15)}		Address	
	15	14	13	12	11	10	9	8	7	6	5	4	3	2	1	0	From	To
RAM #1										X	X	X	X	X	X	X		
RAM #2										X	X	X	X	X	X	X		
RAM #3										X	X	X	X	X	X	X		
ROM #1							X	X	X	X	X	X	X	X	X	X		
ROM #2							X	X	X	X	X	X	X	X	X	X		
ROM #3							X	X	X	X	X	X	X	X	X	X		
PIA #1															RS1	RS0		
PIA #2															RS1	RS0		
PIA #3															RS1	RS0		
ACIA #1																RS		

Fig. 10.9 System layout work sheet (Step 1)

Step 2   Assign the three positive selects of ROM #1 to the appropriate MPU address lines to achieve the proper address. The ROM #1 address range is from 8400 through 87FF. To get an 8000 address, a chip select must be tied to MPU address line A15 (Fig. 10.10). The lowest ROM address, 8400, can be achieved by tying a positive chip select to MPU address line A10. The remaining positive chip select will be tied to +5 V since it is not needed for addressing. Notice in ROM #1 that if A15 and A10 are both high and all remaining address lines low, an address of 8400 is generated. If A15 and A10 are high, and A0 through A9 are also high, an address of 87FF is generated.

Device	\multicolumn{16}{c}{MPU Address Lines (A0-A15)}		Address	
	15	14	13	12	11	10	9	8	7	6	5	4	3	2	1	0	From	To
RAM #1										X	X	X	X	X	X	X		
RAM #2										X	X	X	X	X	X	X		
RAM #3										X	X	X	X	X	X	X		
ROM #1	CS					CS	X	X	X	X	X	X	X	X	X	X	8400	87FF
ROM #2							X	X	X	X	X	X	X	X	X	X		
ROM #3							X	X	X	X	X	X	X	X	X	X		
PIA #1															RS1	RS0		
PIA #2															RS1	RS0		
PIA #3															RS1	RS0		
ACIA #1																RS		

Fig. 10.10 Step 2

Step 3   Assign the three positive and one negative chip selects of ROM #2 to the appropriate MPU address line to achieve the proper address for ROM #2. The ROM #2 address range is from 8800 through 8BFF. Again, a positive chip select must be tied to MPU address line A15. To achieve the beginning address of 8800, a positive chip select must be tied to MPU address line A11. The remaining positive chip select pin must be tied to the +5-V power supply. Now recall the earlier requirement that each device have its own unique address. If A15, A10, and A11 were all high, both ROM #1 and ROM #2 would be addressed. To prevent this from happening, a negative chip select of ROM #1 can be tied to MPU address line A11, and a negative chip select from ROM #2, to MPU address line A10 (Fig. 10.11). Now if

Device	\multicolumn{16}{c}{MPU Address Lines (A0-A15)}		Address	
	15	14	13	12	11	10	9	8	7	6	5	4	3	2	1	0	From	To
RAM #1										X	X	X	X	X	X	X		
RAM #2										X	X	X	X	X	X	X		
RAM #3										X	X	X	X	X	X	X		
ROM #1	CS				C̄S̄	CS	X	X	X	X	X	X	X	X	X	X	8400	87FF
ROM #2	CS				CS	C̄S̄	X	X	X	X	X	X	X	X	X	X	8800	8BFF
ROM #3							X	X	X	X	X	X	X	X	X	X		
PIA #1															RS1	RS0		
PIA #2															RS1	RS0		
PIA #3															RS1	RS0		
ACIA #1																RS		

Fig. 10.11 Step 3

MPU address line A11 goes high, ROM #1 cannot be activated since its A11 pin needs a low signal to activate. The same is true regarding ROM #2 with MPU address line A10. Also notice that with A15 and A11 high and all remaining address lines low, the address of 8800 is achieved. If A15 and A11 are high, A10 is low and A0 through A9 are high; thus address of 8BFF is achieved.

   Step 4   Assign the three positive and one negative chip selects of ROM #3 to the appropriate MPU address lines to achieve addresses 8C00 through 8FFF. If a positive chip select is tied to MPU address lines A15, A11, and A10, the address of 8C00 is achieved (Fig. 10.12). In this case, since the negative chip select of ROM #3 is not used, it must be tied to ground. If A15, A11, and A10 are high, and A0 through A9 all low, the address of 8C00 is achieved. If A15, A11, A10, and A0 through A9 are high, the address of 8FFF is achieved. Also notice that *only* ROM #3 is addressed. (NOTE: Recall that when the MPU puts the address bus at FFFE on restart, a ROM location is addressed. By reviewing the above chart, it should be obvious that when FFFE is on the address bus, the next to last location in ROM #3 is addressed. The MPU will next put all address lines high to address the last location of ROM #3. The contents of these last two locations in the last ROM are placed in the program counter that tells the MPU where to get its first instruction.)

Device	MPU Address Lines (A0−A15)																Address	
	15	14	13	12	11	10	9	8	7	6	5	4	3	2	1	0	From	To
RAM #1										X	X	X	X	X	X	X		
RAM #2										X	X	X	X	X	X	X		
RAM #3										X	X	X	X	X	X	X		
ROM #1	CS				C̄S̄	CS	X	X	X	X	X	X	X	X	X	X	8400	87FF
ROM #2	CS				CS	C̄S̄	X	X	X	X	X	X	X	X	X	X	8800	8BFF
ROM #3	CS				CS	CS	X	X	X	X	X	X	X	X	X	X	8C00	8FFF
PIA #1															RS1	RS0		
PIA #2															RS1	RS0		
PIA #3															RS1	RS0		
ACIA #1																RS		

Fig. 10.12 Step 4

   Step 5   Assign the two positive and one negative chip selects of the PIAs to achieve addresses 4004 through 4007, 4008 through 400B, and 4010 through 4013 by tying the CS1 chip selects of each PIA to MPU address line A14 (Fig. 10.13). If CS0 of PIA #1 is tied to MPU address line A2; CS0 of PIA #2, to MPU address line A3; and CS0 of PIA #3, to MPU address line A4, the above PIA addresses are achieved. By tying the negative chip select of each PIA to MPU address line A15, the PIAs *will not* be addressed if a ROM has been addressed. Again, if A14 and A2 are high and all remaining MPU address lines low, the address of 4004 is achieved. If MPU address lines A14, A2, A1, and A0 are high and the remaining address lines low, the address 4007 is achieved. By going through the same analysis for PIA #2 and PIA #3, it will be seen that the assigned addresses are achieved. (NOTE: Although

CS1 is shown tied to MPU address line A14, this line is really the output of A14 ANDed with VMA, as discussed earlier—see Fig. 10.14).

Device	15	14	13	12	11	10	9	8	7	6	5	4	3	2	1	0	From	To
	MPU Address Lines (A0–A15)																Address	
RAM #1										X	X	X	X	X	X	X		
RAM #2										X	X	X	X	X	X	X		
RAM #3										X	X	X	X	X	X	X		
ROM #1	CS				$\overline{CS}$	CS	X	X	X	X	X	X	X	X	X	X	8400	87FF
ROM #2	CS				CS	$\overline{CS}$	X	X	X	X	X	X	X	X	X	X	8800	8BFF
ROM #3	CS				CS	CS	X	X	X	X	X	X	X	X	X	X	8C00	8FFF
PIA #1	$\overline{CS2}$	CS1												CS0	RS1	RS0	4004	4007
PIA #2	$\overline{CS2}$	CS1											CS0		RS1	RS0	4008	400B
PIA #3	$\overline{CS2}$	CS1										CS0			RS1	RS0	4010	4013
ACIA #1															RS			

Fig. 10.13 Step 5

Fig. 10.14 A14 ANDed with VMA

Step 6   Assign chip select CS0 of the ACIA to MPU address line A5 and CS1 to MPU address line A14 (Fig. 10.15). $\overline{CS2}$ of the ACIA is tied to MPU address line A15 to prevent the ACIA from being addressed when a ROM is addressed. This will achieve the ACIA addresses desired (4020 and 4021).

Device	15	14	13	12	11	10	9	8	7	6	5	4	3	2	1	0	From	To
	MPU Address Lines (A0–A15)																Address	
RAM #1										X	X	X	X	X	X	X		
RAM #2										X	X	X	X	X	X	X		
RAM #3										X	X	X	X	X	X	X		
ROM #1	CS				$\overline{CS}$	CS	X	X	X	X	X	X	X	X	X	X	8400	87FF
ROM #2	CS				CS	$\overline{CS}$	X	X	X	X	X	X	X	X	X	X	8800	8BFF
ROM #3	CS				CS	CS	X	X	X	X	X	X	X	X	X	X	8C00	8FFF
PIA #1	$\overline{CS2}$	CS1												CS0	RS1	RS0	4004	4007
PIA #2	$\overline{CS2}$	CS1											CS0		RS1	RS0	4008	400B
PIA #3	$\overline{CS2}$	CS1										CS0			RS1	RS0	4010	4013
ACIA #1	$\overline{CS2}$	CS1									CS0				RS		4020	4021

Fig. 10.15 Step 6

Step 7   Assign the four negative and two positive chip selects of each RAM to the proper MPU address lines to achieve the desired addresses. Since A15 is high when a ROM is addressed and A14 is high when PIAs and the ACIA are addressed, a negative chip select from each RAM should be tied to MPU address lines A14 and A15 to prevent a RAM from being accidently addressed when a ROM, PIA, or ACIA is addressed. Notice the $\overline{CS}$ assignments in Fig. 10.16 are assigned so that only one RAM can be addressed at any one time. The CS0 of all RAMS is tied to the TTL $\phi2$ signal from the clock. The CS3 on RAM #1 is tied to the +5-V power supply. The $\overline{CS2}$ of RAM #2 and RAM #3 will be tied to system ground.

Device	\multicolumn{17}{c}{MPU Address Lines (A0–A15)}	\multicolumn{2}{c}{Address}
	15	14	13	12	11	10	9	8	7	6	5	4	3	2	1	0	From	To
RAM #1	$\overline{CS5}$	$\overline{CS4}$						$\overline{CS2}$	$\overline{CS1}$	X	X	X	X	X	X	X	0000	007F
RAM #2	$\overline{CS5}$	$\overline{CS4}$						$\overline{CS1}$	CS3	X	X	X	X	X	X	X	0080	00FF
RAM #3	$\overline{CS5}$	$\overline{CS4}$						CS3	$\overline{CS1}$	X	X	X	X	X	X	X	0100	017F
ROM #1	CS				$\overline{CS}$	CS	X	X	X	X	X	X	X	X	X	X	8400	87FF
ROM #2	CS				CS	$\overline{CS}$	X	X	X	X	X	X	X	X	X	X	8800	8BFF
ROM #3	CS				CS	CS	X	X	X	X	X	X	X	X	X	X	8C00	8FFF
PIA #1	$\overline{CS2}$	CS1												CS0	RS1	RS0	4004	4007
PIA #2	$\overline{CS2}$	CS1											CS0		RS1	RS0	4008	400B
PIA #3	$\overline{CS2}$	CS1									CS0				RS1	RS0	4010	4013
ACIA #1	$\overline{CS2}$	CS1								CS0						RS	4020	4021

Fig. 10.16 Step 7

You have now wired up a complete system. If different addresses are to be assigned, start with the first chart in Fig. 10.9 and follow the same procedure.

Problems

1. Using the chart below, configure a system having an MPU, sixteen input and sixteen output lines, 256 bytes of RAM, two ACIAs, and a ROM operating system of 3,980 bytes. The RAM must start at address 0000. The PIAs must start at address 1004, with the ACIAs immediately following the PIAs. The last address of the ROM must be 4FFF. The selection of positive or negative chip selects for the ROM will be determined by you. However, only one device may be addressed at any one time.
2. Using the chart below, configure a system with an MPU, eight input and eight output lines, one ACIA, 128 bytes of RAM for scratchpad memory, and 2,048 bytes of ROM for the operating system. You determine the addresses, but only one device may be addressed at any one time. The ROM chip selects are also your choice.

System Layout Worksheet

Device	\multicolumn{17}{c}{MPU Address Lines (A0-A15)}	\multicolumn{2}{c}{Address}
	15	14	13	12	11	10	9	8	7	6	5	4	3	2	1	0	From	To

11

Example Programs

One of the best techniques for learning about microcomputer systems is to study example programs. In this chapter, several example programs will be presented. Some that don't really do much nevertheless illuminate one aspect or another of such systems. All programs are geared to the M6800 system and are presented for illustrative purposes only.

11.1 Add Four Numbers Program

The purpose of this program for adding four numbers is (1) to show how instructions are structured in a program in machine language, (2) to show how the same program is written in M6800 source language, (3) to show the source program after it has been assembled by the M6800 assembler, and (4) to compare the assembled output, which is in hex, with the machine language solution.

Problem: Write a program, in machine language and in M6800 source language, to add the decimal numbers 25, 35, 50, and 17. Store the answer at RAM location OA. Assemble the source program, and compare the assembled program with the machine language program.

Machine Language Solution

$$
\begin{aligned}
\text{SOLUTION:} \quad 35_{10} &= 100011_2 = 23_{16} \\
50_{10} &= 110010_2 = 32_{16} \\
17_{10} &= 010001_2 = 11_{16} \\
25_{10} &= 011001_2 = 19_{16}
\end{aligned}
$$

MEMORY LOCATION (HEX)	MACHINE LANGUAGE (BINARY)	(HEX)	COMMENT
000B	10000110	(86)	LDA A IMM
000C	00011001	(19)	DATA TO BE PUT IN A
000D	10001011	(8B)	ADD A IMM
000E	00100011	(23)	DATA TO BE ADDED TO A
000F	10001011	(8B)	ADD A IMM
0010	00110010	(32)	DATA TO BE ADDED TO A
0011	10001011	(8B)	ADD A IMM
0012	00010001	(11)	DATA TO BE ADDED TO A
0013	10010111	(97)	STORES A IN LOCATION
0014	00001010	(0A)	0A

Program Written in M6800 Source Language

```
100  NAM  ADD4NR
110  ORG  $A
120  TEMP  RMB  1
130  LDA  A  #25
140  ADD  A  #35
150  ADD  A  #$32
160  ADD  A  #%10001
170  STA  A  TEMP
180  END
```

Notice in the source language statements how the numbers to be added may be listed in decimal, hex, octal, or binary. The assembler will convert them to machine language for you. However, you *must* indicate to the assembler what base system your number is in, that is $32 indicates hex 32. Both 25 and 35 are in decimal, and %10001 indicates that the number is already in binary. The symbol # indicates the immediate mode of addressing.

Previous Source Program Assembled by M6800 Assembler

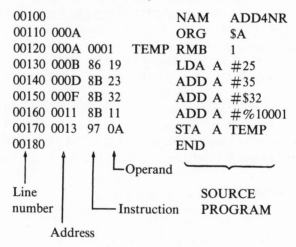

11.2 Program to Clear Nine Memory Locations

This program illustrates how the index register is used to clear consecutive memory locations. The program clears the nine memory locations from hex 70 through 78. A solution with its corresponding flowchart (Fig. 11.1) and two alternative solutions are presented.

Solution

```
100   NAM CLM
110   OPT  M
120   ORG  $500
130   LDX  #$70
140 L1 CLR 0,X
150   INX
160   CPX  #$79
170   BNE  L1
180   END
```

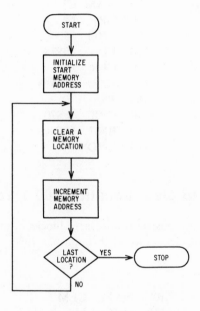

Fig. 11.1 Flowchart of solution

Each time the program comes to the "CPX #$79" instruction, the contents of the index register will be compared with hex number 79. If they are not equal, the "BNE L1" instruction causes the program to return to the instruction that contains the label "L1".

When the index register is equal to hex 79, the program will stop. Notice that the "CPX" instruction resulted in the Z bit of the condition code register being set or reset. The contents of the Z bit determine whether it branches back or goes forward.

Alternative Solution 1

```
100  NAM CLM
110  OPT  M
120  ORG $500
130  LDX  #$9
140 L1 CLR $6F,X
150  DEX
160  BNE  L1
170  END
```

Alternative Solution 2

```
100  NAM CLM
110  OPT  M
120  ORG $500
130  LDS  #$78
140  CLR  A
150 MORE PSH A
160  TSX
170  CPX  #$70
180  BNE  MORE
190  END
```

11.3 Program to Clear Locations 00 Through Hex FF

This program illustrates how large blocks of memory can be cleared (in this case, memory locations 00 through hex FF).

Solution

```
100  NAM  CLM
110  OPT  M
120  ORG  $500
130  LDX  #0
140  CLR  A
150 AGAIN STA A 0,X
160  INX
170  CPX  #$100
180  BNE  AGAIN
190  END
```

Again, the "CPX" instruction sets or resets the bit of the condition code register that the "BNE" instruction will use to determine whether to branch back or continue. This solution uses 12 bytes and takes 4,357 cycles.

Alternative Solution 1

```
100  NAM   CLM
110  OPT   M
120  ORG   $500
130  LDX   #0
140  AGAIN CLR 0,X
150  INX
160  CPX   #$100
170  BNE   AGAIN
180  END
```

This solution uses 11 bytes and takes 4,611 cycles.

Alternative Solution 2

```
100  NAM   CLM
110  OPT   M
120  ORG   $500
130  LDX   #$FF
140  AGAIN CLR 0,X
150  DEX
160  BNE   AGAIN
170  CLR   0,X
180  END
```

This solution uses ten bytes and takes 3,835 cycles.

11.4 Load Memory with a Data Table (Ascending)

This program illustrates how the data table shown below can be loaded into the memory locations given.

ADDR	DATA
0000	00
0001	01
0002	02
0003	03
.	.
.	.
00FD	FD
00FE	FE
00FF	FF

Solution

```
100  NAM  STT
110  OPT  M
120  ORG  $500
130  LDX  #0
140  CLR  A
150  NEXT STA A 0,X
160  INC  A
170  INX
180  CPX  #$100
190  BNE  NEXT
200  END
```

11.5 Load Memory with a Data Table (Descending)

The following two programs illustrate how the data table shown below can be loaded into memory.

ADDR	DATA
0000	FF
0001	FE
0002	FD
.	.
.	.
.	.
00FD	02
00FE	01
00FF	00

Solution 1

```
100  NAM   STT
110  OPT   M
120  ORG   $500
130  LDA   A #$FF
140  LDX   #0
150  AGAIN STA A 0,X
160  INX
170  DEC   A
180  BNE   AGAIN
190  STA   A $FF
200  END
```

Solution 2

```
100   NAM   STT
110   OPT   M
120   ORG   $500
130   LDS   #$FF
140   CLR A
150 AGAIN PSH A
160   INC   A
170   BNE   AGAIN
180   END
```

11.6 Move $80 Bytes of Data

This program moves hex 80 bytes of data from memory locations 0 through 7F (shown below) to memory locations hex 100 through hex 17F.

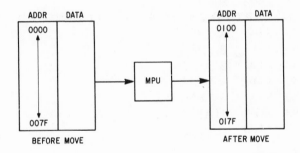

Solution

```
100   NAM MOV
110   OPT   M
120   ORG   $500
130   LDX   #0
140 MORE  LDA A 0,X
150   INX
160   STA   A $FF,X
170   CPX   #$80
180   BNE   MORE
190   END
```

11.7 Program to Move a Constant

Write a program for the following sequence:

1. Begin with data 7F and load it into the A accumulator; then store the data in memory location 50.

2. From location 50, load the data into the B accumulator; then store it in extended memory location 0113.

3. Reload data into the A accumulator from the extended memory location, store it in location 6A, and then jump back to the beginning.

Assume that this program will be used in a microcomputer system with RAM addresses 000 through 200 (512 bytes) and ROM addresses 800 through FFF (2,048 bytes). All numbers in the source program are in hex.

Source Program

```
100   NAM   LTR1
101   OPT   MEM
102   ORG   $6A
103 TEMP   RMB 1
105   ORG   $0800
110 START LDA A #$7F     START OF PROGRAM
120   STA   A $50
130   LDA   B $50
140   STA   B $0113
150   LDA   A $0113
180   STA   A TEMP
190   JMP   START
200   END
```

Assembled Program

```
00100                      NAM   LTR1
00101                      OPT   MEM
00102 006A                 ORG   $6A
00103 006A 0001    TEMP    RMB   1
00105 0800                 ORG   $0800
00110 0800  86 7F  START  LDA A #$7F   START OF PROGRAM
00120 0802  97 50         STA  A $50
00130 0804  D6 50         LDA  B $50   ADDRESS OF DATA
00140 0806  F7 0113       STA  B $0113
00150 0809  B6 0113       LDA  A $0113
00180 080C  97 6A         STA  A TEMP
00190 080E  7E 0800       JMP    START
00200                      END
```

11.8 Program to Subtract Absolute Values of Two Numbers

The purpose of this program is to calculate a quantity Z that will be the absolute value of Y subtracted from the absolute value of W ($|W| - |Y|$). If the result is less than or equal to zero, set Z equal to zero.

$$Z = |W| - |Y| \qquad \text{if } |W| > |Y|$$
$$Z = 0 \qquad \text{if } |W| \le |Y|$$

A flowchart for this program is shown in Fig. 11.2.

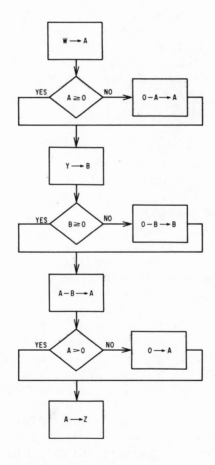

Fig. 11.2 Flowchart of program

Source Program for Absolute Value Problem

```
100   NAM ABS
110   OPT  M
120   ORG  O
130   W RMB 1
140   Y  RMB 1
150   Z  RMB 1
160   ORG  $0500
170   LDA  A W
180   BPL  Z1 IS W POSITIVE?
190   NEG  A W WAS NEG, MAKE POS.
200   Z1 LDA B Y
210   BPL  Z2 IS Y POSITIVE?
220   NEG  B Y WAS NEG, MAKE POS.
230   Z2 SBA SUBTRACT Y FROM W
240   BGT  Z3 IS Z POSITIVE?
250   CLR   A RESULT WAS ZERO OR NEG.
260   Z3 STA A Z STORE ANSWER IN Z.
270   BRA *
280   MON
```

Assembled Program for Absolute Value Problem

```
00100                      NAM    ABS
00110                      OPT    M
00120 0000                 ORG    0
00130 0000  0001    W  RMB     1
00140 0001  0001    Y  RMB     1
00150 0002  0001    Z  RMB     1
00160 0500                 ORG    $0500
00170 0500  96 00         LDA A  W
00180 0502  2A 01         BPL    Z1          IS W POSITIVE?
00190 0504  40            NEG A              W WAS NEG, MAKE
                                             POS.
00200 0505  D6 01  Z1 LDA B  Y
00210 0507  2A 01         BPL    Z2          IS Y POSITIVE?
00220 0509  50            NEG B              Y WAS NEG, MAKE POS.
00230 050A  10     Z2 SBA                    SUBTRACT Y FROM W
00240 050B  2E 01         BGT    Z3          IS Z POSITIVE?
00250 050D  4F            CLR A              RESULT WAS ZERO OR
                                             NEG.
00260 050E  97 02  Z3 STA A  Z               STORE ANSWER IN Z.
00270 0510  20 FE         BRA    *
00280                      MON
```

11.9 Multiplication Subroutine

This subroutine multiplies two eight-bit unsigned binary numbers (producing a 16-bit result). The product of the two eight-bit numbers is formed by shifting the multiplier one bit to the right and checking for a "1" or "0". If a "1" is present, the multiplicand is added to the product (answer). The multiplicand is then shifted one bit to the left. This has the effect of multiplying the multiplicand by two. The multiplier is again shifted one bit to the right and the shifted bit checked for a "1" or "0". If it is a "1", the shifted multiplicand is added to the product. The process is repeated until the multiplier has no more "1"s remaining. When no more "1"s remain in the multiplier, the problem is finished and the product is the final product.

For example, suppose that the decimal numbers 170 and 850 were to be multiplied. Then,

$$170_{10} \times 5_{10} = 850_{10}$$
$$170_{10} = AA_{16}$$
$$5 = 05_{16}$$

| 1010 | 1010 | Multiplicand (M) |
| 0000 | 0101 | Multiplier (N) |

— This 1 requires the multiplicand M to be added to product.

— This 1 requires the multiplicand shifted left twice ($4 \times M$) to be added to the product.

Since all remaining higher bits of the multiplier are zero, the problem is finished.

$$
\begin{array}{c}
1010\ \ 1010\ \ M \\
\underline{10\ \ 1010\ \ 10} \\
11\ \ 0101\ \ 0010\quad 4 \times M \\
3\quad\ \ 5\quad\ \ 2
\end{array}
$$

$$AA_{16} \times 5_{16} = 352_{16} = 850_{10}$$

The flowchart for this multiplication subroutine is shown in Fig. 11.3.

Subroutine

```
100    NAM CMULT
110    OPT M,S
120    * * * * * * * * * * * * * * * * * * * * * *
130    * REV 003 11-10-75 BAINTER
140    *
150    * THIS SUBROUTINE MULTIPLIES TWO 8 BIT BYTES.
160    * THE MULTIPLICAND IS STORED IN BYTE NB1.
```

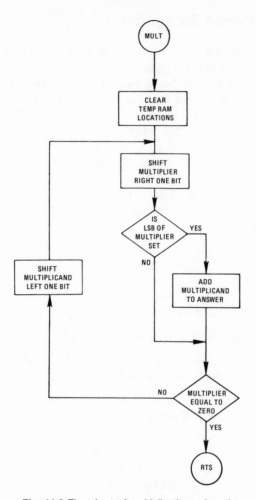

Fig. 11.3 Flowchart of multiplication subroutine

```
170   * THE MULTIPLIER IS STORED IN BYTE NB2.
180   * THE RESULT IS STORED IN BYTES ANS2 AND ANS1.
190   * ANS2 IS THE UPPER BYTE OF THE RESULT.
200   * ANS1 IS THE LOWER BYTE OF THE RESULT.
210   * * * * * * * * * * * * * * * * * * * * * * *
220     SPC   1
230     ORG   0
240   NB1A RMB 1 SHIFT MULTIPLICAND STORE
250   NB1 RMB 1 MULTIPLICAND
260   NB2 RMB 1 MULTIPLIER
270   ANS2 RMB 1 UPPER BYTE OF RESULT
```

```
280   ANS1 RMB 1 LOWER BYTE OF RESULT
290   SPC  1
300   ORG  $10
310   SPC  1
330   MULT CLR A CLEAR ANSWER & SHIFT AREAS
340   STA  A NB1A
350   STA  A ANS1
360   STA  A ANS2
370   LDA  A NB2 NB2 = MULTIPLIER
380   BRA  LOOP1
385   SPC  1
390   LOOP2 ASL NB1 SHIFT MULTIPLICAND LEFT
400   ROL  NB1A UPPER BYTE OF MULTIPLICAND
410   LOOP1 LSR A SHIFT MULTIPLIER RIGHT
420   BCC  NOADD SHIFT AND DON'T ADD
430   LDA  B ANS1 ADD SHIFTED MULTIPLICAND
440   ADD  B NB1 to ANS1 AND ANS2.
450   STA  B ANS1 LOWER BYTE OF RESULT
460   LDA  B ANS2
470   ADC  B NB1A ADD WITH CARRY
480   STA  B ANS2 UPPER BYTE OF RESULT
490   TST  A
500   NOADD BNE LOOP2 START SHIFTING AGAIN
510   RTS  FINISHED!!!
520   MON

READY
```

11.10 System Program—BCD to LED

As an example of a system problem, assume a system composed of a seven-segment LED and a four-wire BCD signal. The object will be to use an M6800 to convert the BCD signal to the seven-segment code necessary to the LED. Even though the same task could be done with one TTL IC (7447), this problem illustrates not only a very simple complete system, but, more important, it demonstrates one method of using a look-up table without getting entangled with more complex concepts. The system configuration is shown in Fig. 11.4.

Source Listing

```
LIST

BCDLED        20:29EST       11/10/75
100   NAM  BCDLED
```

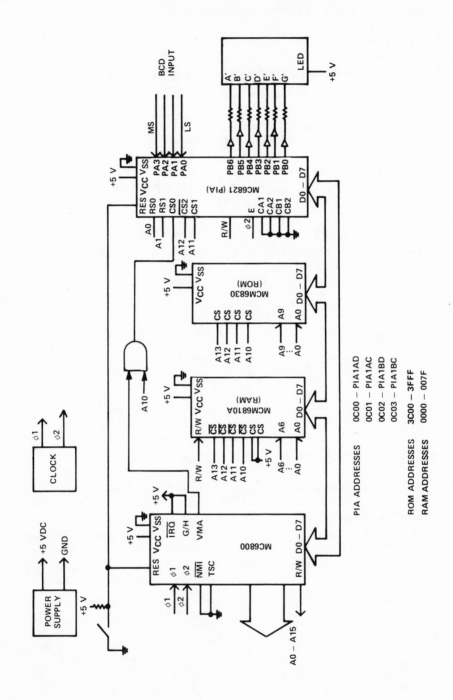

TRUTH TABLE

BCD CODE				SEVEN-SEGMENT CODE							DISPLAY	OUTPUT WORD (HEX)
d	c	b	a	A'	B'	C'	D'	E'	F'	G'		
0	0	0	0	0	0	0	0	0	0	1	0	01
0	0	0	1	1	0	0	1	1	1	1	1	4F
0	0	1	0	0	0	1	0	0	1	0	2	12
0	0	1	1	0	0	0	0	1	1	0	3	06
0	1	0	0	1	0	0	1	1	0	0	4	4C
0	1	0	1	0	1	0	0	1	0	0	5	24
0	1	1	0	0	1	1	0	0	0	0	6	60
0	1	1	1	0	0	0	1	1	1	1	7	0F
1	0	0	0	0	0	0	0	0	0	0	8	00
1	0	0	1	0	0	0	0	1	0	0	9	0C
INVALID CODE				0	1	1	0	0	0	0	E	30

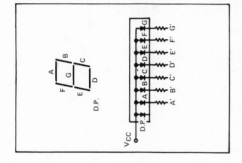

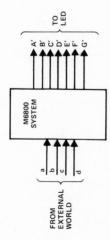

Fig. 11.4 System configuration

```
110    OPT   M
115    SPC   1
120    ORG   0
130    INDEX RMB 2
140    ORG   $0C00 PIA ADDRESSES
150    PIA1AD RMB 1
160    PIA1AC RMB 1
170    PIA1BD RMB 1
180    PIA1BC RMB 1
190    ORG   $3F00 BUILD TABLE
200    TABLE FCB $1,$4F,$12,$6,$4C,$24,$60,$F,,$C
210    FCB   $30,$30,$30,$30,$30,$30 ERROR INPUTS
220    ORG   $3FFE
230    FDB   START RESTART VECTOR
235    SPC   1
240    ORG   $3C00 BEGIN PROGRAM
250    START LDA A #$FF
260    STA   A PIA1BD B-SIDE ALL OUTPUTS
270    LDA   A #%00000100
280    STA   A PIA1AC
290    STA   A PIA1BC
300    LDX   #TABLE GET STARTING ADR OF TABLE
310    STX   INDEX
320    LOOP LDA A PIA1AD READ BCD INPUT
330    AND   A #%00001111 MASK 4 MSB
340    STA   A INDEX+1
350    LDX   INDEX
360    LDA   A 0,X
370    STA   A PIA1BD OUTPUT TO LED
380    BRA   LOOP DO IT AGAIN
390    MON
```

READY

Assembled Listing

```
00100                      NAM   BCDLED
00110                      OPT   M

00120 0000                 ORG   0
00130 0000     0002   INDEX RMB   2
00140 0C00                 ORG   $0C00    PIA ADDRESSES
00150 0C00     0001   PIA1AD RMB  1
00160 0C01     0001   PIA1AC RMB  1
00170 0C02     0001   PIA1BD RMB  1
00180 0C03     0001   PIA1BC RMB  1
```

```
00190 3F00                          ORG    $3F00      BUILD TABLE.
00200 3F00    01        TABLE  FCB    $1, $4F, $12, $6, $4C, $24, $60, $F,, $C
      3F01    4F
      3F02    12
      3F03    06
      3F04    4C
      3F05    24
      3F06    60
      3F07    0F
      3F08    00
      3F09    0C
00210 3F0A    30                     FCB    $30, $30, $30, $30, $30, $30   ERROR INPUT
      3F0B    30
      3F0C    30
      3F0D    30
      3F0E    30
      3F0F    30
00220 3FFE                          ORG    $3FFE
00230 3FFE    3C00                  FDP    START      RESTART VECTOR

00240 3C00                          ORG    $3C00      BEGIN PROGRAM
00250 3C00    86 FF     START  LDA A  #$FF
00260 3C02    B7 0C02          STA  A  PIA1BD   B-SIDE ALL OUTPUTS
00270 3C05    86 04            LDA A  #%00000100
00280 3C07    B7 0C01          STA  A  PIA1AC
00290 3C0A    B7 0C03          STA  A  PIA1BC
00300 3C0D    CE 3F00          LDX    #TABLE GET   STARTING   ADR   OF
                                             TABLE
00310 3C10    DF 00            STX    INDEX
00320 3C12    B6 0C00 LOOP     LDA A  PIA1AD   READ BCD INPUT
00330 3C15    84 0F            AND A  #%00001111     MASK 4 MSB
00340 3C17    97 01            STA  A  INDEX+1
00350 3C19    DE 00            LDX    INDEX
00360 3C1B    A6 00            LDA A  0,X
00370 3C1D    B7 0C02          STA  A  PIA1BD   OUTPUT TO LED
00380 3C20    20 F0            BRA    LOOP     DO IT AGAIN
00390                          MON
```

11.11 Machine Control System Program

The following system description is that of an MC6800 controlling a hypothetical machine. This machine may be part of an industrial or commercial process and could be involved in manufacturing, such as photographic processing or other assembly-line operations. While the application is imaginary, it does serve to illustrate how hardware and software marry and that each has its proper place in any system architecture. Although the system will function if implemented, its purpose is the illustration of techniques and the clarification of the configuring of an entire system.

Function of the System

The input from the machine to be controlled consists of eight switches, manual and/or cam-operated, that provide the input information about the machine's condition. As these switches are mechanical, their output is subject to severe bouncing, which must be eliminated by some method. The driven items (controlled outputs) are four incandescent lamps for operator indication or optical control functions within the machine and four ac motors driving various parts. See Fig. 11.5.

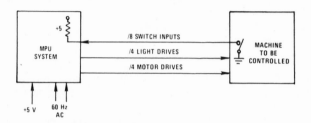

Fig. 11.5 Machine control system

The processor system examines the state of the eight inputs after performing a software debounce and calculates an appropriate output based on this information. It then gives this output to the lamps and motors in a judicious fashion.

System Operation

A system schematic is shown in Fig. 11.6. The clock consists of a cross-coupled monostable MC8602, with an MC3459 driver, and the restart circuit is an MC1455. Interrupts will be given to the system via CA1 and CB1 of the PIA from a one-shot MC74121. The Q output goes high, close to the zero crossing of the ac line, and comes low about 4 ms later, at the peak of the line cycle.

The restart routine (Fig. 11.7) sets the stack pointer, initializes the PIA, clears out some RAM locations, clears the interrupt mask, then falls into the executive code. The executive code is a loop that runs continuously, looking at the eight inputs and comparing them to a look-up table. This table is composed of two-byte pairs. The first byte of a pair is indicative of a certain input combination, and the second byte is the corresponding output pattern that would be given to the lights and motors if the first byte should be a match with the actual inputs. The reader should notice that the executive code takes its input word not from the PIA, but from RAM—at EXINP—and gives its output not to the PIA, but to RAM—at EXOUT. Therefore, the executive code does not handle the system tasks of I/O; these are taken care of in the interrupt routines.

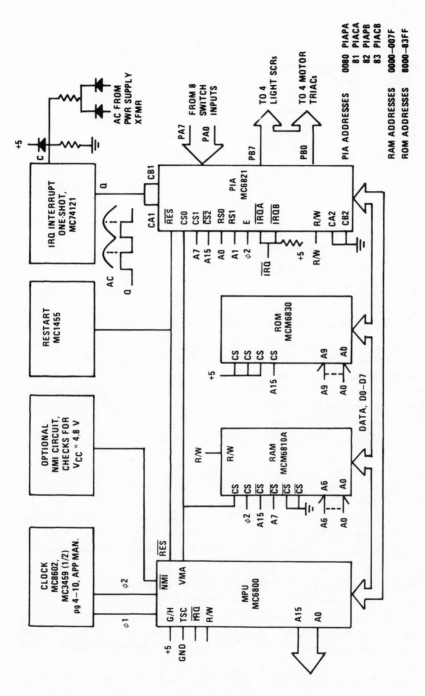

Fig. 11.6 System configuration

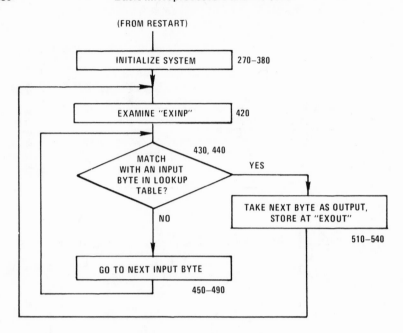

Fig. 11.7 Software flow

Notice in Fig. 11.6 that CA1 and CB1 are tied together and are driven by the A output of the one-shot. Line CA1 has been programmed to be sensitive to a rising edge, and CB1, to a falling edge. Since the one-shot is driven by the ac line, we have indicators in terms of interrupts corresponding to the zero-crossing (CA1) and peak (CB1) times of the line cycle.

The system makes use of three interrupts: Valley, Peak, and NMI (Fig. 11.8).

The Valley interrupt comes from CA1 and occurs near the zero-cross of the ac line. The lights are turned on at this zero-current time, greatly increasing their life and reducing in-rush stress on the SCRs. This output data is taken from RAM location EXOUT, the executive output. Valley has the second function of bringing in the input information from PIAPA, conditioning (debouncing) it, and storing it at EXINP, the input for the executive. Debouncing is performed by checking the inputs at 8-ms intervals. If they are equal for three consecutive times, the data is stored in EXINP, thus eliminating the external hardware that would otherwise be required.

The Peak interrupt comes from CB1 and occurs near the peak of the line cycle. This is the optimum time to turn off inductive loads, and the only function of this interrupt is to output the four bits of motor data from EXOUT to PIAPB.

There is a third interrupt, NMI. Here it is used to indicate the impeding loss of power. In order not to leave the motors and lights running uncon-

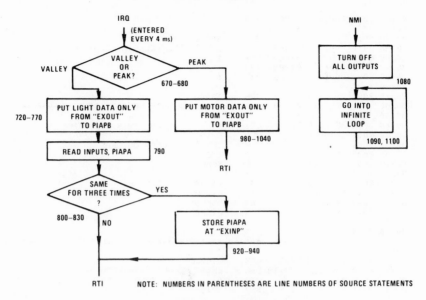

Fig. 11.8 Interrupt routines

trolled because of a power supply or other failure, NMI turns off all outputs and goes into an infinite loop with no escape.

If an oscilloscope were hung on the IRQ line, it would look like an inverted picket fence timed to the line frequency (Fig. 11.9).

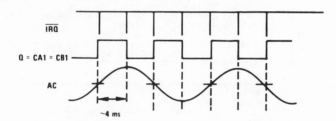

Fig. 11.9 Result of oscilloscope being hung on IRQ line

It is obvious that a processor such as the MC6800 is not fully utilized in this application. It could perform several other functions in addition to controlling this machine, or it could control many of them simultaneously.

Assembled Listing

```
00100                    NAM    HYDER    10/30/75  REV 002
00110                    OPT    M=MF9,S,O=TAPE,NOG
00120  0000              ORG    0000
00130  0000 0001  EXINP  RMB    1           LABEL RAM LOCATIONS
00140  0001 0001  COUNT  RMB    1
00150  0002 0001  EXOUT  RMB    1
```

```
00160 0003 0001    TEMP    RMB     1
00170              •
00180 0030                 ORG     $0030
00190 0030 0001    PIAPA   RMB     1         LABEL PIA LOCATIONS
00200 0031 0001    PIACA   RMB     1
00210 0032 0001    PIAPB   RMB     1
00220 0033 0001    PIACB   RMB     1
00230              •
00240 3000                 ORG     $3000
00250              ••••••••••••••••••••••••••••••BEGIN RESTART ROUTINE•••••••
00260              •
00270 3000 8E 007F RESTRT  LDS     #$007F    LOAD STACK POINTER
00280 3003 7F 0000         CLR     EXINP
00290 3006 7F 0001         CLR     COUNT     CLEAR OUT RAM
00300 3009 7F 0002         CLR     EXOUT
00310 300C 7F 0003         CLR     TEMP
00320              •
00330 300F CE 0007         LDX     #$0007    SET UP PIA
00340 3012 DF 80           STX     PIAPA
00350 3014 CE FF05         LDX     #$FF05
00360 3017 DF 82           STX     PIAPB
00370              •
00380 3019 0E              CLI
00390              ••••••••••••••••••••••••••••••BEGIN EXECUTIVE ROUTINE••
00400              •
00410 301A CE 3033 EXEC    LDX     #TABLE
00420 301D 96 00   CONTIN  LDA A   EXINP     GET DATA FROM RAM
00430 301F A1 00           CMP A   0,X       IS THERE A MATCH?
00440 3021 27 09           BEQ     MATCH
00450 3023 08      CHECK   INX
00460 3024 08              INX
00470 3025 8C 3049         CPX     #ENDTAB+2  END OF TABLE?
00480 3028 26 F3           BNE     CONTIN    NO? CONTINUE
00490 302A 20 EE           BRA     EXEC      YES? BEGIN AGAIN
00500              •
00510 302C E6 01   MATCH   LDA B   1,X       GET DATA TO OUTPUT
00520 302E D7 02           STA B   EXOUT     STORE IT IN RAM
00530 3030 3E              WAI               NOTHING ELSE TO DO
00540 3031 20 E7           BRA     EXEC      RETURN TO EXEC LOOP
00550              •
00560              ••••••••••••••••••••••••••••••••••••••••••••••••••••••••••
00570              •TABLE FOLLOWS: FORM IS: DATA BYTE FOLLOWED
00580              •BY AN OUTPUT BYTE INDICATIVE OF THE OUTPUT BYTE
00590              •TO BE GIVEN TO THE PIAPB
00600              •
00610 3033 0000    TABLE   FDB     $0000,$0103,$0277,$0381,$4201,$A42F
00620 303F D311            FDB     $D311,$3B29,$FF11,$FEC8
00630 3047 4D88    ENDTAB  FDB     $4D88      END OF TABLE
00640              •
00650              •••••••••••••••••IRQ POLLING ROUTINE•••••••••••••••••••••••
00660              •
00670 3049 96 33   POLL    LDA A   PIACB     GET CB
00680 304B 2B 27           BMI     PEAK      VALLEY OR PEAK INTERRUPT?
00690              •
00700              •••••••••••INTERRUPT FOR VALLEY (LIGHTS & INPUTS)•
00710              •
00720 304D 86 F0   VALLEY  LDA A   #$F0
00730 304F 94 02           AND A   EXOUT     OUTPUT 4 BITS OF LIGHT
00740 3051 D6 82           LDA B   PIAPB     DATA ONLY W/O CHANGING
00750 3053 C4 0F           AND B   #$0F      MOTOR OUTPUTS
00760 3055 1B              ABA
00770 3056 97 82           STA A   PIAPB
00780              •
00790 3058 96 80           LDA A   PIAPA     INPUTS SAME AS
00800 305A 91 03           CMP A   TEMP      LAST TIME? CLEARS INTERRUPT
00810 305C 27 06           BEQ     SAME
00820 305E 97 03           STA A   TEMP      STORE NEW DATA
00830 3060 7F 0001         CLR     COUNT     ZERO COUNTER
00840 3063 3B              RTI               GO BACK TO EXEC
00850              •
00860 3064 C6 01   SAME    LDA B   #01       THIRD TIME MATCH?
00870 3066 D1 01           CMP B   COUNT
00880 3068 27 04           BEQ     GOODIN    IF SO, GO TO GOODIN
00890 306A 7C 0001         INC     COUNT     IF NOT, JUST INC COUNTER
```

```
00900 306D 3B              RTI              AND RETURN
00910              *
00920 306E 97 00  GOODIN STA A  EXINP       PUT GOOD DATA IN RAM
00930 3070 7F 0001        CLR   COUNT
00940 3073 3B              RTI
00950              *
00960              **********INTERRUPT FOR PEAK (MOTOR) OUTPUTS*****
00970              *
00980 3074 36 0F   PEAK   LDA A  #$0F       OUTPUT 4 BITS OF
00990 3076 94 02          AND A  EXOUT      MOTOR DATA W O CHANGING
01000 3078 D6 32          LDA B  PIAPB      LIGHT DATA. ALSO CLEARS INT
01010 307A C4 F0          AND B  #$F0
01020 307C 1B             ABA
01030 307D 97 32          STA A  PIAPB
01040 307F 3B             RTI
01050              *
01060              ******************OPTIONAL NMI INTERRUPT*******
01070              *
01080 3080 7F 0032 NMI    CLR    PIAPB      TURN OFF ALL OUTPUTS
01090 3083 01      HANGUP NOP
01100 3084 20 FD          BRA    HANGUP     GO TO SLEEP
01110              *
01120              ******************SET VECTORS IN UPPER ROM*******
01130              *
01140 33F8                ORG    $33F8
01150 33F8 8049           FDB    POLL,0000,NMI,RESTRT
01160              *
01170                     MON
```

11.12 Time Delay Program (Short Delay)

It is often desirable to program time delay loops into your program, and there are several ways to do so. One technique is to load the A accumulator with a number and decrement it to zero. It takes two cycles to decrement the A accumulator and four cycles to determine if it has been decremented to zero, or a total of six cycles per decrement. A program to load the A accumulator and then decrement it to zero is shown below, and a flowchart is given in Fig. 11.10.

Program:

			Cycles
100	NAM	TMR	
110	OPT	M	
120	ORG	$8000	
130	LDA	A #$FF	2
140	DAGN	DEC A	2
150	BNE	DAGN	4
160	END		

Since hex FF is equal to 255_{10}, the program will make 255 loops at six cycles each plus the two original cycles to load the A accumulator:

$$
\begin{array}{rl}
255 \text{ loops @ 6 cycles ea.} & = 1{,}530 \text{ cycles} \\
1 \text{ loop @ 2 cycles ea.} & = \underline{\quad 2} \text{ cycles} \\
& 1{,}532
\end{array}
$$

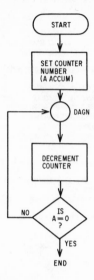

Fig. 11.10 Flowchart of time delay program (short)

If each cycle takes 1 microsecond, then 1,532 cycles results in a delay of 1,532 microseconds.

11.13 Time Delay Program (Long Delay)

A longer time delay may be needed to perform some function such as flashing a light every two seconds. Such functions can be accomplished with the following program. A flowchart is given in Fig. 11.11.

Program

			Cycles
100	NAM LTC		
105	OPT M		
110	ORG $3000		
115	LOOP1 LDA A	#4	2
120	LOOP2 LDX	#$FFFF	3
130	AGN DEX		4
140	BNE	AGN	4
145	DEC	A	2
150	BNE	LOOP2	4
155	END		

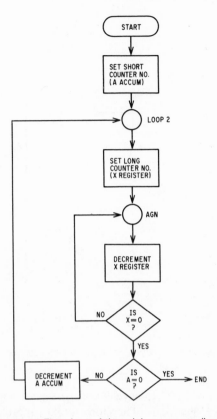

Fig. 11.11 Flowchart of time delay program (long)

The label LOOP1 is shown as a means of branching from some other location to this routine when the time delay is needed. To calculate the time required to go through this time delay, just add up the number of cycles and multiply the result by the time for each cycle. For example, if one cycle = 1 ms, then:

Instruction	No. of Times Executed	No. of Cycles Each Time	Total Cycles
LDA A #4	1	2	2
LDX #$FFFF	4	3	12
DEX	65535 × 4	4	1048560
BNE AGN	65535 × 4	4	1048560
DEC A	4	2	8
BNE LOOP2	4	4	16

Total No. of Cycles 2097158

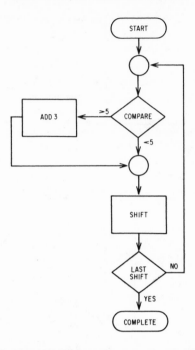

Fig. 11.12 Binary to BCD conversion flowchart

The product of 2,097,158 cycles and 1 μs per cycle is approximately 2,097,158 μs or 2.09158 seconds. Therefore, it takes approximately 2 seconds to go through this loop. By changing the number loaded in the "short counter" (A register) or the index register, the delay time can be varied.

11.14 Binary to BCD Conversion Program*

A standard technique for binary-to-BCD conversion is that of the Add 3 algorithm. The technique requires a register containing the N-bit binary number and enough four-bit BCD registers to contain the maximum equivalent BCD number for the initial binary number. The conversion starts by checking each BCD register for a value of 5 or greater. If this condition exists in one or all of these registers (initially this condition cannot exist), then a 3 is added to those registers where the condition exists. Next, the registers are shifted left, with the carry out of the previous register being the carry in to the next register. Again each BCD register is checked for values of 5 or greater. This sequence continues until the registers have been shifted N times, where N is the number of bits in the initial binary word. The BCD registers then

*Reprinted from *Motorola AN-757, Analog-to-Digital Conversion Techniques with the M6800 Microprocessor System,* by Don Aldridge.

contain the resulting BCD equivalent of the initial binary word. The example below starts with an eight-bit binary word consisting of all "1"s. This word is converted to the BCD equivalent of 255 by this technique. After eight shifts, the last binary bit has been shifted out of the binary register, and the hundreds, tens, and units registers contain a 255.

The M6800 source program for performing this technique of binary to BCD conversion follows. The initial binary number is a 16-bit number and occupies memory locations MSB and LSB; this number is converted (see Figs. 11.12 and 11.13) to the equivalent BCD number in memory locations TENTSD, HNDTHD, and UNTTEN. Each of these memory locations contains two BCD digits. Eighty-three memory locations are required for program storage, with a maximum conversion taking 1.8 ms.

Hundreds	Tens	Units	8-Bit Binary	
			1 1 1 1 1 1 1 1	
		1	1 1 1 1 1 1 1	Shift
		1 1	1 1 1 1 1 1	Shift
		1 1 1	1 1 1 1 1	Shift
		1 0 1 0	1 1 1 1 1	Add 3 to Units
	1	0 1 0 1	1 1 1 1	Shift
	1	1 0 0 0	1 1 1 1	Add 3 to Units
	1 1	0 0 0 1	1 1 1	Shift
	1 1 0	0 0 1 1	1 1	Shift
	1 0 0 1	0 0 1 1	1 1	Add 3 to Tens
1	0 0 1 0	0 1 1 1	1	Shift
1	0 0 1 0	1 0 1 0	1	Add 3 to Units
1 0	0 1 0 1	0 1 0 1		Shift
2	5	5		Total Shifts 8

Fig. 11.13 Binary to BCD conversion

Source Program

```
 10   NAM DWA21
 20   OPT M
 30   ORG 0              INITIAL BINARY NUMBER
 40   MSB RMB 1             MOST SIGNIFICANT 8 BITS
 50   LSB RMB 1             LEAST SIGNIFICANT 8 BITS
 60   ORG $0010         BCD RESULTS
 70   UNTTEN RMB 1         UNITS AND TENS DIGITS
 80   HNDTHD RMB 1         HUNDREDS AND THOUSANDS
 90   TENTSD RMB 1         TENS OF THOUSANDS DIGIT
100   ORG $0F00         **BEGINNING OF PROGRAM**
110   CLR UNTTEN
```

```
120   CLR HNDTHD
130   CLR TENTSD
140   LDX #$0010
150   BEGIN LDA A UNTTEN          UNITS COMPARISON
160   TAB
170   AND A #$0F
180   SUB A #$05
190   BMI AT
200   ADD B #$03
210   AT TBA                      TENS COMPARISON
220   AND A #$0F0
230   SUB A #$50
240   BMI BT
250   ADD B #$30
260   BT STA B UNTTEN
270   LDA A HNDTHD                HUNDREDS COMPARISON
280   TAB
290   AND A #$0F
300   SUB A #$05
310   BMI CT
320   ADD B #$03
330   CT TBA                      THOUSANDS   COMPARISON
340   AND A #$0F0
350   SUB A #$50
360   BMI DT
370   ADD B #$30
380   DT STA B HNDTHD
390   LDA A TENTSD                TENS OF THOUSANDS COMPARISON
400   TAB
410   SUB A #$05
420   BMI ET
430   ADD B #$03
440   ET STA B TENTSD
450   ASL LSB
460   ROL MSB
470   ROL UNTTEN
480   ROL HNDTHD
490   ROL TENTSD
500   DEX
510   BNE BEGIN                   END OF CONVERSION CHECK
520   END
530   MON
```

11.15 ACIA Memory Load/Dump Program

Assume that there are three 128×8 MCM6810 RAMs in a system. It is desired to load a 256-byte program into the two upper RAMs starting with address 0080. Then,

Hand load:

	RAM Loc.	Value
	0000	00
	0001	80
	0002	01
	0003	80

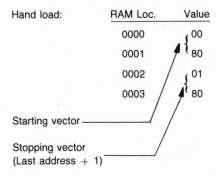

Starting vector

Stopping vector
(Last address + 1)

After the hand-loading of the starting and stopping vectors, the *load program* is executed by starting the MPU at program address 0900. When the program has finished loading, the CA2 line of PIA1 will go low. This signal can be used to stop the tape recorder or turn off a lamp to indicate the end of the loading process.

The *memory dump program* works as follows: The start-and-stop memory dump addresses or vectors are hand-loaded into RAM locations 0000, 0001, 0002, and 0003 in the same manner as in the previous load program. Program execution begins at memory address 094B. The characters AA and 55 are first dumped or placed on the tape in order to indicate the beginning of memory dump or listing. Each program character or byte is dumped via the ACIA and modem until the last memory location has been addressed and dumped. When the dump operation is complete, the CA2 lead of PIA1 will go low, indicating dump complete. (See Figs. 11.14 and 11.15 for load and dump flowcharts.)

Source Program

```
1.000   NAM LDBOOT
2.000   OPT M
3.000   ◆THIS PROGRAM LOADS OR DUMPS MEMORY
4.000   ◆PLACE START ADDRESS IN LOC 00 & 01
5.000   ◆PLACE END ADDRESS + 1 IN LOC 02 & 03
6.000   ◆IF ERROR OCCURS, CHECK LOC 04 & 05 FOR ADDRESS.
7.000   ◆CA2 STOPS DRIVE AT EOT OR ERROR.
8.000   ◆CB2 GIVES ERROR INDICATION.
9.000   ◆DUMP PROGRAM STARTS AT LOC 094B.
10.000  PIA1AC EQU $0805
11.000  PIA1BC EQU $0807
12.000  ACIAC EQU $0806
```

```
13.000 ACIAD EQU $0809
14.000   ORG $0900
15.000   LDA A #$03
16.000   STA A ACIAC ACIA MASTER RESET
17.000   LDX $00 LOAD START ADDRESS
18.000   LDA A #$19 ACIA 8 BITS EVEN PARITY
19.000   STA A ACIAC
20.000 LOOP LDA A ACIAC
21.000   ROR A
22.000   BCC LOOP RECEIVER FULL?
23.000   LDA A ACIAD
24.000 CMPAA CMP A #$AA IS FIRST CHAR "AA"?
25.000   BNE LOOP BRANCH IF NOT
26.000 LOOP1 LDA A ACIAC
27.000   ROR A
28.000   BCC LOOP1
29.000   LDA A ACIAD
30.000   CMP A #$55 IS SECOND CHAR "55"?
31.000   BNE CMPAA IF NOT, TRY FOR AN "AA"
32.000 LOOP2 LDA A ACIAC
33.000   TAB TRANSFER A TO B
34.000   AND B #$70
35.000   BNE ERROR BRANCH IF ERROR
36.000   ROR A
37.000   BCC LOOP2
38.000   LDA A ACIAD LOAD A CHAR FROM TAPE
39.000   STA A 0,X STORE IN MEMORY
40.000   INX INCREMENT ADDRESS
41.000   CPX $02 LOAD COMPLETED?
42.000   BNE LOOP2 GO GET MORE
43.000 END LDA A #$30
44.000   STA A PIA1AC TURN OFF CA2
45.000   BRA ◆
46.000 ERROR LDA A #$36
47.000   STA A PIA1BC TURN ON ERROR LIGHT
48.000   STX $04 STORE ADR OF ERROR
49.000   BRA END
50.000   PAGE
51.000   LDX $00        ◆START OF DUMP PROGRAM
52.000   LDA A #$19
53.000   STA A ACIAC
54.000   LDA A #$AA        ◆OUTPUT CONTROL CHAR
55.000   STA A ACIAD
56.000 LOOP5 LDA A ACIAC
57.000   ROR A
58.000   ROR A
59.000   BCC LOOP5        ◆XMIT BUFFER EMPTY?
60.000   LDA A #$55        ◆OUTPUT SECOND CONTROL CHAR
61.000   STA A ACIAD
62.000 LOOP6 LDA A ACIAC
63.000   ROR A
64.000   ROR A
65.000   BCC LOOP6        ◆XMIT BUFFER EMPTY?
```

```
66.000 LOOP4 LDA A 0, X
67.000   STA A ACIAD      ◆OUTPUT CHAR TO TAPE
68.000 LOOP3 LDA A ACIAC
69.000   ROR A
70.000   ROR A
71.000   BCC LOOP3        ◆XMIT BUFFER EMPTY?
72.000   INX
73.000   CPX $02
74.000   BNE LOOP4
75.000   BRA END
76.000   MON
```

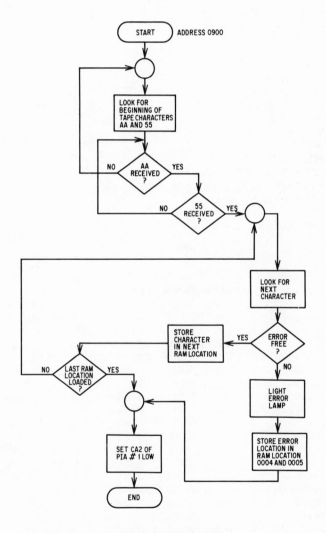

Fig. 11.14 Load flowchart

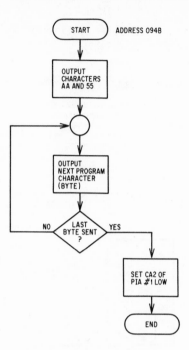

Fig. 11.15 Dump flowchart

Assembled Program

```
00010                          NAM     LDBOOT
00020                          OPT     M
00030                    ◆ THIS PROGRAM LOADS OR DUMPS MEMORY
00040                    ◆ PLACE START ADDRESS IN LOC 00 & 01
00050                    ◆ PLACE END ADDRESS + 1 IN LOC 02 & 03
00060                    ◆ IF ERROR OCCURS, CHECK LOC 04 & 05 FOR ADDRESS.
00070                    ◆ CA2 STOPS DRIVE AT EOT OR ERROR.
00080                    ◆ CB2 GIVES ERROR INDICATION.
00090                    ◆ DUMP PROGRAM STARTS AT LOC 094B.
00100       0805         PIA1AC  EQU     $0805
00110       0807         PIA1BC  EQU     $0807
00120       0806         ACIAC   EQU     $0806
00130       0809         ACIAD   EQU     $0809
00140 0900                       ORG     $0900
00150 0900 86 03                 LDA A   #$03
00160 0902 B7 0806               STA A   ACIAC     ACIA MASTER RESET
00170 0905 DE 00                 LDX     $00       LOAD START ADDRESS
00180 0907 86 19                 LDA A   #$19      ACIA 8 BITS EVEN PARITY
00190 0909 B7 0806               STA A   ACIAC
00200 090C B6 0806       LOOP    LDA A   ACIAC
00210 090F 46                    ROR A
00220 0910 24 FA                 BCC     LOOP      RECEIVER FULL?
00230 0912 B6 0809               LDA A   ACIAD
```

```
00240 0915 81  AA      CMPAA  CMP A  #$AA      IS FIRST CHAR "AA"?
00250 0917 26  F3             BNE    LOOP      BRANCH IF NOT
00260 0919 B6  0806    LOOP1  LDA A  ACIAC
00270 091C 46                 ROR A
00280 091D 24  FA             BCC    LOOP1
00290 091F B6  0809           LDA A  ACIAD
00300 0922 81  55             CMP A  #$55      IS SECOND CHAR "55"?
00310 0924 26  EF             BNE    CMPAA     IF NOT, TRY FOR AN "AA"
00320 0926 B6  0806    LOOP2  LDA A  ACIAC
00330 0929 16                 TAB              TRANSFER A TO B
00340 092A C4  70             AND B  #$70
00350 092C 26  14             BNE    ERROR     BRANCH IF ERROR
00360 092E 46                 ROR A
00370 092F 24  F5             BCC    LOOP2
00380 0931 B6  0809           LDA A  ACIAD     LOAD A CHAR FROM TAPE
00390 0934 A7  00             STA A  0, X      STORE IN MEMORY
00400 0936 08                 INX              INCREMENT ADDRESS
00410 0937 9C  02             CPX    $02       LOAD COMPLETED?
00420 0939 26  EB             BNE    LOOP2     GO GET MORE
00430 093B 86  30     END     LDA A  #$30
00440 093D B7  0805           STA A  PIA1AC    TURN OFF CA2
00450 0940 20  FE             BRA    ◆
00460 0942 86  36     ERROR   LDA A  #$36
00470 0944 B7  0807           STA A  PIA1BC    TURN ON ERROR LIGHT
00480 0947 DF  04             STX    $04       STORE ADR OF ERROR
00490 0949 20  F0             BRA    END
00510 094B DE  00             LDX    $00       ◆START OF DUMP PROGRAM
00520 094D 86  19             LDA A  #$19
00530 094F B7  0806           STA A  ACIAC
00540 0952 86  AA             LDA A  #$AA      ◆OUTPUT CONTROL CHAR
00550 0954 B7  0809           STA A  ACIAD
00560 0957 B6  0806    LOOP5  LDA A  ACIAC
00570 095A 46                 ROR A
00580 095B 46                 ROR A
00590 095C 24  F9             BCC    LOOP5     ◆XMIT BUFFER EMPTY?
00600 095E 86  55             LDA A  #$55      ◆OUTPUT SECOND CONTROL
                                                CHAR
00610 0960 B7  0809           STA A  ACIAD
00620 0963 B6  0806    LOOP6  LDA A  ACIAC
00630 0966 46                 ROR A
00640 0967 46                 ROR A
00650 0968 24  F9             BCC    LOOP6     ◆XMIT BUFFER EMPTY?
00660 096A A6  00     LOOP4   LDA A  0, X
00670 096C B7  0809           STA A  ACIAD     ◆OUTPUT CHAR TO TAPE
00680 096F B6  0806    LOOP3  LDA A  ACIAC
00690 0972 46                 ROR A
00700 0973 46                 ROR A
00710 0974 24  F9             BCC    LOOP3     ◆XMIT BUFFER EMPTY?
00720 0976 08                 INX
00730 0977 9C  02             CPX    $02
00740 0979 26  EF             BNE    LOOP4
00750 097B 20  BE             BRA    END
00760                         MON
```

Appendix A
M6800 Instruction Set Summary

JUMP AND BRANCH INSTRUCTIONS

JUMP AND BRANCH OPERATIONS	MNEMONIC	RELATIVE OP	~	#	INDEX OP	~	#	EXTND OP	~	#	INHER OP	~	#	BRANCH TEST	5 H	4 I	3 N	2 Z	1 V	0 C
Branch Always	BRA	20	4	2										None	•	•	•	•	•	•
Branch If Carry Clear	BCC	24	4	2										$C = 0$	•	•	•	•	•	•
Branch If Carry Set	BCS	25	4	2										$C = 1$	•	•	•	•	•	•
Branch If = Zero	BEQ	27	4	2										$Z = 1$	•	•	•	•	•	•
Branch If ≥ Zero	BGE	2C	4	2										$N \oplus V = 0$	•	•	•	•	•	•
Branch If > Zero	BGT	2E	4	2										$Z + (N \oplus V) = 0$	•	•	•	•	•	•
Branch If Higher	BHI	22	4	2										$C + Z = 0$	•	•	•	•	•	•
Branch If ≤ Zero	BLE	2F	4	2										$Z + (N \oplus V) = 1$	•	•	•	•	•	•
Branch If Lower Or Same	BLS	23	4	2										$C + Z = 1$	•	•	•	•	•	•
Branch If < Zero	BLT	2D	4	2										$N \oplus V = 1$	•	•	•	•	•	•
Branch If Minus	BMI	2B	4	2										$N = 1$	•	•	•	•	•	•
Branch If Not Equal Zero	BNE	26	4	2										$Z = 0$	•	•	•	•	•	•
Branch If Overflow Clear	BVC	28	4	2										$V = 0$	•	•	•	•	•	•
Branch If Overflow Set	BVS	29	4	2										$V = 1$	•	•	•	•	•	•
Branch If Plus	BPL	2A	4	2										$N = 0$	•	•	•	•	•	•
Branch To Subroutine	BSR	8D	8	2										See Special Operations	•	•	•	•	•	•
Jump	JMP				6E	4	2	7E	3	3					•	•	•	•	•	•
Jump To Subroutine	JSR				AD	8	2	BD	9	3				Advances Prog. Cntr. Only	•	•	•	•	•	•
No Operation	NOP										01	2	1		•	•	•	•	•	•
Return From Interrupt	RTI										3B	10	1		⑩	⑩	⑩	⑩	⑩	⑩
Return From Subroutine	RTS										39	5	1	See special Operations	•	•	•	•	•	•
Software Interrupt	SWI										3F	12	1		•	S	•	•	•	•
Wait for Interrupt	WAI										3E	9	1		•	⑪	•	•	•	•

252

INDEX REGISTER AND STACK MANIPULATION INSTRUCTIONS

INDEX REGISTER AND STACK

POINTER OPERATIONS	MNEMONIC	IMMED OP	~	#	DIRECT OP	~	#	INDEX OP	~	#	EXTND OP	~	#	INHER OP	~	#	BOOLEAN/ARITHMETIC OPERATION	H (5)	I (4)	N (3)	Z (2)	V (1)	C (0)
Compare Index Reg	CPX	8C	3	3	9C	4	2	AC	6	2	BC	5	3				$(X_H/X_L) - (M/M+1)$	•	•	⑦↕	↕	⑧	•
Decrement Index Reg	DEX													09	4	1	$X - 1 \rightarrow X$	•	•	•	↕	•	•
Decrement Stack Pntr	DES													34	4	1	$SP - 1 \rightarrow SP$	•	•	•	•	•	•
Increment Index Reg	INX													08	4	1	$X + 1 \rightarrow X$	•	•	•	↕	•	•
Increment Stack Pntr	INS													31	4	1	$SP + 1 \rightarrow SP$	•	•	•	•	•	•
Load Index Reg	LDX	CE	3	3	DE	4	2	EE	6	2	FE	5	3				$M \rightarrow X_H, (M+1) \rightarrow X_L$	•	•	⑨↕	↕	R	•
Load Stack Pntr	LDS	8E	3	3	9E	4	2	AE	6	2	BE	5	3				$M \rightarrow SP_H, (M+1) \rightarrow SP_L$	•	•	⑨↕	↕	R	•
Store Index Reg	STX				DF	5	2	EF	7	2	FF	6	3				$X_H \rightarrow M, X_L \rightarrow (M+1)$	•	•	⑨↕	↕	R	•
Store Stack Pntr	STS				9F	5	2	AF	7	2	BF	6	3				$SP_H \rightarrow M, SP_L \rightarrow (M+1)$	•	•	⑨↕	↕	R	•
Indx Reg → Stack Pntr	TXS													35	4	1	$X - 1 \rightarrow SP$	•	•	•	•	•	•
Stack Pntr → Indx Reg	TSX													30	4	1	$SP + 1 \rightarrow X$	•	•	•	•	•	•

CONDITION CODE REGISTER MANIPULATION INSTRUCTIONS

CONDITIONS CODE REGISTER

OPERATIONS	MNEMONIC	INHER OP	~	#	BOOLEAN OPERATION	H (5)	I (4)	N (3)	Z (2)	V (1)	C (0)
Clear Carry	CLC	0C	2	1	$0 \rightarrow C$	•	•	•	•	•	R
Clear Interrupt Mask	CLI	0E	2	1	$0 \rightarrow I$	•	R	•	•	•	•
Clear Overflow	CLV	0A	2	1	$0 \rightarrow V$	•	•	•	•	R	•
Set Carry	SEC	0D	2	1	$1 \rightarrow C$	•	•	•	•	•	S
Set Interrupt Mask	SEI	0F	2	1	$1 \rightarrow I$	•	S	•	•	•	•
Set Overflow	SEV	0B	2	1	$1 \rightarrow V$	•	•	•	•	S	•
Acmltr A → CCR	TAP	06	2	1	$A \rightarrow CCR$	⑫	⑫	⑫	⑫	⑫	⑫
CCR → Acmltr A	TPA	07	2	1	$CCR \rightarrow A$	•	•	•	•	•	•

CONDITION CODE REGISTER NOTES:

(Bit set if test is true and cleared otherwise)

① (Bit V) Test: Result = 10000000?

② (Bit C) Test: Result ≠ 00000000?

③ (Bit C) Test: Decimal value of most significant BCD Character greater than nine? (Not cleared if previously set.)

④ (Bit V) Test: Operand = 10000000 prior to execution?

⑤ (Bit V) Test: Operand = 01111111 prior to execution?

⑥ (Bit V) Test: Set equal to result of N ⊕ C after shift has occurred.

⑦ (Bit N) Test: Sign bit of most significant (MS) byte of result = 1?

⑧ (Bit V) Test: 2's complement overflow from subtraction of MS bytes?

⑨ (Bit N) Test: Result less than zero? (Bit 15 = 1)

⑩ (All) Load Condition Code Register from Stack. (See Special Operations)

⑪ (Bit I) Set when interrupt occurs. If previously set, a Non-Maskable Interrupt is required to exit the wait state.

⑫ (ALL) Set according to the contents of Accumulator A.

ACCUMULATOR AND MEMORY INSTRUCTIONS

ACCUMULATOR AND MEMORY OPERATIONS	MNEMONIC	IMMED OP	IMMED ~	IMMED #	DIRECT OP	DIRECT ~	DIRECT #	INDEX OP	INDEX ~	INDEX #	EXTND OP	EXTND ~	EXTND #	INHER OP	INHER ~	INHER #	BOOLEAN/ARITHMETIC OPERATION (All register labels refer to contents)	H (5)	I (4)	N (3)	Z (2)	V (1)	C (0)
Add	ADDA	8B	2	2	9B	3	2	AB	5	2	BB	4	3				$A + M \rightarrow A$	↕	•	↕	↕	↕	↕
	ADDB	CB	2	2	DB	3	2	EB	5	2	FB	4	3				$B + M \rightarrow B$	↕	•	↕	↕	↕	↕
Add Acmltrs	ABA													1B	2	1	$A + B \rightarrow A$	↕	•	↕	↕	↕	↕
Add with Carry	ADCA	89	2	2	99	3	2	A9	5	2	B9	4	3				$A + M + C \rightarrow A$	↕	•	↕	↕	↕	↕
	ADCB	C9	2	2	D9	3	2	E9	5	2	F9	4	3				$B + M + C \rightarrow B$	↕	•	↕	↕	↕	↕
And	ANDA	84	2	2	94	3	2	A4	5	2	B4	4	3				$A \bullet M \rightarrow A$	•	•	↕	↕	R	•
	ANDB	C4	2	2	D4	3	2	E4	5	2	F4	4	3				$B \bullet M \rightarrow B$	•	•	↕	↕	R	•
Bit Test	BITA	85	2	2	95	3	2	A5	5	2	B5	4	3				$A \bullet M$	•	•	↕	↕	R	•
	BITB	C5	2	2	D5	3	2	E5	5	2	F5	4	3				$B \bullet M$	•	•	↕	↕	R	•
Clear	CLR							6F	7	2	7F	6	3				$00 \rightarrow M$	•	•	R	S	R	R
	CLRA													4F	2	1	$00 \rightarrow A$	•	•	R	S	R	R
	CLRB													5F	2	1	$00 \rightarrow B$	•	•	R	S	R	R
Compare	CMPA	81	2	2	91	3	2	A1	5	2	B1	4	3				$A - M$	•	•	↕	↕	↕	↕
	CMPB	C1	2	2	D1	3	2	E1	5	2	F1	4	3				$B - M$	•	•	↕	↕	↕	↕
Compare Acmltrs	CBA													11	2	1	$A - B$	•	•	↕	↕	↕	↕
Complement, 1's	COM							63	7	2	73	6	3				$\overline{M} \rightarrow M$	•	•	↕	↕	R	S
	COMA													43	2	1	$\overline{A} \rightarrow A$	•	•	↕	↕	R	S
	COMB													53	2	1	$\overline{B} \rightarrow B$	•	•	↕	↕	R	S
Complement, 2's (negate)	NEG							60	7	2	70	6	3				$00 - M \rightarrow M$	•	•	↕	↕	①	②
	NEGA													40	2	1	$00 - A \rightarrow A$	•	•	↕	↕	①	②
	NEGB													50	2	1	$00 - B \rightarrow B$	•	•	↕	↕	①	②
Decimal Adjust, A	DAA													19	2	1	Converts Binary Add. of BCD Characters into BCD Format, A ACCUM	•	•	↕	↕	↕	③
Decrement	DEC							6A	7	2	7A	6	3				$M - 1 \rightarrow M$	•	•	↕	↕	④	•
	DECA													4A	2	1	$A - 1 \rightarrow A$	•	•	↕	↕	④	•
	DECB													5A	2	1	$B - 1 \rightarrow B$	•	•	↕	↕	④	•
Exclusive OR	EORA	88	2	2	98	3	2	A8	5	2	B8	4	3				$A \oplus M \rightarrow A$	•	•	↕	↕	R	•
	EORB	C8	2	2	D8	3	2	E8	5	2	F8	4	3				$B \oplus M \rightarrow B$	•	•	↕	↕	R	•
Increment	INC							6C	7	2	7C	6	3				$M + 1 \rightarrow M$	•	•	↕	↕	⑤	•
	INCA													4C	2	1	$A + 1 \rightarrow A$	•	•	↕	↕	⑤	•
	INCB													5C	2	1	$B + 1 \rightarrow B$	•	•	↕	↕	⑤	•
Load Acmltr	LDAA	86	2	2	96	3	2	A6	5	2	B6	4	3				$M \rightarrow A$	•	•	↕	↕	R	•
	LDAB	C6	2	2	D6	3	2	E6	5	2	F6	4	3				$M \rightarrow B$	•	•	↕	↕	R	•
Or, Inclusive	ORAA	8A	2	2	9A	3	2	AA	5	2	BA	4	3				$A + M \rightarrow A$	•	•	↕	↕	R	•
	ORAB	CA	2	2	DA	3	2	EA	5	2	FA	4	3				$B + M \rightarrow B$	•	•	↕	↕	R	•

Operations	Mnemonic	IMMED OP	IMMED ~	IMMED #	DIRECT OP	DIRECT ~	DIRECT #	INDEX OP	INDEX ~	INDEX #	EXTND OP	EXTND ~	EXTND #	INHER OP	INHER ~	INHER #	Boolean/Arithmetic Operation	H	I	N	Z	V	C
Push Data	PSHA													36	4	1	$A \to M_{SP}, SP - 1 \to SP$	•	•	•	•	•	•
	PSHB													37	4	1	$B \to M_{SP}, SP - 1 \to SP$	•	•	•	•	•	•
Pull Data	PULA													32	4	1	$SP + 1 \to SP, M_{SP} \to A$	•	•	•	•	•	•
	PULB													33	4	1	$SP + 1 \to SP, M_{SP} \to B$	•	•	•	•	•	•
Rotate Left	ROL							69	7	2	79	6	3				M	•	•	↔	↔	⑥	↔
	ROLA													49	2	1	A	•	•	↔	↔	⑥	↔
	ROLB													59	2	1	B	•	•	↔	↔	⑥	↔
Rotate Right	ROR							66	7	2	76	6	3				M	•	•	↔	↔	⑥	↔
	RORA													46	2	1	A	•	•	↔	↔	⑥	↔
	RORB													56	2	1	B	•	•	↔	↔	⑥	↔
Shift Left, Arithmetic	ASL							68	7	2	78	6	3				M	•	•	↔	↔	⑥	↔
	ASLA													48	2	1	A	•	•	↔	↔	⑥	↔
	ASLB													58	2	1	B	•	•	↔	↔	⑥	↔
Shift Right, Arithmetic	ASR							67	7	2	77	6	3				M	•	•	↔	↔	⑥	↔
	ASRA													47	2	1	A	•	•	↔	↔	⑥	↔
	ASRB													57	2	1	B	•	•	↔	↔	⑥	↔
Shift Right, Logic.	LSR							64	7	2	74	6	3				M	•	•	R	↔	⑥	↔
	LSRA													44	2	1	A	•	•	R	↔	⑥	↔
	LSRB													54	2	1	B	•	•	R	↔	⑥	↔
Store Acmltr.	STAA				97	4	2	A7	6	2	B7	5	3				$A \to M$	•	•	↔	↔	R	•
	STAB				D7	4	2	E7	6	2	F7	5	3				$B \to M$	•	•	↔	↔	R	•
Subtract	SUBA	80	2	2	90	3	2	A0	5	2	B0	4	3				$A - M \to A$	•	•	↔	↔	↔	↔
	SUBB	C0	2	2	D0	3	2	E0	5	2	F0	4	3				$B - M \to B$	•	•	↔	↔	↔	↔
Subract Acmltrs.	SBA													10	2	1	$A - B \to A$	•	•	↔	↔	↔	↔
Subtr. with Carry	SBCA	82	2	2	92	3	2	A2	5	2	B2	4	3				$A - M - C \to A$	•	•	↔	↔	↔	↔
	SBCB	C2	2	2	D2	3	2	E2	5	2	F2	4	3				$B - M - C \to B$	•	•	↔	↔	↔	↔
Transfer Acmltrs	TAB													16	2	1	$A \to B$	•	•	↔	↔	R	•
	TBA													17	2	1	$B \to A$	•	•	↔	↔	R	•
Test, Zero or Minus	TST							6D	7	2	7D	6	3				$M - 00$	•	•	↔	↔	R	R
	TSTA													4D	2	1	$A - 00$	•	•	↔	↔	R	R
	TSTB													5D	2	1	$B - 00$	•	•	↔	↔	R	R

LEGEND:

OP	Operation Code (Hexadecimal);	M_{SP}	Contents of memory location pointed to be Stack Pointer;
~	Number of MPU Cycles;	+	Boolean Inclusive OR;
#	Number of Program Bytes;	⊕	Boolean Exclusive OR;
+	Arithmetic Plus;	$\overline{M}$	Complement of M;
–	Arithmetic Minus;	→	Transfer Into;
•	Boolean AND;	0	Bit = Zero;
		00	Byte = Zero;

H	Half-carry from bit 3;	R	Reset Always
I	Interrupt mask;	S	Set Always
N	Negative (sign bit);	↔	Test and set if true, cleared otherwise
Z	Zero (byte);	•	Not Affected
V	Overflow, 2's complement;	CCR	Condition Code Register
C	Carry from bit 7;	LS	Least Significant
		MS	Most Significant

Appendix B
Powers of 2 and 16

POWERS OF 2				POWERS OF 16		
2^n	n			16^n	n	2^n
256	8		$2^0 = 16^0$	1	0	
512	9		$2^4 = 16^1$	16	1	
1 024	10		$2^8 = 16^2$	256	2	8
2 048	11		$2^{12} = 16^3$	4 096	3	12
4 096	12		$2^{16} = 16^4$	65 536	4	16
8 192	13		$2^{20} = 16^5$	1 048 576	5	20
16 384	14		$2^{24} = 16^6$	16 777 216	6	24
32 768	15		$2^{28} = 16^7$	268 435 456	7	28
65 536	16		$2^{32} = 16^8$	4 294 967 296	8	32
131 072	17		$2^{36} = 16^9$	68 719 476 736	9	36
262 144	18		$2^{40} = 16^{10}$	1 099 511 627 776	10	40
524 288	19		$2^{44} = 16^{11}$	17 592 186 044 416	11	44
1 048 576	20		$2^{48} = 16^{12}$	281 474 976 710 656	12	48
2 097 152	21		$2^{52} = 16^{13}$	4 503 599 627 370 496	13	52
4 194 304	22		$2^{56} = 16^{14}$	72 057 594 037 927 936	14	56
8 388 608	23		$2^{60} = 16^{15}$	1 152 921 504 606 846 976	15	60
16 777 216	24					

Handwritten additions:

33 554 432   25
67 108 864   26

15 14 13 12 11 10 9 8 | 7 6 5 4 3 2 1 0

8 BIT MAX = $2^8 - 1$ = 255
16 BIT MAX = $2^{16} - 1$ = 65,536

2^n	n
1	0
2	1
4	2
8	3
16	4
32	5
64	6
128	7

DEC	4
10	A
11	B
12	C
13	D
14	E
15	F

HEX

X 0
X 16
X 256
X 4096

Index

Index